S0-AFR-647

The Witches of Early America

The Witches
of Early America

by Sally Smith Booth

HASTINGS HOUSE • PUBLISHERS

New York 10016

LIBRARY OF CONGRESS CATALOGING IN PUBLICATION DATA

Booth, Sally Smith.
　The witches of early America.

　　1.　Witchcraft—United States.　I.　Title.
BFL573.B66　　133.4'0973　　75-2068
ISBN 0-8038-8072-3

Published simultaneously in Canada by
Saunders of Toronto, Ltd., Don Mills, Ontario

Printed in the United States of America

To the three witches
hanged at sea:

Katherine Grady
Mary Lee
Elizabeth Richardson

Contents

The Colonial Experience

To the eye of the casual traveler, life was good in the colonies of the seventeenth century. Although physically demanding, the toil of America was far better than the deprivation of England's tenement cities or upcountry, where farmers were but a step beyond fiefdom.

Each day new cabins sprang up in the forest clearings, pushing the frontier farther from the sea. Land was plentiful. The earth fertile. Here outcasts from the Old World could begin anew.

But the early years had left their mark on the transplanted Britishers settled in footholds along the Atlantic's western shore. Beneath the surface of America's bright promise was an undercurrent of dread, created by ceaseless threats to survival. Some of the dangers came from external forces. Unfriendly Indians ringing pioneer villages might launch surprise attacks at any moment. Droughts or floods could bring on "starving times," such as those that had caused the first residents at Jamestown to eat rats and ants. Warships from France and Spain, together with marauding pirate vessels, hovered offshore, ready to make lightning raids against settlements on waterways. Disease was an everpresent calamity that struck suddenly and mortally.

Perhaps the worst fears, however, came from the mind. In a time when many were too weak to live, the future was uncertain for all. At any moment, even the most hearty might be felled without warning or reason. The uncertainty of survival linked provincials of all faiths, stations, and regions and contributed to the most uncontrollable of all fears, dread of the unknown. Belief in a powerful, supernatural world was a basic part of the philosophy of early Americans. But the attitude did not spring totally from conditions in the new land. Just as immigrants had retained many European customs and traditions, so had they transported across the ocean a deep and unquestioned conviction in the reality of an unknown realm.

An environment of superstition shrouded even the most trivial occurrences in the everyday life of early colonizers. Untrained in the methods of scientific thought that were budding in Europe, provincials viewed almost every physical event as a "sign." Any out of the ordinary happening was interpreted as concrete proof that the netherworld forces of good and evil were at work. The birth of a healthy baby, a good harvest, or a fair wind were all presumed to be gifts of a Christian God showing pleasure with his obedient flock. The sudden death of a pig, a corn blight, or an overturned hay wagon were judged grave warnings of the Trinity's wrath or indications that the devil was about.

In response to these "preternatural" omens, colonists altered their manner of conduct, for to ignore the teachings of a sign was to court personal or community disaster. Days of prayer and fasting were ordered in New England following the appearance of a phenomenon such as a comet, an ominous token thought to portend the coming of a particularly important crisis. Even the most pious Puritans delved deeper into self-confession after witnessing lightning storms, for the bright flashes were seen as "heaven's arrows" sent to strike down the wicked. An attitude of equal alarm resulted from the observation of meteorites. These missiles were presumed to be harbingers of death or weapons flung down from above by a displeased deity.

Although most settlers believed themselves helpless in controlling the world's mystical forces, a small band of immigrants were credited with possessing special powers to alter the moves of fate. These were witches, mortals so skilled in the black arts that each could harness the forces of the spirit kingdom in order to inflict pain or death.

These magic workers prompted fear rather than awe among the citizenry, for underlying the entire concept of witchcraft was the principle of maleficium, the idea that enchanters existed solely to perform acts of evil and harm. The English belief in a special band of good or "white" witches, who used their secrets for the benefit of society, was not accepted in the colonies.

Also absent from American witchlore was the elaborate nomenclature by which magic workers in Europe were classified according to their specialties. In Britain and on the continent, precise distinctions were made between soothsayers, wizards, conjurers, charmers, and divines. For the pioneer, however, such definitions were not needed. All those who chose to work in the darkness of evil were known as witches, and their powers were virtually unlimited.

A witch's harm could be as minor as a lame foot caused by the evil eye, or as devastating as a death created by voodoo torture on puppet dolls. Witches could conjure demon spirits, raise sudden winds, or make objects disappear. Through divining they could solve past crimes and foretell the future. They could change men into boars or "hagride" innocent victims throughout the countryside night after night. With the aid of secret charms, fish could be stolen from the nets of seamen, milk curdled as it came from the udder, and crops spoiled on the vine. Magical herbs could be ground into love potions or agonizing ointments. Witches could soar through the air on broomsticks, deform unborn children in the womb, or assume the shape of grotesque creatures. No colonial, no animal, and no object was immune to their power.

A fascination with mysticism marked the American scene from the earliest days of exploration. Elaborate reference books on witchcraft, magic, and sorcery were treasured possessions of the first immigrants, but the traditional doctrines of Europe were soon altered to meet the needs of the primitive environment. A time and culture lag separated the New World from the Old as surely as did the waters of the Atlantic, and ideas pertinent in the wide avenues of London were often unsuitable on the wagon paths of Virginia.

Sophisticated theological arguments, which consumed European scholars of witchcraft, were of little relevance to the pioneer struggling with a possessed hog or an enchanted cow. Just as the American experience necessitated the development of different forms of law, politics, and economics, so the mysteries of a virgin continent resulted in the formation of a unique and functional witchcraft creed. Although the new body of beliefs retained many of the doctrines framed by learned mind, it was rooted in the uncomplicated, daily fears of simple farm folk.

The American experience did not lessen the harsh legal penalties that had been imposed for centuries upon witches, but a more cautious approach did develop in prosecuting those suspected of being in league with the devil. With the exception of the Salem delusion in 1692, the colonial atmosphere was not plagued by the climate of hysteria that underlay European attitudes from the fifteenth to the eighteenth century, when an estimated one million witches were burned. The indiscriminate "turning off" of human lives was considered both a social and economic waste in the sparsely settled colonies.

However, the zeal of American witch-hunters was not tempered as sharply as was the country's legal punishments. Long after nations such as England had ceased their sweeping purges of sorcerers, provincials were diligently ferreting out and destroying citizens deemed to be magic workers.

Several distinct methods of confronting the issue of witchcraft emerged in seventeenth-century America. The most radical approach dealt with enchanters as heretical members of a demonic cult involved in a conspiracy to destroy the Puritan outposts west of the Atlantic. A more moderate viewpoint, similar to English concepts, portrayed witches as isolated individuals whose magical spells were primarily self-motivated and unconnected with an organized Satanist plot. A final philosophy accepted the existence of witchcraft, but held that the actual practice of magic was so extraordinary an event as to be of little real import.

The demonic cult theory was most popular in New England, where the powerful Puritan clergy instilled in the citizenry a deep and everpresent fear of mass destruction by witchcraft. Boston's Cotton Mather, a prominent advocate of this attitude, preached that witches were direct agents of the devil and had entered into a compact to destroy God's chosen people, the Puritans.

Mather, author of more than 450 books and pamphlets, possessed what may have been the most scientific mind in the colonies, but despite his intellectual achievements, the minister never waivered in his prophesies concerning the dangers of the supernatural world. The threat to life was real and imminent according to Mather, who preached that an "army of devils" was poised to sweep down upon the religious enclaves of New England. By acting against witches, Satan's human instruments, frontier settlers would be fighting a holy war, according to the minister. Battle lines were clearly drawn. Belligerents in the conflict would be the Massachusetts "saints" and the "incarnate legions" of evil.

Extremist members of the clergy maintained that the Puritans had been targeted for attack by the devil for two major reasons. First, the sect's form of worship was supposedly closest to the wishes of God and thus represented a far greater threat to evil than the less holy Catholics, Anglicans, or pietist devotions. Perhaps even more important a cause in the minds of the ministers was the belief that for many ages America had been the devil's homeland and sanctuary. Here Satan dwelled, served by his evil followers, the new-world Indians.

In attempting to rally his congregation, Mather emphasized the importance of the invasion into the "devil's territories," and explained:

> It was a rousing alarm to the Devil, when a great company of English Protestants and Puritans came to erect evangelical churches in a corner of the world where he had reign'd without any control for many ages. . . . The Indian powawes used all their sorceries to molest the first planters here. . . .

As a result of clerical influences, witchcraft in New England was conceived not as merely a civil crime, but as a religious heresy of the highest magnitude. Enchanters were judged not only guilty of infringing upon the codes of the State, but as perpetrators against the holy laws of God. Justice against those accused of delving into the black arts was swift and harsh. In the villages of the northeast the issue of Satanism was a constant preoccupation that reached obsessive heights. Suspicion of neighbor against neighbor was commonplace and routinely translated into court action. Approximately ninety percent of all witchcraft trials held in seventeenth-century America took place in New England. Ninety-five percent of all executions came in the saint's communities where both courts and citizens unhesitatingly obeyed the biblical admonitions that witches and workers with familiar spirits should be destroyed.

The fanaticism of the Puritans, although unbounded philosophically, was restrained geographically. A more lenient attitude toward witchcraft predominated in the tidewater areas of the mid-Atlantic. In the intellectually active communities around Chesapeake Bay and in the casual pioneer settlements on the western frontier, citizens accepted the realness of witchcraft, but discarded the religious notion of demonic conspiracy.

Instead of satanistic plotters, witches were viewed as eccentric hags who worked alone to cast spells aimed at harassing or annoying their enemies. At no time were witches considered threats to society or conspiratorial agents of the devil. Their existence was real, but their danger was slight.

In Maryland and Virginia, witchcraft was legally recognized as a capital felony, but the courts generally considered accusations of sorcery as trivial. Instead of prosecuting the suspects in criminal trials, citizens alleged to be witches were permitted to sue their accusers in civil actions of slander or defamation of character. This approach, coupled with high fines for defamers, significantly limited the number of witchcraft cases that came before the bar.

The Dutch reform patroons of New Netherland and the Quakers under William Penn were even less concerned with netherworld matters than were the southern colonists. The possibility of witchcraft was acknowledged by these tolerant immigrants, but actual instances of preternaturally inspired events were considered rare. Rather than punishing settlers whose deviate behavior would have created evidence of guilt in New England or in the South, officials in New Netherland, East and West Jersey, Pennsylvania, and Delaware opened their territories as safe havens for any fleeing the excesses of witch-hunters in less enlightened areas.

Yet even the most intellectually sophisticated settlements of the seventeenth century were not inured to the influences of witchlore. Centuries-old superstitions, bred in the dark times of medieval Europe, were not easily discarded. Each colonist, whether born on the soil of America or uprooted from a nation beyond the sea, was a child of old-world heritage. For most provincials, witchcraft was perceived not as an outmoded fantasy, but as a real and threatening presence.

CHAPTER I

The Devil and Possession

WHEN Boston's Mercy Short met the devil in 1692, he was a short, black man about the height of a walking stick and was instantly recognizable by his cloven feet. Mary Lancey agreed he was black, but added that the prince of darkness could be distinguished by the high crowned hat perched upon his head.

Christopher Browne, who "discoursed" with the devil at Salem, announced that Satan had come to their rendezvous tastefully disguised as a "gentleman," while Connecticut's Hugh Crotia said the devil presented himself in the form of a young boy.

Mary Osgood confessed that Satan had crept into her Salem orchard in the specter of a cat. In the same village, Ann Foster insisted that he approached as a white bird and, after promising her prosperity, transformed himself into a black one. A similar transfiguration was seen by Catreen Branch, a possessed servant girl, to whom the devil appeared as both a black cat and a white dog. Rebecca Greensmith, described by contemporaries as a "lewd, ignorant, and considerably aged woman," assured the court at Hartford that the evil worker was actually a fawn or deer that skipped about.

Discrepancies in the physical description of Satan by those who claimed to have visited with him supported the contention that the demon of Hades could appear in any form, at any time or place. However, there was no conflict among witnesses regarding the purpose of such a call. Satan, all agreed, was anxious to recruit human converts, binding them as witches by a formal and unbreakable contract. In exchange for their commitment, the devil promised to bestow pleasing gifts on his followers—gifts such as good fortune, happiness, great wealth, or the ability to perform magical spells.

Rewards could be altered to fit the particular whims of a prospective witch. Groton's Elizabeth Knapp was reportedly promised "such things as suited her youthful fancey—money, silkes, fine clothes, ease from labor," and travel throughout the world. A particularly honorable present was said to have been requested by Martha Carrier, who asked to be crowned Queen of Hell in exchange for her service.

In most cases, the devil approached potential witches when illness or dissatisfaction made them most susceptible to temptation. Connecticut servant Mary Johnson admitted at her 1648 witchcraft trial that during such a period of "discontent," a sly demon had come to seize her soul. According to Mary, in an offguarded moment she had wished that Satan would help her perform the day's farm chores. Almost immediately after this blasphemy had been voiced, a specter materialized and asked what services could be rendered. Mary's requests were simple, and according to the court record the devil was delighted to accommodate the girl:

> Her master blamed her for not carrying out the ashes, and a devil afterwards would clear the hearth of ashes for her. Her master sending her to drive out the hogs that sometimes broke into their field, a devil would scare the hogs away, and make her laugh to see how he scared them. She confessed that she had murdered a child, and committed uncleanness both with men and with devils.

Mary paid a high price for the assistance of the demon helper. On the basis of her confession she was found guilty of witchcraft and condemned to hang. After bearing a child in prison, Mary was carted to the gallows and, according to one account, "died in a frame extremely to the satisfaction of them that were spectators of it."

Verbal agreements, such as that between Mary and the devil, were a common practice in England, but in the colonies, witchcraft contracts were usually framed in more formal terms. For example, it was thought that after conditions of a bargain had been agreed upon, Satan produced a large black book, which the witch was then compelled to sign or mark. As well as satisfying any legal necessities of the underworld, the written verification was necessary so that future converts might be able to identify others in the area who were similarly bound. The signature could be written in either black ink, which appeared magically out of the air, or with the blood of the new recruit.

Agreements were usually open-ended, with the devil's service terminating only in the event of the witch's death. However, Elizabeth Knapp's contract was not as liberal as the norm, for Satan agreed to assist the woman for a specific period of only six years.

Although no complaints were ever reported from the representative of evil, the unholy alliances were not always satisfactory to the mortal partner. Mary Osgood was one dissatisfied customer who complained that the bargain had been reneged upon. Mary claimed that although she had been promised "satisfaction and quietness" in exchange for her soul, no favors at all had been granted during her eleven years of servitude.

The concept that an individual had voluntarily agreed to become a witch was an important factor in supporting the harsh attitudes that developed in Early America toward enchanters. Because Satan was believed to have no powers to either compel or conscript devotees, the full responsibility for becoming a sorcerer was credited entirely to the mortal. No excuses or mitigating circumstances were sufficiently valid to alleviate the punishment prescribed for a convicted worker of magic. But while the decision to enter the devil's service was considered voluntary, it was thought some tools were available to help the demon in persuading the undecided or unwilling. Torture was the most valuable weapon.

Confessing witches often attempted to defend themselves by claiming that long and painful torment had been the cause of their ultimate surrender. Such a proposition did not diminish the evilness of the bargain in the eyes of the court or population. The Puritan could conceive of no pain so great as to compel a godly citizen into the crime of serving the devil. Death was to be preferred to the alternative of treason to God.

Persistent threatening was also helpful in converting the hesitant. In some cases, a concerted period of harassment was continued for months and occasionally stretched into years. Joseph Ring claimed to have been courted by Satan for more than two years. During the period, Ring was carried about the countryside as a prisoner and subjected to various ill treatments. Not only was he repeatedly struck mute, but the settler maintained that he was also forced to attend witch ceremonies, where he was knocked in the head and chained during the revelous feasting and dancing. With true stoicism, the provincial steadfastly refused the "delectable things" that were offered as temptations and never consented to sign a devil's contract.

Prayer and fasting were considered the only effective weapons for those who struggled against the power of the supernatural procurers. Besieged individuals such as Joseph Ring could seek to combat the evil persuasions by surrounding themselves with friends who conducted long prayer sessions aimed at bringing the forces of good into battle against the devil's seduction.

The failure of Elizabeth Goodman to accept such assistance was interpreted by the New Haven courts as incriminating evidence that perhaps the pressures had already proved successful. Elizabeth escaped punishment for witchcraft in a 1653 court action, but damaging evidence was presented against her when sorcery charges were renewed in 1655.

Stephen Goodyeare, deputy governor of the colony and Elizabeth's landlord, testified that the woman had admitted that she was undergoing a period of strong demonic temptation. Not only did Elizabeth announce that she had witnessed supernatural apparitions and unexplained flashes of light, but she also reported seeing an assortment of other "strange sights which affrighted her." In order to calm his lodger's fears and provide courage in the fight against the pursuing evil, Goodyeare suggested that members of his own family should keep day and night vigil with Elizabeth. She refused the offer, preferring to trust in the "spiritual armour" that she claimed protected her from harm. In a more mundane explanation, Elizabeth added that her bed was too weak to support two people.

The court looked with suspicion on this scorning of assistance and was even more concerned with evidence indicating that Elizabeth was having contact with spirits of the darkness.

According to Goodyeare, late one night his entire household was awakened by thunderous noises and clamoring. Upon investigating, the official discovered Elizabeth stealthfully creeping about the dwelling. When confronted, Elizabeth admitted that she had been roaming about, but claimed that she was merely attempting to light a candle so that she might hunt for two grapes previously dropped on the floor. Her fear was that mice would discover the fruit and play with them all night, thus disturbing the Goodyeares' sleep. The incident was ruled by the court to be suspicious enough to commit Elizabeth to prison until further evidence of witchcraft could be gathered.

After a prospective witch had signed Satan's black book, one final procedure was thought necessary before the bargain became operational. This was the placing of a devil's mark upon the new convert. In addition to enabling Satan to recognize his followers, the mark allowed individual witches to identify each other as authentic believers and to expose imposters who might attempt to penetrate into the clan.

Even the most learned theoreticians were unable to agree on an exact description of a "witches' mark." Scars, birthmarks, unusual skin pigmentations, even insect bites could have been identified as devil signs under the vague definitions ascribed as possible proof of witchcraft. English jurist Richard Bernard in his 1627 *A Guide to Grand-Jury Men* suggested:

> A witch in league with the Devil is convicted by . . . a witches *mark;* which is on the baser sort of witches; and this, by the Devil's either sucking or touching of them. Tertullian says, *It is the Devil's custom to mark his.* And note, that this mark is insensible, and being prick'd, it will not bleed.

Bernard's work was read widely by the intellectual classes in America, but his suggestion that marks appeared only on the "baser sort of witches" was not accepted. American enchanters of any social standing were assumed to carry the secret blemish concealed somewhere on their bodies. This liberal interpretation was partially supported by Michael Dalton, whose 1618 work *Countrey Justice* was perhaps the most popular treatise in colonial circles of justice. Dalton believed that by thoroughly searching a suspect's body, devil's marks would invariably be discovered. In describing this important means of witch detection, the jurist wrote:

> Sometimes [it is] like a blew spot or red spot, like a flea-biting, sometimes the flesh sunk in and hollow (all which for a time may be covered, yea, taken away, but will come again to their old form). And these, the Devil's marks, be insensible, and being pricked will

not bleed, and be often in their secretest parts, and therefore require diligent and careful search.

Unlike the devil's mark, a demonical "fact" accepted by both Americans and Europeans, the Black Sabbath was viewed with significantly different attitudes on the two continents. The sabbath, a mass celebration by demons and witches, was an integral part of the supernatural lore in the Old World. However, the concept was little known in the colonies.

Not until the Salem outbreak in the last decade of the seventeenth century was the theory publicly discussed that witches might meet together in midnight gatherings. Even in New England, where the conspiratorial cult theory was dominant, witches were viewed as lone figures who acted independently of other converts. Although a sorcerer was indeed in league with the devil, the relationship was a limited, two-party agreement. Enchanters had no social or professional ties with other mortals who had made similar bargains.

The American concept of witches as individual offenders was consistent with the attitudes popular in England during most of the mother country's period of prosecution. No indication of communal aspects appeared in British courts until the Lancashire trials of 1612, when a confessed witch admitted consuming a midnight meal in the company of the devil and another enchanter.

In Scotland and the catholic nations of Europe, however, associative demonology was a prime tenet. Sabbaths were conceived as mass revels and sexual orgies in which a large and closely knit demonic community plotted against Christian society. These gatherings were bloody affairs, according to report, where enchanters performed black masses and mock sacraments, using human sacrifices such as unbaptized infants. The netherworld rites were identical to those of the accepted church, but each was performed backward, a not particularly subtle symbol that the realm of the devil was the reverse in every way of God's heavenly environment.

Accompanying the sacraments were great feasts of exotic food and human flesh. Wild dances by the witches and their demon partners were supposedly performed around blazing fires representing the flames of hell. Instead of the somber atmosphere of the traditional church, the entire sabbath was a chaotic form punctuated by the shrieks and howls of the participants. As dawn approached, the witches anointed themselves with magical potions made from ingredients such as the bodies of infants or pulverized bones of hanged men. The enchanters then flew away into the night on poles.

Several aspects of the primitive environment of the New World made the idea of voluptuous sabbaths difficult to accept. First, colonists were greatly influenced by English customs, which traditionally ignored the communal aspects of witchery. Even more important, the struggle for survival made most settlers pragmatic and skeptical toward concepts that seemed ludicrous in the frequently destitute conditions of America.

In the hundreds of incidences of witchcraft recorded in the early colonies, only one case prior to the Salem period included mention of what could be interpreted as a Black Sabbath. This evidence came in the 1662 trial of Hartford's Rebecca Greensmith.

Rebecca, an elderly woman considered by some to be "distempered" of mind, confessed to attending two meetings during her tenure as a practicing witch. Neither of the gatherings were identified by name as "sabbaths," and the description of the modest affairs bore little resemblance to the tales of bloody alliances considered routine in Europe. Instead of human flesh and opulent dainties, the Connecticut cult of Rebecca Greensmith was content to split a bottle of sherry. Rather than framing a plot to overthrow God's entire kingdom, the American witch conspiracy seemed to consist of a tearful neighbor standing in an orchard while cursing another neighbor for some slight.

Like the Connecticut affairs, the witch parleys described at Salem thirty years later seem to have been docile events. In the bay colony hearings, seven-year-old Sarah Carrier asserted she had been baptized by her mother in the presence of several witches grouped in one Andrew Foster's pasture. In a more gory account, accuser Abigail Williams claimed to have seen a vision of a mass mock sacrifice attended by many Salem residents, whom she suggested "had bread as red as raw flesh and red drink." Presumably, the liquid was meant to represent blood. Although another witness claimed that the town's witches were summoned to their sabbaths by former minister George Burroughs, who sounded the welcoming call on a trumpet, few accusers were able to provide concrete details of actual gatherings.

Ann Foster presented what was perhaps the most comprehensive description. The Andover woman explained that she had been taken prisoner by the devil and forced to undertake a harrowing journey to attend a sabbath. Along with the devil and Martha Carrier, Ann flew through the air on a pole. At one point the stick was broken and, "hanging about Carrier's neck," the trio fell to the ground. Despite the temporary setback, Ann arrived at the council where she saw about twenty-five persons conducting an unholy ceremony involving the use of bread and wine. According to Ann, before disbanding the group agreed to "set up the devil's kingdom" in Massachusetts. However, no practical strategy for accomplishing the task was discussed.

Levitation or nightriding was also mentioned in connection with Martha Carrier's son Richard. Accuser Mary Lancey declared that together with Carrier, she often soared above the trees on a stick. Tibula, a servant and the first alleged witch at Salem, also partook of the pleasures of flight. In describing one journey on which she was accompanied by two confederates, the black woman stated: "I ride upon a stick or a pole, and Good and Osburn behind me. We ride taking hold of one another. [I] don't know how high we go, for I saw no trees nor path . . . ." An even more crowded flight was described by confessed witch Mary Osgood, who claimed she flew to her baptism on a pole that held not only herself, but also the devil and four other witches.

Conveniences such as poles, fireplace spits, and broomsticks were the most common means of propulsion, but the items were not considered essential for all witches. Hadley's Mary Webster, for example, was accused of being able to fly without the aid of any tangible object. Salves or ointments, believed necessary in Europe to enable enchanters to perform their soaring feats, were not thought essential in America. Similarly, the candles Europeans assumed were attached to the end of broomsticks to light the way were also ignored in provincial witchlore.

Instances of air riding were described more often by self-confessed witches than by witnesses who claimed to have seen sorcerers in flight. One reason for this pattern may have been that admitted witches became so entranced with the mystique of magic that they were hesitant to confirm that their arrival at a sabbath had been on foot or horseback. In order to glamorize the profession, more unique means of transportation were proposed.

Divergences from centuries-old concepts were also apparent in the realm of witch morality. Sexual intercourse between humans and devils was an essential part of continental witchlore, where scores of citizens claimed to have consummated a union with spirits of the underworld. But in America, instances of liaisons between mortals and representatives of the devil were virtually unknown. There is no indication that colonists accepted the concept of "succubus," the mating of male humans with female demons, and only isolated references were made to "incubus," the pairing of females with devil men.

Mary Johnson was one settler who confessed to having committed "uncleanness" with devils, but she did not elaborate on the experience. Rebecca Greensmith admitted that Satan had "frequent use of her body," but perhaps because of her somewhat unbalanced mental state, she was not pressed for precise evidence in the matter.

Since the Middle Ages it had been believed that such illicit unions might result in the birth of half-human, half-demon offspring. Criteria were developed so that the children of such a liaison could be readily identified by the public and the church. One trait supposedly common to devil-sired children was the sprouting of horns. Another was gross misshaping of appendages, which produced a "monster-like" appearance.

In 1531, a witch in Augsburg, Germany, was reported to have given birth to a two-footed serpent as the result of a mating with Satan. A less obvious distortion occurred on the continent in a situation involving the child of a human and a cow-devil. The infant was born physically perfect, but after reaching adulthood, the unfortunate youth experienced uncontrollable desires to wander through the farm meadows and intermingle with grazing steers.

Colonial sources make no references to even a single instance of devil-sired births. In 1637, the delivery at Boston of a severely deformed child was given wide publicity and the infant was described as an unnatural "monster." However, citizens did not credit the baby's distortions to fathering by Satan, but instead assumed that the infant had been bewitched by evil spirits.

The almost complete rejection of exotic doctrines such as the Black Sabbath, incubus, and succubus illustrates the adaptive process under which a unique witch creed was devised. The Americanization of traditional beliefs was a subconscious process, for settlers did not intentionally choose to disregard the old-world dogma, which was incompatible with the colonial environment. In no area is this informal selection so evident as in the realm of demonology.

To most Americans, the forces of evil were represented by a single, personal Satan, just as goodness was personified by one, Christian God. Although it was believed that Satan was served by many lesser devils and demons, neither the number nor the powers and importance of these minor figures was given particular consideration by the general population. Only a small band of clerics chose to speculate even briefly on the more obscure aspects of demonology. Cotton Mather, the most learned and scholarly of this group, delved into the organization of the underworld, but his investigations were significant only because they were unique, not because the resulting theories were widely accepted and gained public popularity.

Mather made no effort to determine the total number of demonic characters, but the clergyman was convinced that their legions were mighty. In his *The Wonders of the Invisible World*, Mather warned:

> The devils they swarm about us, like the frogs of Egypt, in the most retired of our chambers. Are we at our boards? Beds? There will be devils to tempt us into carnality. Are we in our shops? There will be devils to tempt us into dishonesty. Yea, though we get into the church of God, there will be devils to haunt us in the very temple itself, and there tempt us to manifold misbehaviors. I am verily persuaded that there are very few human affairs whereinto some devils are not insinuated.

> 'Tis to be supposed that there is a sort of arbitrary, even military, government among the devils. . . . These devils have a prince over them, who is king over the children of pride. 'Tis probable that the devil . . . is now the general of those hellish armies . . . and the rest are his angels, or his soldiers. . . . 'Tis to be supposed that some devils are more peculiarly commission'd, and perhaps qualify'd for some countries, while others are for others. . . . It is not likely that every devil does know every language; or that every devil can do every mischief. 'Tis possible that the experience, or, if I may call it so, the education of all devils is not alike, and that there may be some difference in their abilities . . . .

Even Mather's deductions, published as the last vestiges of witch-hunting were dying, were considered primitive when compared to the level of sophisticated ideas circulating in Europe. Here demonology had been a preoccupation among theologians and jurists since the early sixteenth century. Hundreds of volumes of minutia had been produced by scholars who devoted their entire lives to the study of Satan and his followers. Despite the years of thought, experts frequently disagreed on even the most fundamental issues. For example, the exact number of devils in operation was heatedly debated.

Reginald Scot, in his 1584 treatise on the discovery of witches, listed the names of sixty-eight diabolical chiefs who helped rule the underworld. Included in the roll call were devils such as Barbatos, Zepar, Sabnacke, Asmoday, Scox, Murmur, and Amy. According to Scot, these princes controlled exactly 14,198,580 lesser demons. Mightiest of all was Bileth, who reigned over eighty-five legions, each including 6,666 members. French thinkers disagreed not only with English calculations, but with the figures of their own countrymen. The most commonly accepted estimate, however, was 7,409,127 devils controlled by seventy-nine chiefs, a total calculated in the sixteenth century by Jean Wier, physician to the Duc de Cleves.

While Americans largely ignored the more esoteric details of demonology, the practical impact of devilism was a matter of great concern. Most unexplained calamities automatically gave rise to speculation that Satan's disciples were at work. But even the most unusual natural event did not result in the wonderment that was stirred by demonic possession, the most intriguing facet of demonology.

Possession involved the supposed inhabiting of a human body by demons who inflicted great pain and suffering on the victim. The condition was believed to be caused by witches who instructed devils in the manner of torture to be provided and identified the mortal target. By accepting this theory, colonials rejected the traditional doctrine that Satan could be solely responsible for a possession and needed no witch intermediary.

Instances of possession were limited almost entirely to New England, but even in this receptive atmosphere there was wide disagreement as to the degree and frequency in which the condition occurred. Many adhered to the radical view that the mentally retarded, physically deformed, blind, deaf, or insane were actually "demoniacks," whom witches had assigned devils to attack. This encompassing theory stemmed from the prescientific presumption that all disease was magically created. A companion axiom held that self-destructive acts such as suicides were actually caused by temporary possession and occurred when devil torture became too great to be borne.

The most widely held sentiment suggested that possession was not an attack directed solely toward a single individual, but was actually part of a wider struggle between the forces of good and evil. Under this philosophy, the person possessed was considered merely an innocent vehicle, usually chosen at random, to play a role in a theological battle. Only in rare instances had the victims singled themselves out as targets by offending the witch, who in turn retaliated by summoning devils. A clear distinction was made in the public mind between spontaneous and voluntary possession. The afflicted, being possessed through no fault of their own, were blameless for any blasphemous actions or declarations made while under the demon's inhabitation. No stigma of sin or guilt was attached to anyone whose body was under the compulsory control of a foreign spirit. A far different view was taken of witches who occasionally displayed traits similar to those possessed. Because enchanters had voluntarily chosen to associate with Satan, no compassion tempered the repugnance in which they were held.

Instances of diabolical possession were viewed as exciting community events in Early America. The possibilities for social contact inherent in an affliction were so significant that the religious connotations were frequently relegated to a secondary role.

As soon as word was announced that a suspected incidence of possession had been discovered, local ministers, government officials, and other interested spectators flocked to observe the bewitched person. Customarily, every unusual action by the afflicted one was thoroughly discussed in the crowded sickroom. There was usually continuing chaos about the patient's bed as visitors arrived or departed, noisily exchanging places so that others might obtain a full view of the goings-on. The most advantagous positions were reserved for those elders who were considered knowledgeable in the subtleties of possession and the implications of physical symptoms.

In urban areas where trained medical practitioners were available, a doctor's examination was deemed necessary before the final conclusion could be made that the patient was indeed possessed. Such was the case with Elizabeth Knapp, reportedly attacked in 1671. In describing the happening, Groton minister Samuel Willard wrote:

> On the Sabbath the physician came, who judged a main part of her distemper to be natural, arising from the foulness of her stomack, and corruptness of her blood, occasioning fumes in her brain, and strange fansyes, whereupon . . . she was removed home and the succeeding weeks she took physick and was not in such violence handled in her fits as before, but enjoyed intermission and gave some hopes of recovery.

Eight days later, however, Elizabeth was again struck by the strange seizures and the physician, unable to cure her "distemper," pronounced it diabolically originated.

Undoubtedly a small number of doctors, whose cures had not proved effective against stubborn physical illness, chose to mask their failures by declaring the patient possessed and thus beyond the realm of human help. But most healers genuinely believed that their clients were inhabited by demons. Medical practitioners were subject to the same climate of superstition and prejudice that guided the attitudes of average citizens. Within such a framework, the outbreak of a rare or unidentified disease, which responded to no known cure, may well have seemed to be of supernatural cause.

A more realistic explanation is that the afflictions of some "possessed" persons were organic in origin, while others were psychological. A small number were probably related to epilepsy or schizophrenia, conditions whose origins were shrouded in mystery during the seventeenth century. Others may have suffered from severe manic-depression, a syndrome that could have been the "disease of astonishment" mentioned by doctors of the era. Huntington's disease, a neurological condition that produces uncontrolled motor activity similar to the convulsive seizures of possession, possibly accounted for a limited number of incidents. The greatest number of cases can be attributed to hysteria—or fraud. The lack of scientific knowledge eliminated medical explanations as a course of action for most physicians. For the health "experts" of the seventeenth century, a diagnosis of demonic attack, rather than physical illness, was an acceptable course.

After all hope of medical care had been exhausted, suspected victims were scrutinized for telltale signs considered indisputable evidence that demons had invaded the body. Scores of such signs had been identified and, although the symptoms were not expected to occur in every case, the presence of a significant number was considered sufficient to prove that the sickness was due to demons rather than disease.

In *Countrey Justice,* Michael Dalton chronicled the seven most important signs, and according to the jurist, indications that a "sick party be bewitched" included:

1. When a healthy body shall be suddenly taken &c without probable reason, or natural cause appearing.

2. When two or more are taken in the like strange fits in many things.

3. When the afflicted party in his fits doth tell truly many things, which the witch, or other parties absent are doing or saying and the like.

4. When the parties shall do many things strangely, or speak many things to purpose, and yet out of their fits know not anything thereof.

5. When there is a strength supernatural, as that a strong man or two shall not be able to keep down a child, or weak person, upon a bed.

6. When the party doth vomit up crooked pins, needles, nails, coal, lead, straw, hair, or the like.

7. When the party shall see visibly some apparition, and shortly thereafter some mischief shall befall him.

Dalton's guides were primarily aimed at assisting English courts and clerics in dealing with possession, but six of the suggested signs were also considered valid proof in the colonies. The sole exception involved item three. Clairvoyance was not recognized in the provinces as an indication of possession, but rather as a power reserved for witches.

In the colonies, as in England, some of Dalton's symptoms were regarded as more significant than others. The most important sign was the sudden onset of fits or seizures in a previously healthy individual. These spells of deviate motor activity lasted from periods of several minutes to lengthy bouts continuing for days. Each spasm was characterized by severe physical contortions of the body, in which the patient's limbs were twisted or knotted into positions considered impossible to be impostured by trickery. During the convulsions, the victim was also subject to grotesque writhing similar to epileptic fits, which alternated with periods of total paralysis identified as "catalepses" or "catoche." At unpredictable intervals, the paroxysms would suddenly stop and the afflicted person would return to normal. The only traces left of the possession would be extreme physical and mental exhaustion.

Graphic accounts of this deviate behavior were recorded by settlers who witnessed cases of supposed demonic attack. The most extensive accounts were provided by participants in the most highly publicized possession occurring in Early America. This incident involved four children of John Goodwin, a respected resident of North Boston, described by some as a "good liver."

Goodwin, a wealthy member of the Massachusetts community, had led a quiet and uneventful life in the years before the summer of 1688. At that time, however, an insignificant event occurred that would interrupt his unextraordinary existence and blossom into a major public controversy.

The incident began when Goodwin's oldest daughter, thirteen-year-old Martha, accused the family's washerwoman of stealing a supply of household linen. The servant's mother, an Irish woman named Glover, was enraged by the charge and openly attacked Martha in a near violent confrontation.

Soon after the argument, Martha became "indisposed in her health and visited with strange fits." Contemporary accounts note that she displayed the "stiffness and posture of one that had been two days laid out for dead." Soon Martha's seven-year-old sister was similarly seized, and two brothers, ages eleven and five, also succumbed. The rapid spreading of symptoms was interpreted as an extremely serious sign and doctors were summoned to examine the patients. All medical efforts to heal the illness proved futile, and at last Dr. Thomas Oakes, an eminent physician, announced that the maladies were caused by "hellish witchcraft."

The diagnosis was immediately accepted as valid, despite substantial evidence that the children may have been strongly influenced by outside suggestions. Most of the victims' symptoms and descriptions of torture corresponded to those revealed at a series of well-publicized witch trials held in 1684 at Suffolk, England. Details of the

Suffolk action were so widely discussed in the Massachusetts colony that the children were undoubtedly aware of the facts in the case. But instead of concluding that the youths had patterned their behavior on the English model, Bostonians viewed the coincidence as proof that the Goodwins' possession was authentic and supported by precedent. Equally important a factor in reinforcing the possession diagnosis was Goody Glover's past reputation as a dealer in magic. Rumors of her supernatural abilities were so pervasive that even her own husband had proclaimed her to be an enchanter. Goody Glover's connection with the incident was considered indeed suspicious, and she fell under attention as the probable cause of the children's affliction.

Cotton Mather, a constant visitor in the Goodwin household, carefully recorded the symptoms suffered by the children and published a complete account in his *Memorable Providences*. According to the tract:

> The variety of their tortures increased continually; and tho about nine or ten at night they always had a release from their miseries, and ate and slept all night for the most part indifferently well, yet in the day time they were handled with so many sorts of ails, that it would require of us almost as much time to relate them all, as it did of them to endure them. Sometimes they would be deaf, sometimes dumb, and sometimes blind, and often, all this at once. Once-while their tongues would be drawn down their throats; another-while they would be pull'd out upon their chins, to a prodigious length. They would have their mouths opened unto such a wideness that their jaws went out of joint; and anon they would clap together again with a force like that of a strong spring-lock. The same would happen to their shoulder-blades, and their elbows, and hand-wrists, and several of their joints.
>
> They would at times lie in a benummed condition; and be drawn together as those that are ty'd neck and heels; and presently be stretched out, yea, drawn backwards, to such a degree that it was fear'd the very skin of their bellies would have crack'd. They would make most pitteous out-cries, that they were cut with knives, and struck with blows that they could not bear. Their necks would be broken, so that their neck-bone would seem dissolved unto them that felt after it; and yet on the sudden, it would become again so stiff that there was not stirring of their heads, yea, their heads would be twisted almost round; and if main force at any time obstructed

a dangerous motion which they seem'd to be upon, they would roar exceedingly.

Although the appearance of convulsive distortions was sufficient to create a strong suspicion of possession, a second symptom, the displaying of great physical prowess, was also considered incriminating. The unusual powers were not credited to the patient, but explained as the preternatural strength of the possessing demon.

Elizabeth Knapp repeatedly demonstrated superhuman strength. According to eye witnesses, "she was violent in body motions, leapings, strainings, and strange agitations, scarce to be held in bounds by the strength of three or four; violent also in roarings and screamings . . . ." Even more spectacular abilities were demonstrated by Boston's Margaret Rule in 1693. In formal affidavits, several settlers declared that Margaret had performed numerous feats of levitation. One document asserted:

> I do testify that I have seen Margaret Rule in her afflictions from the invisible world, lifted up from her bed, wholly by an invisible force, a great way towards the top of the room where she lay; in her being so lifted, she had not assistance from any use of her own arms or hands or any other part of her body, not so much as her heels touching her bed, or resting on any support whatsoever. And I have seen her thus lifted, when not only a strong person hath thrown his whole weight across her to pull her down; but several other persons have endeavoured, with all their might, to hinder her from being so raised up, which I suppose that several others will testify as well as myself, when call'd unto it.

A third important sign of possession was transmogrification. In this process, the victim underwent radical physical changes that supposedly resulted from the taking over of the body by a demon. After the transfer became complete, the victim's mind and body were believed to be completely under the control of the invading devil. Thus the external changes that occurred were thought to mirror the characteristics of the evil being inside. Horrifying facial grimaces were considered a reflection of the countenance of the possessing spirit. Gnarled hands suggested a devil's claw-like appendages. A change in body shape or size indicated the particular stature of the inhabiting demon.

Samuel Holly claimed to have seen Catreen Branch undergo a

temporary period of transmogrification and reported that "in her fit
. . . she did swell in her breasts (as she lay on her bed) and they rose
as like bladders and suddenly passed into her belly, and in a short time
returned to her breasts, and in a short time her breasts fell . . . ." A
similar incident was recorded in the possession of Martha Goodwin,
whose "belly swelled like a drum" and emitted loud croaking noises.

In addition to alterations in physical appearance, possessed persons might also experience changes in voice tenor and language
fluency. Afflicted persons were constantly described as "roaring out"
in deep or piercing tones. Such vocal frequencies were thought to be
the accustomed means of communication used by underworld spirits.

The ability to converse in a language previously unknown to the
patient and the faculty to speak in unknown tongues were further
indications that a demon was in control. Ann Cole of Hartford cried
out nonsensical passages, such as "Ah, she runs to the crock," during
her 1662 affliction. In one instance, just before she lapsed into Dutch,
a language unknown to her before the possession, Ann's inner voice
purportedly called out: "Let us confound her language, that she may
tell no more tales." Sarah Kecham observed Catreen Branch singing
merrily in French, and Martha Goodwin developed sudden fluency
not only in Greek and Latin but in classical Hebrew as well.

Elizabeth Knapp, described as a "ventriloqua" because of the
curious voices crying out during her 1671 possession, was more suc-
cinct in her mutterings. Her most frequent cries were constant repeti-
tions of the word "money."

The crying out of unintelligible or seemingly senseless phrases
was interpreted in two ways. In one explanation, although the spoken
words had no meaning to human ears, the messages were believed to
be easily understood by possessing demons, who also conversed in
"devil language." The second theory was that demons intentionally
garbled the tongue of their victims in order to hamper interrogation,
which might lead to a possible cure.

Occasionally, voices spoke in "labial letters." In this manifesta-
tion, victims showed no physical signs of speaking, but distinct words
could be heard coming from parts of their body, such as the throat.

When demonic voices changed mid-sentence in tenor or when
several inner spirits seemed to be carrying on a private conversation,
the case was considered one of dual possession. In Early America, the

record for this particular form of bewitchment was held by Margaret Rule, whose illness was attributed to eight separate specters operating simultaneously.

Afflicted persons could also take on the characteristics of beast-like devils. This animal possession or zooanthropy was introduced into the colonies from continental Europe, where it had previously become a widespread phenomenon. Many people became so convinced that they had been bewitched into were-animals that they chose to leave their homes and live in the forests. Bestial possession was recognized in America, but the practice never resulted in the extreme preoccupation that developed on the continent. Colonial incidences were usually limited to brief periods in which animal characteristics were displayed. During a 1659 possession at Branford, Connecticut, a young boy who had earlier associated with conjurers was heard to bark like a fox and hiss like a serpent. Elizabeth Knapp not only produced canine growls but also bleated like a calf and crowed like a cock.

The four Goodwin children exhibited a wide range of zooanthropical characteristics. According to Mather:

> They would bark at one another like dogs, and again purr like so many cats. . . . Yea, they would fly like geese and be carried with an incredible swiftness thro the air, having but just their toes now and then upon the ground, and their arms waved like the wings of a bird. One of them, in the house of a kind neighbour and gentleman (Mr. Willis), flew the length of the room, about twenty foot, and flew just into an infant's high-armed chair (as 'tis affirmed), none seeing her feet all the way touch the floor.

Afflicted persons who descended into dream-like trances were described as suffering from unconscious possession. In this form, victims emerged from their seizures unaware of events that took place during the convulsions. More frequently, however, bewitched persons suffered non-somnambulistic possession and were thus able to provide graphic descriptions of the tortures to which they had been exposed. Mercy Short maintained that she had been forced to swallow a whitish poison, which caused her abdomen to swell painfully. The servant girl also exhibited stigmatas in the form of skin lesions. These "witches' wounds," considered evidence that the victim had been engaged in battle with the possessing demons, could take the form of bruises, burns, cuts, or other marks of unknown origin. They were identified as "supernatural" primarily because of the rapidity with which they healed or became invisible.

In almost every instance of conscious possession, victims claimed to have seen visions of spirits either preceding or during a fit. Sometimes the apparition was of the devil, who attempted to recruit the individual as a witch. Failure to sign the black book resulted in the onset of more severe pain. Such a situation confronted Catreen Branch, who announced that during one seizure Satan had threatened to "tear her in pieces" if she did not consent to join his service. Mercy Short, who had been taken captive in an Indian massacre of her entire family, also saw a vision of the devil. According to her description, the demon was a tawny man with straight black hair and cloven feet.

One of the most elaborate post-convulsive tales was told by Elizabeth Knapp, who announced she had been taken on a guided tour of hell. When Elizabeth asked her demon escort to transport her to heaven for a similar inspection, the devil refused, confiding that it was "an ugly place, and that none went thither but a company of base rogues."

Victims also saw apparitions of the witches who were supposedly responsible for the possession. In Hartford, Ann Cole spied the specter of Rebecca Greensmith, who later confessed to instigating the affliction. Catreen Branch saw not one, but six witches in ghostly form.

Other signs of possession were chronicled, but most were experienced with far less frequency than the traditional occurrences of seizures, unnatural strength, and transmogrification.

The vomiting of pins or other sharp objects, though common in England, was rarely mentioned in the colonies. The symptom may have been the basis for an important class of provincial signs involving convulsive swallowing, gagging, or a strong sense of strangulation. In extreme cases, possessed persons were so choked that the eating of solid food was impossible. Forced fasts lasting as long as several weeks often resulted from the throat obstructions and were presumably aimed at weakening the will of the victim so that the temptations of the devil would appear more attractive. More than two centuries after the symptoms were observed in the colonies, such constrictions of the throat were medically classified as classic signs of hysteria.

The European theory that possession usually occurred in large groups rather than with a single individual was not recognized as a basic American concept. Although the Goodwin children did suffer simultaneously, their possession was an exception to the general custom, where affliction was considered an isolated incident limited to a single victim.

Clues suggesting demonic inhabitation could also be found in a victim's sickroom. Spectral flames observed about the bed represented the fires of hell. The smell of brimstone or musk was seen as being left behind by hell-dwelling spirits. Bedclothes that mysteriously flew about without human instigation were believed to be evidence that a physical struggle was being waged by the inhabiting forces against the holy powers attempting to cleanse the victim.

Several signs common in Europe were not recorded in America. One of these involved the theory that during seizures, victims of possession routinely made lewd exposure of their bodies while shouting obscene or blasphemous curses. The absence of these symptoms may have been due to the sexually repressive atmosphere of staid New England, which contrasted significantly to the bawdy customs of seventeen-century Europe.

Foretelling or divining was also not evidenced in the provinces. Afflicted persons neither displayed nor were expected to have any special ability to foresee the future. Instead, these powers were proofs of witchcraft and gifts of the devil. The ability of possessed persons to relate events that took place when they were physically absent was also not included as a possession symptom. Like clairvoyance, this ability was credited only to enchanters, who were able to transmogrify or become invisible in order to observe others without being detected.

When supernatural symptoms had proved beyond a doubt that a patient was under the influence of diabolical possession, the case passed into the hands of the clergy. For centuries in England and Europe, holy men and saints had performed miraculous cures of possession. Victims were often committed to monasteries or took vows of the clergy in an attempt to break the spells of bewitchment.

Dependence upon the ministry was equally important in the colonies, where it was presumed that the powers of the devil would be broken only by the intervention of God, brought to bear through the supplications of the clergy. But unlike Europe, where flagellation, fumigation, and formal rites of exorcism were routinely prescribed for treatment, colonial clergymen had no formal procedures for producing cures.

Generally, large prayer sessions were considered the most efficacious means of eliminating possession. These bedside vigils were usually attended by crowds of pious folk who were led by a local minister. Long prayers and oratories that called upon God to free the soul of the sufferer were the core of this approach. In the partially successful exorcism of Margaret Rule, for example, an estimated forty supplicants crowded into the sickroom to take part in the healing. Private prayers might also be offered, but they were preferred less than the mass gatherings, which coordinated the collective pleadings of many citizens.

Attempts at exorcism usually resulted in the display of an additional symptom. This sign was based on the concept that any reference to God or a reading from a holy book would severely wound the inhabiting spirit. In order to ease the pain, the devil countermanded the exorcism by inflicting the most terrible tortures on the victim. Through this means the spirit sought to capitalize on the sympathies of the healers who, unwilling to submit their patient to continued abuse, would cease their petitions to God. An additional benefit to the devil was that the shrieking of the pained individual usually drowned out oral Bible readings and disturbed the meditation of the supplicants.

Not all religious works, however, produced such dire reactions. By coincidence, Boston's puritan clergy discovered that only those books endorsed by their religion resulted in torment to the demons. The very appearance of the puritan Bible or catechism was sufficient cause to set off wild activities on the part of the possessed. No reaction, however, was given when "heathen" materials, such as tracts by Quakers, "papists," or Anglicans, were produced. This finding proved entirely consistent with the New England concept that the writings of other religions were expressions of the devil, while the saints references were those of God.

Fastings could be used in conjunction with prayer to promote recovery. Denial of food was a self-sacrifice traditionally recommended as a means of bringing one closer to God. Special days of abstinence and humiliation were decreed in colonial New England, so that citizens might reevaluate their sinful lives and become more worthy followers. The use of fasting by possessed persons was aimed at enabling the victim to focus clean and holy thoughts upon the evil spirit.

Despite their unrefinement, the healing techniques of the clergy were remarkably effective, and the recovery rate for possessed provincials was nearly a hundred percent. The rate of the cures ranged from dramatic to near imperceptible. In some instances, all signs of possession suddenly ceased during a prayer session and never returned. In others, recovery involved a gradual lessening in the frequency and severity of attacks. Sessions of prayer and fasting were continued until the symptoms disappeared entirely.

In the case of the Goodwin children, a day-long prayer session attended by ministers from Cambridge and Boston resulted in the "cure" of the youngest girl, but the remaining three children were for the most part not affected at that time. Puritan attempts at exorcism proved more beneficial in the case of Mercy Short. A three-day meeting temporarily relieved all symptoms, and a complete healing was accomplished when the procedure was repeated a second time.

After prayer, time was the most common healer. Just as signs of possession tended to increase with heightened public interest, so did symptoms lessen when the initial elation and curiosity abated. In many instances, the victim's torment disappeared completely after several months of inattention by local residents. Like more spectacular recoveries, these healings were credited to a victory of God over the devil.

CHAPTER II

Familiars and
Other Witch Helpers

A LL along the eastern coast, from Puritan New England to the Anglican colonies of the South, Early Americans agreed that witchcraft was closely interwoven with the animal world. Cutting across differences in religion, language, and homeland was the firm belief that witches, unlike normal humans, had special powers to control both real and unearthly creatures. The evolution of this concept was simple. Most immigrants viewed the country's wildlife with a puzzlement and fear similar to that accorded to the supernatural world.

Ignorance was a major factor contributing to the mystical awe in which animals were viewed, for life in Europe had little prepared pioneers to cope with a primitive environment. Unlike the crowded urban areas of the Old World, colonial settlements were surrounded by an abundance of strange and unknown creatures. Few of the immigrants, as former city dwellers, possessed even the most elementary knowledge of the types, habits, and behavior of the animals that dwelt in America.

More subtle influences were the exaggerated but enthusiastic reports published in Europe by early explorers. These accounts no doubt created preconceived notions in prospective settlers that the areas across the Atlantic were havens of magical creatures. Equally fantastic were the descriptions found in promotional literature distributed by land-grant holders in an attempt to promote large-scale immigration. These seventeenth century pamphlets describing North America asserted that lobsters grew to be five feet long and crabs were so gigantic that a single specimen could feed four people. The bodies of birds were credited with possessing the ingredients to effect miraculous cures and rattlesnakes were described as being able to fly through the air and kill with a single breath.

Interchange with the Indians may have reinforced the immigrants' concepts concerning the preternaturalness of animals. In the eastern colonies, where settlers often viewed red people as servants of the devil, animal worship played an important part in the religion of many tribes. Various beasts were considered vessels in which lived the spirits of the gods. Deers, snakes, and insects were shown homage by the Indians, who courted animal spirits in an attempt to gain success in love, war, or hunting.

Members of most tribes conversed with animals and expected replies in return. Colonials, observing the "pagan" conversations, may well have been further persuaded that certain creatures were representatives of Satan.

The traditions of Europe, when coupled with the ignorance of colonists and the new-world environment, convinced even the most educated that beasts should be regarded with caution. The wariness sometimes extended to domestic animals as well. Massachusetts Governor John Winthrop trembled as he wrote in his journal the news that a six-eyed calf had been born in the colony. Winthrop's consternation stemmed from his fear that the event portended some awful calamity.

The most important creatures in American witchlore were familiars, demon servants that took the form of living animals in order to surreptitiously serve the enchanters. Familiars were indispensable in the practice of magic. Not only did the creatures assist witches in casting spells, but by disguising themselves as normal beasts of the wilderness, the spirits could move undetected through the countryside, spying upon innocent citizens and performing evil assignments.

While the existence of familiars was subject to no dispute, the spirits' physical makeup was the subject of some disagreement. One school of thought held that the helpers were actually transmogrified demons, presented by Satan as gifts to newly recruited witches. A second group held that the familiars were conjured by enchanters through magic. In these instances, the powers of the familiars came not from Satan but from the witches. A final belief was that familiars were not demon spirits at all, but were actual animals that had been bewitched into performing supernatural acts.

Although the familiar could take the appearance of any beast, some visages were preferred to others. Usually the forms chosen were those that would be most inconspicuous in a rural environment. Foxes, rabbits, weasels, rats, mice, and groundhogs were common forms. Frogs and toads, long symbols of inspiration and good luck, were also favorites, as were such insects as wasps, moths, and flies.

The presumption that domestic pets and barnyard stock such as hogs, dogs, and cats could be familiars was a distinctly Anglo-American belief. In order to separate innocent animals from demons in disguise, several items of suspicion were devised. Any black animal was immediately suspect, for ebony was considered the traditional color favored by evil forces. The giving of names to pets or livestock was also incriminating. The bestowing of such a title was considered a show of respect and personification implying connotations of human rather than animal qualities. Persons seen speaking to non-human creatures were instantly suspect. Rather than merely an owner displaying tender affection for a pet, the conversation was thought to reveal a witch ordering her familiar to perform some evil deed.

A familiar's most important function was to perform magical tasks requested by the witch, but helpers might also serve as messengers between enchanters or between witches and the devil. In Europe it was believed that familiars carried invitations to the Black Sabbath and that larger animals transported witches through the air to the unholy gatherings. The idea of familiars as messengers and conveyers was not present in America, where collaboration between witches was virtually unknown and sabbaths were rare events. Instead of animals, colonial enchanters preferred to nightride on broomstaffs, fireplace spits, or poles. Such items were more practical modes of supernatural locomotion, for American familiars were usually smaller animals than those popular in Europe. The difficulties in flying above the ground on a small mouse or miller fly were evidently too great for even the powers of sorcerers.

Birds, long an object of superstition and mystery to primitive people awed by flight, were occasionally identified as familiars. Massachusetts' Sarah Good was accused of having both a cat and a yellow bird as helpers. Sarah's daughter claimed that the woman had not one, but three familiars who specialized in inflicting pain upon young children. Black birds, crows, and ravens, all signified as harbingers of death, were particularly menacing familiars and created the most severe dread of any demon spirit.

In addition to familiars who took the form of identifiable animals, witches would also be aided by helpers who took unknown forms. Accused witch Sarah Osburn of Salem was presumed to possess an extremely hairy familiar about three feet high. The spirit sported a long nose and resembled no natural animal. The helper of Sarah's reported colleague Sarah Good was rumored to be "a thing all over hairy."

One of the most spectacular descriptions of familiars came at the trial of suspected witch Alice Parker. The woman's accuser, a local tavern keeper, maintained that soon after an argument with the defendant, he was attacked by several shadowy animals with gleaming eyes. The story not only demonstrates that supernatural specters were part of colonial witchlore, but also gives some credence to the theory that in heavy-drinking Early America, visions of specters were sometimes the result of delirium tremens.

In 1682, Antonio and Mary Hortado of Salmon Falls, Maine, had an experience with a particularly grotesque familiar. While crossing a river near their home, the pair saw a dismembered spirit swimming just in front of their canoe. The animal showed "the head of a man new shorn, and the tail of a white cat, about two or three foot distant from each other." The most amazing part of the vision, according to the witnesses, was that no body joined the two parts together.

Familiars, whether shaped as ghastly specters or as everyday animals, were not thought capable of sustaining themselves without nourishment. Their food, however, was not normal animal fare, but consisted of a secretion that was produced only in the body of the witch whom they served. Thus, each day, familiars were forced to return to their owners in order to suck the necessary substance.

Because of this widespread superstition, the existence of an unusual protuberance on the body of a suspected enchanter was conclusive evidence of guilt. These blemishes, called "teats," were thought to be nipple-shaped portions of skin from which the familiars fed. Like the devil's marks, teats could be found on any part of the anatomy, but were usually hidden in unobtrusive locations so that accidental discovery would be difficult.

Court-ordered body searches aimed at uncovering teats were frequently conducted by provincial juries especially selected for the task because of their knowledge of witchlore. However, the hunt for supernatural nipples was not always so formally conducted. Mary Parsons claimed to have thoroughly searched her husband for teats while he slept. The investigation did not prove particularly fruitful, for Mary admitted to finding nothing except what she said could be hidden on his "secret privates."

In some instances, teats were discovered accidentally. Charles Browne, a witness in the trial of John Godfrey, maintained that seven years earlier he had spied a nipple beneath Godfrey's tongue as the suspected witch opened his mouth to yawn in church. A similar unintentional discovery was made by the constable of Salisbury. The lawman, while stripping enchanter Eunice Cole for a flogging, noted a suspicious "blue thing" on one breast. A local court was promptly informed and asked to order a more conventional examination of Eunice.

When a teat was discovered, the blemish was watched for twenty-four hours by observers anxious to detect any change in size or shape. If the nipple enlarged during that period, it was assumed to be filling with a day's supply of the familiar's food. If it decreased, spectators concluded that a familiar had managed to suck its daily meal without detection. No change in the teat's appearance indicated it was a natural infirmity.

Because folk beliefs were not codified and tended to vary among different segments of the population, confusion was sometimes created when an incriminating sign was identified. For example, unless indisputable evidence could be presented that proved ownership of a supposed familiar by a specific individual, charges and countercharges were likely to become so involved that the entire matter was dropped. Such a situation took place in 1659 when allegations of witchcraft were made against John Godfrey.

The dispute began when four members of the Job Tylar family presented an affidavit describing an incident that they considered damaging to the suspect. In the joint document, Tylar, his wife Mary, and their children Moses and Mary reported that

> they saw a thing like a bird to come in at the door of their house with John Godfrey in the night about the bigness of a black bird or rather bigger, to wit as big as a pigeon, and did fly about, John Godfrey labouring to catch it and the bird vanished, as they conceived, through the chink of a cojointed board, and being asked by the man of the house wherefore it came, he [Godfrey] answered: "It came to suck your wife." This was (as they remember) about five or six years since.

In the Tylars' opinion, the simultaneous entry of Godfrey and the magical bird was suspicious indeed and a clear illustration of a witch on the prowl with his familiar. But, according to deposition, the opposite conclusion was drawn by Godfrey. He, upon entering the Tylar house and seeing the bird vanish, deduced that the family was harboring a devil's servant, which had come to suck its mistress. The court, confused by the conflicting accusations, was unable to reach a decision. All charges were dismissed.

The existence of familiars had been acknowledged in Europe since classical times, but the spirits played a much larger role in the witchlore of England and the colonies than on the continent. Puritans were particularly interested in the subject, perhaps because of the many biblical references dealing with animal helpers. Among the most specific passages which helped frame the harsh New England position were verses in the book of Leviticus that announced:

> Regard not them that have familiar spirits, neither seek after wizards, to be defiled by them: I am the Lord your God.

> And the soul that turneth after such as have familiar spirits, and after wizards, to go a whoring after them, I will even set my face against that soul, and will cut him off from among his people.

> A man also or woman that hath a familiar spirit, or that is a wizard, shall surely be put to death: they shall stone them with stones: their blood shall be upon them.

Supernatural animals were not always familiars, for witches were assumed to have the power of transfiguration or the ability to change into bestial form. This metamorphosis enabled witches to roam about undetected by humans and to do foul deeds without fear of discovery. In England, witches supposedly preferred to assume shapes of small insects, such as bees or flies, and required a special ointment in order to accomplish the change. The magical salve was not an item of speculation in the colonies. Citizens either did not consider the matter important enough for speculation or believed the witch possessed powers so great that the change could be made by will alone.

The legends dealing with a witch's power to metamorphose may have developed during medieval times or in early pagan cultures, where members of primitive cults donned animal skins and horns as part of tribal rites. As centuries passed, believers in witchcraft may have elevated the custom to a more sophisticated level, involving not a superficial disguise, but an actual change into human form. Like familiars, witch transfiguration was supported by biblical "evidence," such as the story of Lot's wife, who was changed into a pillar of salt by supernatural intervention.

Two old-world theories on transfiguration did not receive wide acceptance west of the Atlantic. The continental belief in harpies, heinous birds with human faces, may have been completely unknown. However, a somewhat similar creature was described by Salem's J. Louder, who claimed to have been attacked by an animal with the body of a monkey, the feet of a fowl, and the face of a man. When Louder struck at the specter it flew away and disappeared behind an apple tree. The classical concept of lycanthropy, the changing of humans into wolves, was also rejected in America. With the exception of Salem's Sarah Good, who was alleged to have assumed the shape of a wolf, lycanthropy was of no importance in the colonies.

The transfigured forms preferred by colonial witches were not exotic creatures, but beasts common in the lives of simple pioneers. The most unusual metamorphosis was that credited to Salisbury's Mary Bradbury, who was accused of turning herself into a blue boar.

Hampton's Eunice Cole, a woman whose various witchcraft trials covered a period of twenty-five years, was said to have appeared in the shape of a dog, an eagle, and a cat in order to lure Anne Smith to live with her. According to irate neighbors of Portsmouth's Jane Walford, a supernatural cat was also active in that community.

Susannah Trimmings testified that during an argument, Jane changed into a cat and disappeared into the air. As the feline faded from view, Susannah was "struck, as with a clap of fire on the back." The attack was presumably a bolt of lightning or a ball of flames conjured by the angered witch. At least three other citizens reported seeing Jane in animal form. Goody Evans, who claimed to be followed wherever she went by a yellowish cat, took refuge in the home of Agnes Puddington. Agnes also saw the apparition and called her husband John to drive away the evil spirit. According to court records, the attempt was only partially successful:

> John came and saw a cat in the garden, took down his gun to shoot her. The cat got upon a tree, and the gun would not take fire and afterward the cock would not stand. She afterwards saw three cats. The yellow one vanished away on the plain ground, and she could not tell which way they went.

The saga of the disappearing cat and crippled rooster was damaging indeed. Lower courts twice found evidence against Jane sufficient for referral to a higher court, but the cases against her were ultimately dismissed. Thirteen years later, however, the suspected enchanter was back in court, this time as the complainant in a slander action against Robert Couch. Couch, a healer, had stated that during the two years he had been practicing in Portsmouth, he had seen many persons "strangely distempered." Their illnesses, he concluded, were not naturally inspired, but the result of diabolical agents. Although Couch maintained that he had not directly charged Jane with instigating the afflictions, the court ruled otherwise. Couch was found guilty of defamation and sentenced to pay £5 in damages and all court costs.

The charm of transfiguration had one major drawback for the witch. Any injuries inflicted upon the enchanter while in animal form would appear in the same location when the change back to human shape was made. Thus, important evidence of guilt could be discovered by searching the bodies of suspects for wounds that offended citizens believed they had inflicted upon familiars.

Newberry's Jonathan Woodman declared that Elizabeth Morse had shown incriminating wounds. At Elizabeth's witchcraft trial Woodman testified to a strange experience that had happened one dark night as he walked through the forest. Woodman observed:

> I met with a white thing like a cat, which did play at my legs, and I did often kick at it, having no weapon in my hand; at last [I] struck it with my feet against the fence ere I saw Webster's house, and there it stopped with a loud cry after the manner of a cat and I see it no more.

I further testify, that William Morse of Newberry did owne that he did send for a doctor for his wife the same night and same time that I was troubled with that cat abovementioned, which was some grounds for suspicion.

John Pressy of Amesbury reported a similar incident that took place in 1668. Pressy announced that one evening as he headed home, a strange supernatural light began to pursue him. In order to defend himself, Pressy beat unmercifully at the spirit. The following day, the settler discovered that rumored enchanter Susannah Martin was indisposed because of a severe thrashing. Pressy and others concluded that the beating had been that which he administered to the ghostly form.

While only a small percentage of the animal population was considered to be supernatural in origin, all creatures were thought to be susceptible to control by witches. A small number of reports dealing with bewitched animals involved wild creatures, such as the swarm of bees captured through the special powers of witch Katherine Harrison. Wild animals also played a role in the 1626 hearing against Virginia's Goodwife Wright, probably the first colonial to be formally accused of witchcraft. According to complainant Sargeant Booth, Goody Wright, out of vindictiveness, had cast a protective spell over all the animals in the forest. According to the minutes of the colonial court: "Booth went forth with his peece, and came to good game and very fayre to shoot at, but for a long tyme after, he could never kill anything."

Because of the rarity and importance of domestic livestock, tales involving bewitchment of cattle were the most frequently circulated stories. Enchanters supposedly could steal milk directly from a cow's udder or make the animals go dry in the bag. These tricks could be accomplished while the witch remained safely home, simulating the milking process by tugging on stool legs, pot hooks, ropes, or other objects resembling an udder. Wilmot Redd of Marblehead was accused not only of turning milk into "blue wool"—probably mold—but also of curdling the liquid as it was squeezed into the pail.

Most provincial legends involving the disappearance or change in quality of milk could be explained rationally. Milk theft was a common crime and frequently curdling or spoiling could result from the lack of adequate refrigeration. Goody Redd's blue mold was probably natural bacterial growth; changes in the color of milk can also be accounted for by the varied diet of the stock, which often grazed on wild plants and berries. But colonial farmers, non-expert owners of a family cow, saw such unusual happenings not as explainable incidents, but as the evil retributions of some offended sorcerer.

Hugh Parsons of Springfield was one victim of this lack of scientific knowledge. Sarah Edwards, testifying at Parsons' 1651 witchcraft trial, stated that some two years earlier one of her prize cows had been supernaturally afflicted. According to Sarah, the bewitchment was spurred when she refused to sell Parsons a large quantity of milk. The animal customarily produced three quarts per meal, but after the disagreement was able to give only one quart, and that "yellow as saffron." The cow's production continued to decline and turn various strange colors. A week after the argument, presumably when Parsons' wrath had cooled, the animal returned to normal.

In addition to milk stealing, the maiming or killing of cattle by magic was also considered a serious threat. John Pressy reported that during a fight with Susannah Martin, she had prophesied that he would never prosper or own more than two cows. Twenty years passed and, according to Pressy, during the entire period he had never been able to keep more than a pair of livestock alive at any one time. J. Howe, in charging his sister-in-law Elizabeth Howe with witchery, reported that after an argument between the couple, several of his healthy stock leaped into the air about three feet and then collapsed dead. Mercy Disborough was accused of venting her anger in a similar manner. Thomas Benit declared that during one fracas, Mercy threatened to make him "bare as a bird's tail." He lost four calves and thirty lambs as a result of the curse.

Stories involving the bewitchment of horses were only slightly less frequent than those dealing with cattle. Under one common charm, the steeds could be "pixeyled" or prevented from walking in a straight line from point to point. Instead, horses bewitched in this manner merely circled about continuously until the spell was broken.

Horses could also provide companionship for traveling witches. Mary Parsons, accusing her husband of sorcery, testified that often just before he arrived home at night, a roar like "forty horses" filled the air. Mary, who would later be acquitted of witchcraft allegations but hanged for murder, suggested that the eerie sound was the galloping of Hugh's spiritual companions.

All witches possessed the power of magical flight, but sometimes enchanters chose to undertake journeys on horseback. These secret jaunts always occurred at night and an animal taken on such a trip was identified as being "hagridden."

In 1692, Isaac Cummins testified in Salem court that defendant Elizabeth Howe had either ridden or bewitched his mare. Although the witness had no real proof to substantiate the claim, he related a chain of circumstances that were considered indeed incriminating.

The incident began when Elizabeth's son asked to borrow Cummins' mare. The request was refused. The horse, which seemed normal and healthy, changed dramatically just two days after young Howe's visit. The alteration was drastic to owner Cummins, who explained:

> The said mare as I did apprehend did show as if she had been much abused by riding, and her flesh, as I thought, much wasted, and her mouth much seemingly to my apprehension much abused and hurt with ye bridle bits. I, seeing ye mare in such a sad condition, I took up the said mare and put her into my barn and she would eat no manner of things as for provender or anything which we gave her.

Cummins, concerned with the sudden change in condition, sent for Thomas Andros, a man evidently considered somewhat of an amateur veterinarian. After Andros' medical remedies failed to revive the animal, he suggested that the mare was suffering from either a serious "baly ach" or was bewitched and thus beyond medical cure.

In order to settle the matter, Andros proposed that a test be conducted, which would prove if witchcraft was involved. The trial was a well-known procedure that involved the placing of a lighted pipe or fire near the rear end of the horse. If the animal had been ridden by a witch, some of the traces of hell would remain and burn bright blue. To colonials, the telltale hue represented the color of brimstone, but the indigo tint was actually caused by nitrogenous gases escaping from the animal's digestive tract.

Cummins was not enthusiastic about the suggested test, which he considered illegal. Andros calmed the owner's fears and at last Cummins agreed to conduct the experiment. He reported:

> I took a clean pipe and filled it with tobacco and did light it and went with the pipe lit to the barn. Then the said Andros used the pipe

as he said before he would and the pipe of tobacco did blaze and burn blue. Then I said to my brother Andros: "You shall try no more, it is not lawful." He said: "I will try again once more," which he did and then there arose a blaze from the pipe of tobacco which seemed to me to cover the buttocks of the said mare. The blaze went upward towards the roof of the barn and in the roof of the barn there was a great crackling as if the barn would have fallen or been burnt, which seemed so to us which were within and some that were without and we had no other fire in the barn but only a candle and a pipe of tobacco. And then I said I thought my barn or my mare must go.

Although the results of Andros' experiment indicated that magic was indeed involved in the mare's sickness, Cummins was not completely satisfied. Instead, he called in John Hunkins, another expert, who suggested that an attempt be made to break the magical charm that had been cast. Hunkins' counterspell involved cutting off and throwing into the fire a bit of flesh from the horse. This procedure was believed to serve as an undeniable summons, calling whomever had created the harmful spell back to the scene of the crime. A visitor appearing unexpectedly and unbidden after such a test had been conducted was immediately suspect in the affair. In order to avoid discovery, it was assumed that the witch would lift any charm that had been set.

Cummins was not enthralled with the idea of participating in still another dubious test and testified:

> The next day, being Lord's Day, I spoke to my brother Andros at noon to come to see the said mare, and said Andros came and what he did I say not. The same Lord's Day at night, my neighbor John Hunkins came to my house and he and I went into my barn to see this mare. Said Hunkins: "If I were you, I would cut off a piece of this mare and burn it." I said: "No, not today," but if she lived til tomorrow morning, he might cut off a piece of her and burn [it] if he would. Presently as we had spoken these words, we stepped out of the barn and immediately the said mare fell down dead and never stirred as we could perceive, after she fell down, but lay dead.

The unexpected death of the horse coming just after the burning test had been discussed could have been interpreted as a further indication of witchcraft. The enchanter, although not present in the barn, knew that a test was being contemplated. In order to thwart the procedure, the mare had been bewitched to death.

The death of an afflicted animal did not completely hamper the conduct of such countermagic. At a 1684 hearing into the behavior of Pennsylvanian Margaret Matson, witness Annakey Coolin testified that the heart of a calf believed to be enchanted had been boiled in an effort to discover the identity of the guilty sorcerer. According to Annakey, soon after the organ had been placed on the fire, Margaret appeared unexpectedly and "visibly decomposed."

Human excrement and urine as well as inanimate objects could be burned. In Springfield, a slice of pudding, which citizens thought was under a magical spell, was cast into the fire. When Hugh Parsons stumbled uninvited onto the scene one hour later, he was deemed undeniably guilty of sorcery.

If real horses were unavailable for hagriding, colonials believed that witches would substitute human beings for natural steeds. Sometimes the victims were physically transformed into horses, but in most cases the unfortunate settlers were left in human form while being compelled to gallop about. In either situation, the experience was known as a "nightmare." The condition always occurred during periods of sleep and was thought akin to dreams, considered during the seventeenth century to be messages from the unknown world.

Nightmares were particularly common in Virginia, where settlements were farther apart than in compact New England and horses were a vitally important means of transportation. The condition was characterized by an overwhelming sensation of flying or falling through the air. A feeling of suffocation was frequently experienced, together with an awareness that great weights were being placed on the body. Fear was always present and was sometimes accompanied by palpitations of the heart.

In England the condition was called "the mare" and was believed to be caused by the entering into the body of a foreign spirit. The inhabitation could be prevented or ended by the presence of a common herb named St. John's Wort. In the colonies, nightmares were not associated with the temporary possession of a body by a demon, but instead centered on the mere transportation of a witch from one place to another.

Anne Ball in King and Queen County, Virginia, seemed particularly susceptible to being hagridden. Anne claimed not only that Nell Crane had saddled her twice, but added that Eleanor Morris had galloped her about so vigorously that she was tired almost to death. The jury, after hearing Anne's story, was not favorably impressed, and instead of finding Nell and Eleanor guilty of witchcraft, the officials convicted Anne of defamation of character.

In the local court of Princess Anne County, Virginia, John Byrd and his wife, Anne, sued Charles Kinsey for defamation and spreading damaging rumors. The complainants alleged that Kinsey had "falsely and scandalously defamed them, saying that the said Anne did ride him from his house to Elizabeth Russell's, and that by such his discourse, she was reported and rendered to be a witch or such like person . . . ."

Kinsey's gossip had set other tongues to wagging. In a corresponding action, the Byrds filed suit against John Pitts, who had said they "rid him along the seaside and home to his own house."

Kinsey and Pitts, when called before the bar to either prove their accusations or face legal penalty, modified their tales. Kinsey admitted that he might have only "dreamed" the incident. Pitts said that the hagriding had happened according to his "thoughts apprehension."

In both cases, the jury found in favor of the defendants, thus ruling that the men believed they had been ridden by Anne. No judicial comment was made as to whether the incident had happened and no award of damages was made to any party in the dispute. The fact that no further attempts were made to investigate the allegations of witchcraft lodged against the Virginia woman indicates that accusations of nightriding were not considered a particularly damaging slander in the colony. The superficial manner in which the case was handled substantiates the view that the charge was made so often it had lost all fearful connotations.

Allegations of witchcraft were not limited only to the tobacco colony. In Southampton, Long Island, Edward Lacy spread the rumor that he had been ridden for three nights by a Mrs. Thomas Travally. Goodman Travally sued Lacy for defamation, but an out-of-court settlement was evidently reached and no additional action was taken. As late as 1724, when most formal charges of witchcraft had disappeared from the American scene, rumors involving hagriding were still circulating. The eighteenth-century action involved Sarah Spencer of Colchester, New Hampshire, who was accused of "riding and pinching" Elizabeth Ashley. Elizabeth's husband retaliated for his wife's mistreatment by making threats against the supposed sorcerer. Sarah's husband promptly sued the Ashleys, asking £500 damages for the harming of her good name. Although the court ruled that Sarah's reputation had been injured, only £5 was awarded. This figure was later reduced to a token settlement of one shilling. As in Virginia, the New Hampshire authorities seemed to view hagriding accusations as only minor slights and considered those making such charges as somewhat mentally unbalanced. In the case of Sarah Spencer, for example, officials ordered that a formal examination be made into the sanity of the Ashleys. Both were found compos mentis.

A final area in which witches were believed to be involved with the world of creatures included the activities of animal-like spirits known as poltergeist.

No physical description of poltergeist was recorded in the colonies and settlers seemed undecided as to exactly what form was taken by these witches' agents. The spirits may have been conceived as imps with no recognizable shape, or perhaps the demons were judged as amorphous masses. It was agreed, however, that their purpose was less sinister than that of familiars. Instead of seeking to do lasting harm, poltergeist were creators of mischief, whose most common activity was the disruption of daily activities.

The concept of poltergeist was primarily Anglo-American; it had little weight in the theological creed of the continent. The basic concept may have been derived from ancient Celt and Welsh folk tales, for in pre-medieval Britain, imps and elves played important roles in mythology.

The most famous colonial poltergeist were called "lithobolia," or stone-throwing devils. The spirits' usual mode of operation involved the bombarding of dwellings with thick showers of rocks or stones. Using "invisible hands," the poltergeist created confusion that lasted for periods as long as a year.

A particularly well-documented incident of lithobolia began on the night of June 11, 1682, when the home of Portsmouth farmer George Walton was suddenly pelted with a deluge of stones. As soon as the attack began, visitors in the household ran outside in an attempt to discover the source of the barrage. In the darkness, nothing could be identified as the direct cause of the disruption and all were quickly driven back inside by the continuing cascade.

According to eyewitness Richard Chamberlain, secretary of the province of New Hampshire, the stones were as hot as if they had just come from a fire and were thrown with great force. Curiously, however, when a rock did hit one of the observers, the blow was feather light and no burns resulted.

The attack lasted four hours and then ceased, only to begin again later in the night. No longer were the missiles confined to striking the roof and outside walls of the house. The stones rained down in the interior of the dwelling and the door to Chamberlain's bedroom was knocked in by one rock weighing an estimated eight and a half pounds.

Other strange pranks accompanied the stoning. A gate was wrenched from its hinges, candlesticks leaped about on a table, cheese was taken out of a press and strewed on the floor, metal objects grew red hot, and several items disappeared. Brickbats, crowbars, spits, and hammers sailed through the air propelled, according to Chamberlain, by "unseen hands or agents."

The incidents continued intermittently for three months, during which time the Waltons adjusted to the interruption of their previously peaceful lives. After a morning of bombardment, the family would go to work in the fields, there to be occasionally pelted by rocks.

The source of the attacks was subject to repeated discussion. Ultimately, Chamberlain's conclusion that the "lapidary salutations" were "praeternatural and not assignable to, or the effect of, natural causes" was accepted. A local woman who specialized in "diabolical tricks and practices" came under heavy suspicion for causing the acts by witchcraft.

Like many unexplained events attributed to witchcraft, the Walton episode had been preceded by a personal argument between the victim and the accused. In this case, the alleged instigator was aged Hannah Jones, who lived adjacent to the besieged house and was involved in a boundary dispute with Walton. On July 4, 1682, Hannah complained to the colonial council that Walton had falsely accused her of evildoing and that his horse had several times broken into her pasture and "doth her damage."

Council members shared the general suspicion that Hannah lay at the root of the lithobolia. Because sufficient evidence of guilt was not available, the woman was allowed to remain free, subject only to a bond to insure good behavior. Despite the precaution, the attacks on Walton continued.

For some time, many in the neighborhood had considered the widow Jones to be a witch. One of the most damaging proofs against her was that she was the daughter of Jane Walford, who had been tried for witchery in 1656. Close relatives and particularly the children of known enchanters were automatically suspected of practicing the black arts. It was supposed that all witches were required to recruit others into the devil's service and the most easily persuaded were their own children.

As the stoning continued unabated throughout the summer months, the personal confrontation between Hannah and Walton waxed more heated. On August 31, Elizabeth Clark testified that the farmer had said that "Grandma Jones," presumably Hannah, was a witch and that he would continue to maintain that fact until his death. Walton retorted that Hannah had accused him of being a wizard and said that if he further defamed her mother, she would throw rocks at his head.

Several suspicious signs were witnessed that tended to confirm the existence of supernatural spirits in the area. A black cat that appeared during one stone throwing session was branded a familiar. The snorting and trotting of an invisible horse was heard, along with an eerie whistling that came from the air. When two girls saw a distant figure hurling rocks at the house, Chamberlain pronounced the visages not human, but devilish.

Growing increasingly perturbed, the Walton family decided to perform a counterspell. Many in the folk class firmly believed in the powers of these charms, but the practice was considered borderline witchcraft by most intellectuals and the clergy. These groups held that although one could indeed combat a sorcerer's power by mystical means, to do so involved using methods that also called upon forces of the supernatural. Such an act might corrupt the individual performing the counterspell and make the experimenter more susceptible to the devil's temptations.

Urine boiling was selected as the means by which the devils would be dispelled from the Walton farm. This counterspell was a simple one that involved the heating of a pot of urine into which pins or needles had been placed. In theory, the temperature of the red hot pins would be transferred to the witch and would cause such pain that the charmer would be forced to end the stoning in order to halt the torment.

All did not go as expected. According to witnesses, as soon as the pot began to boil, "a stone came and broke the top or mouth of it, and threw it down and spilt what was in it. . . . " The Waltons were not deterred by the setback, which was interpreted as an effort by the witch to stop the counterspell. A second vessel was filled and placed on the fire. Once more a mysteriously thrown stone rent the container. When a third try met with the same results, the Waltons conceded defeat.

In September, the colonial council agreed to examine the facts of the case once more. Walton, while traveling to testify at the hearing, was pelted on the road by three unusually large stones. One, he claimed "broke his head," while the others inflicted severe pain on his back.

The new meeting accomplished little, for again the council was unable to resolve the matter. However, during the days following the council session, the lithobolic attacks lessened. The inquiry had evidently dampened the vigor of the perpetrating prankster.

By spring, no new stoning had been reported, but occasional mischievous acts continued to occur. In August of 1683, Portsmouth minister Joshua Moody wrote the latest from the Walton house to Increase Mather, father of Cotton. "The last thing I have heard," wrote Moody, "was the carrying away of several axes in the night, notwithstanding they were laid up, yea, locked up very safe, as the owner thought at least. . . . "

As the Walton episode was fading from view, a more serious visitation of poltergeist began in Hartford. Here, the house of Nicholas Desborough was not only pelted with stones and earth, but with cobs of Indian corn as well. The invisible hands also kindled a fire that destroyed part of the victim's property. Although the incident was credited to supernatural forces, a practical solution was found to halt the harassment. Just before the lithobolic bombardment had begun, Desborough was accused by a neighbor of stealing a trunk of clothing. As soon as the goods were restored to their rightful owner, the stone-throwing attacks ceased as suddenly as they had begun.

No such obvious motivation was involved in the case of Mary Hortado of Salmon Falls. The first sign of trouble occurred in August of 1683 when Mary, busy with her household chores, heard a dismembered voice calling out: "What do you here?" A short while later, Mary was struck in the eye by an invisible fist.

Several uneventful days passed before, without warning, a large stone was thrown down the chimney of Mary's house, striking a frying pan with such force that its ring was heard by neighbors a hundred rods away.

The settlerwoman was attacked in her yard by spirits who hit her on the head with a rock and then beat and scratched her on both arms and one breast. The impression of many "male" teeth were left as evidence of the bout, as well as several bruises that had no natural cause. Twice Mary glimpsed visions of a spirit moving about her. One apparition was of a woman dressed in a short blue cloak and white cap. The following day, the apparition reappeared, but the specter now sported a gray gown with a white apron.

The sighting and attacks proved too much for the Hortado family, who left their home for temporary safety elsewhere. When the settlers returned, their corn patch fence had been razed and the field was covered with the tracks of milling cattle. Mysteriously, however, the great herd that had trampled the earth had not disturbed a single stalk of corn.

Poltergeist continued to work inside the dwelling. Footsteps were heard, but no figure was seen to account for the sounds. Floorboards were observed to buckle as if under the pressure of an invisible foot. Mary, like members of the Walton family, decided to break whatever spell had beset her house. But instead of urine boiling, she chose an herbal charm. All around the dwelling she planted a protective row of bay bushes, a plant which supposedly would set up a barrier against both witches and their powers. As long as the shrubs stayed green and healthy, the house was free from disturbances. However, in the fall, as the bay plants began to wither and drop their leaves, the strange harassment began again.

Although poltergeist were generally thought to be near-harmless pranksters, who performed annoying rather than dangerous activities, the spirits inhabiting the house of William Morse appeared to be borderline demons.

In 1679, Morse, a Newberry shoemaker, his wife, Elizabeth, and their grandson, John Stiles, were confronted by perhaps the most vindictive poltergeist in colonial history.

Not only did the spirits throw bricks, stones, and wood against the Morses' house, but on one occasion a cat was hurled at Elizabeth. Chaos reigned inside the structure. A chair flew about in the air. A chest moved unaided from place to place. A spit clattered noisily up and down the chimney.

At mealtimes the poltergeist were particularly active. As the family attempted to eat, ashes were thrown into their food or dumped on their heads. Boxes were tossed about and a mysterious force beat the victims with boards. At their prayers, William, Elizabeth, and John were hit on the head with brooms, and once a chamberpot with its contents was dumped on their heads as they lay in bed.

John Stiles was singled out for special treatment. At night his cap was pulled off and his hair jerked. His body was pinched, struck with awls and pins and hurled around the house. One observer noted that the youth was "flung about at such a rate that it was feared his brains would be beaten out." The list of harms grew longer. John was stabbed in the back with three-tined fork and stuck with an iron spindle. As he ate, food flew out of his mouth, and ashes, sticks, and yarn flew in. During one attack, Stiles began to bark like a dog and cluck like a hen.

Neighbor Caleb Powell, a sailor who claimed vast knowledge of astronomy and astrology, offered to fight the demons by sheltering John. During the period in which the youth lodged with Powell, all harassment ended at the Morses' dwelling and John was free from torment. Rather than delight, William Morse demonstrated anger at the new turn of events. He promptly accused Powell of using witchcraft to both create and halt the unexplained incidents.

On March 30, 1680, Powell was brought before the court at Ipswich to answer the sorcery charges. John Stiles, one of the principal witnesses, claimed that Powell had once caused him to fly over the roof of a house and land against a cart wheel. The fall reportedly caused the youth to become temporarily mute and lame. Another witness, relying on hearsay, testified that many years before a rumor had circulated that Powell had received instructions in the black arts from a famous European witch named Norwood.

The court ruled the evidence insufficient to proceed against the sailor, and Powell was released. But such strong suspicions had been created by the facts and oral testimony that the defendant was not entirely exonerated. The officials ruled that Powell was liable for part of the court costs, a levy usually applied only to those found guilty. In announcing their action, the judges explained that the accused "hath given such ground of suspicion, of his so dealing, that we cannot so acquit him, but that he justly deserves his own share and the cost of the prosecution of the complaint."

CHAPTER III

Sea Witches

P ORT towns were the strongholds of witch superstition in Early
America. Not only were these settlements the most populated and
culturally diversified communities in the new land, but each seacoast
villager was influenced by the great mass of maritime folklore in
which witches for centuries had played a prominent role.

The seafaring life, a profession in which the unknown was a
constant factor, was a breeding ground for mystical legends. Despite
obstacles such as uncharted waters, pirates, hidden shoals, and enemy
ships, the most feared of all ocean dangers was the witch. Whether
battling the fierce Atlantic, or sailing the fishing waters of coastal
bays, Amercian mariners were constantly aware that evil enchanters
might cast away their vessels with a mere nod of the head.

Many of the superstitions of the sea were assimilated into the
witchlore of land-based colonists who dwelt near colonial ports. Even
those immigrants who resided far inland retained portions of the tales
to which they had been exposed on the transatlantic passage.

Some of the legends told by American seamen stretched back in
origin to the ancient sailors of Egypt and Greece. Like most folk
stories, the mariners' witchlore had been passed from generation to
generation, growing with each retelling in scope and strength. Many
of the charms used on seventeenth-century vessels to allay a sorcerer's
power had been in practice since long before the Romans first invaded
England.

Almost every facet of life aboard ship was tightly governed by convention based on superstition. Even the most innocuous action could be important in either courting good luck or inviting the presence of evil. For example, black objects were to be avoided as possible possessions of the devil. Finger and toenail clippings were to be carefully hidden so that the items could not be stolen by witches, who might use the relics in magical potions. Animals, particularly cats, were shunned, for the creatures could be familiars attending witches who were ship passengers. Horseshoes must be nailed to the mast to conceal any evil spell that might be set upon the vessel.

Perhaps the strongest protection against witches' magic could be gained by carrying religious fetishes. More cautious sailors, fearing that loss of their charms would leave them vulnerable, chose to have protective signs etched into their skin in the form of tattoos. Presumably a witch at sea would be powerless to act against a seaman who displayed a good omen permanently marked on his body.

Friday, the time of the Witches' Sabbath, was considered particularly unlucky for a sailor. Voyages were rarely begun on this day, for it was feared ill luck would follow the entire passage. Similarly, a ship whose keel was laid, mainmast stepped, or hull launched on the fifth day was supposed forever marked for disaster.

One of the most universally accepted notions concerned the power of witches to raise storms and control the natural elements at sea. A woman whistling on board was silenced and suspected of being a witch calling up a tempest. In England, witches of "white" magic were courted by mariners, who considered their powers helpful in controlling the forces of nature. As early as the fourteenth century, British enchanters openly sold knotted ropes to help seamen master the winds during a voyage. If the knots were left securely tied, the weather would be calm. If slightly loosened, a light breeze would spring up. Further releasing of the bond would provide a strong wind increasing to gale force. If the rope was completely untied, the ship would become engulfed in a hurricane. By reversing the process, sailors could supposedly diminish any torrential winds met in passing.

Some witches specialized in selling trunks of winds to merchants who wished a speedy voyage for their fleet. These kits were based on the principle of Pandora's Box. When the lid was cracked a breeze escaped, which increased in velocity as the cover was raised higher.

Although American witches did not usually traffic in wind controlling items, the practice was known to settlers connected with the sea. Colonial William Byrd II, one of the wealthiest and best-educated men in Virginia, firmly believed in the power of witches to control the winds. In a 1735 letter to London merchant John Hanbury, Byrd wrote:

> I am glad to hear your ship the *Williamsburg* got home well, and that Crane agreed with a witch at Hampton for a fair wind all the way. The new tobacco she carry'd surely will make your smokers jump at it as the French at Canada at a fresh cargo of women, and I hope, like them, they will be persuaded to pay a good price for it.

Merchants and seamen were not the only provincials to voice concern of water witches. The entire company of the *Ark,* a transport vessel bringing Maryland's first settlers from England in 1634, was beset by fears when the vessel was confronted with an incredibly powerful gale. One passenger noted that the torrent had unnaturally risen in the midst of a quiet passage, when clouds "gathered in a fearful manner, terrible to the beholders, so that ere it began to blow it seemed all the spirits and witches of Maryland were now set in battle array against us."

Immigrants such as the *Ark*'s passengers were at least partially prepared for the supernatural events thought likely to occur during the weeks-long transatlantic passage. Before the ocean crossing had become routine, warnings of dire consequences that might result from tempting the sea demons were widely circulated. Among the most common tales was that passengers of vessels sailing the Atlantic would be turned black before arriving in America. It was also believed that all women undertaking the trip would be made sterile.

Amateur scientist John Josselyn was not deterred by the dire warnings of danger and set off for America in 1638. Although Josselyn was not directly attacked by witches, he did observe evidence that spirits were at work nearby. Aboard the *New Supply,* bound for Boston, the traveler noted in his journal:

> About eight of the clock at night, a flame settled upon the mainmast, it was about the bigness of a great candle, and is called by our seamen St. Elme's Fire. It comes before a storm, and is commonly thought to be a spirit. If two appear, they prognosticate safety.

Josselyn's supernatural sign, known as St. Elmo's Fire, was considered a particularly important omen. The phenomenon, however, was not devil-inspired as Josselyn believed, but a charge of electricity that passed through the end of a yardarm or masthead before a lightning storm. Colonial mariners, unaware of the scientific explanation, conceived of the glow as a portend of future danger. Similar omens were the phosphorescent slicks that were observed on the crests of waves. This condition was called "witches' oil" and, like St. Elmo's Fire, was judged to be a warning sign from the spirit world.

The safe arrival of a ship and its crew was heralded with much thankfulness in both new- and old-world ports. If it became known that the company had managed to complete the trip despite opposition from supernatural forces, the joy was particularly bountiful. For English citizens, caught in the excitement of the mass immigrations of the seventeenth century, the deliverance of a vessel from the clutches of the devil and his witches was an event of wonderment. Instead of crediting the survival of a periled ship to rational causes, the escape was usually deemed an "illustrious providence," during which the forces of good had once more triumphed over evil.

Perhaps the most famous delivery from witches took place on the *Margaret* during a 1695 voyage out of Boston. Survivors of the *Margaret* maintained that the ship's passage had been beset from the first by the activities of the devil, who was seeking to recruit witches from the vessel's crew. The *Margaret* set out on December 28 bound for Barbados, loaded with a cargo of fish, beef, and lumber. Several days out of port, helmsman Winlock Curtis shouted from the wheelroom that the rudder would not respond to command. When helpers rushed to assist, Curtis announced that just before the boat had become uncontrollable, a demon had appeared on the binnacle. The spirit announced that several in the crew had agreed to become witches and urged Curtis to follow their example. When the sailor refused to sign the spirit's large black book, the ship foundered.

Curtis was relieved from his post and was given a Bible to read in an attempt to combat the devil's onslaught. The volume was largely ineffective against the tortures of mind and body the sailor claimed to be experiencing. As Curtis' resolution weakened, he attempted to jump overboard, explaining that he wished to join the demons in the sea. Eventually he was taken below and bound. Conditions on the vessel returned to normal.

On the evening of January 17, as the *Margaret* sailed quietly through a calm sea, the ship unexpectedly lurched to starboard. Water poured through the unbattened hatches and portholes. Under normal circumstances, the vessel would have sunk under the pressure of the flooded hull, but the cargo of lumber kept the ship buoyant and barely above water.

The near-capsizing was merely the first in a series of strange happenings. A passenger named Dibbs announced that an apparition had summoned him from the mast. Within days, both Dibbs and helmsman Curtis disappeared, supposedly carried away by unseen hands. Other members of the company were also lost, most to large waves, which periodically swept the unfortunates overboard. In some cases, just before the waves appeared, those marked for death claimed to have heard "various and wonderous noises, like the voices of birds, turkeys, and other fowl."

For eleven weeks a tiny band of survivors clung to the wounded hull. Their number gradually decreased, until at last only three remained. On Monday, April 6, at two o'clock, the trio was saved by an illustrious providence, when the ship ran ashore on Guadeloupe.

Although the opening of transatlantic traffic served to spread the superstitions of maritime witchlore to great numbers of the general population, at least one long-standing fear was ended as a result of colonization. This was a legend that involved the Bermuda Islands, long considered to be inhabited by witches and devils, who cavorted about enticingly upon the rocky coast.

Early explorers avoided that landfall at all costs, for many reliable captains claimed to have seen hundreds of evil enchanters scampering about in residence. Named the Isles of the Devils, Bermuda was thought to be somewhat of an illusion, or a crusty trap that would sink into the sea as soon as an unsuspecting mortal set foot on the shore.

But as colonists poured across the Atlantic in increasing numbers, several ships at last braved a landing and came face to face with the spirits seen by less hardy mariners. To the surprise of the seafaring community, the visitors lived to return. One of the first described what the invaders of the devil's territories had found:

Of the Bermudas, the example such,
Where not a ship until this time darst touch,
Kept, as suppos'd by hell's infernal dogs;
Our fleet found there most honest, courteous hogs.

A second explorer who braved the curse explained: "These islands of the Bermudas have long been accounted an enchanted place, and a desert inhabitation for devils; but all the fairies of the rock were but a flock of birds, and all the devils that haunted the woods were but herds of swine."

Within several years after the first forays, Bermuda's reputation as a haven for witches and spirits had been discarded. The Isles of the Devils, once the feared home of netherworld spirits, became an important, safe haven, providing protection for ships caught in ocean storms.

Superstitions such as St. Elmo's Fire and the witches of Bermuda were evolved and spread in the semi-rational manner that underlay all folk legends. Both tales of lore were based on real situations that were viewed and reported by dependable witnesses. In an attempt to explain the puzzling occurrences, seventeenth-century minds turned to the only realm with which they were familiar, the supernatural world. Thus ignorance, rather than fraud, changed a scientifically explainable happening into a preternaturally inspired superstition.

By interpreting the electrical charge of St. Elmo's Fire as a spirit-produced sign, and the hogs of Bermuda as romping devils, the mariners of the Atlantic were not manufacturing false tales, but merely misassessing real events in order to provide a rationale for the unknown. Today, many of the visions seen at sea are accepted as optical illusions, natural phenomena, mirages, or products of imagination or hallucination, but to those who witnessed the same sensations in the loneliness of the seventeenth-century Atlantic, the sights were terrifying indeed.

Massachusetts merchant Samuel Endicott was one of those who returned safely from a harrowing voyage to tell strange tales of apparitions and unholy spirits. But, unlike most mariners, Endicott was able to fight back against the witch he suspected had worked magic on the high seas.

The merchant's story was related at the witchcraft trial of Salisbury's Mary Bradbury, a devil's servant who supposedly specialized in casting spells upon ships. Endicott testified that two firkins of butter, purchased from Mary by one of his captains, had been be-witched and caused dire effects on the seamen's voyage. The first sign of trouble came soon after the vessel passed Barbados. As the ship sped through the warm waters of the Caribbean, the butter turned sour just before an unexpected storm arose. The vessel was saved, but severe damage was caused by the gale. Not only was the mainmast lost, but the hull sprang a leak so large that much of the hold's cargo of salt was destroyed. The eeriest event was yet to come.

Endicott, sitting on deck one night and no doubt contemplating the disastrous voyage, happened to glance upward into the moonlight. There, perched jauntily on the windlass, was Mary Bradbury, or the spirit of Mary Bradbury, dressed as she customarily appeared, in a white cap and neckcloth. The apparition was undoubtedly one of a vindictive witch gloating over the harm wracked by her handiwork.

The merchant's testimony, coupled with statements of other citizens who alleged that Mary was a worker in charms, proved costly for the seventy-five-year-old defendant. Mary was found guilty of practicing magic and was sentenced to be executed.

Because of the uncertainties of the ocean, colonial courts gave wide discretion to ship captains forced to deal with supposed witchcraft at sea. The transatlantic passage was a difficult one even in the best of seasons but its importance to the colonial economy was inestimable. Supplies and immigrants from England were vitally necessary to sustain and populate the provinces. So virtually any measure deemed necessary by a master to assure successful completion of his voyage was accepted by civil authorities as just.

In good weather, the trip from England could be completed in a minimum of six to seven weeks, but if strong headwinds were encountered, the journey might stretch to as long as four months. In such extended voyages, both food and tempers ran short. Fears increased in periods of rough weather and the prospect of abandoning ship was apt to create mutiny among both passengers and crew. Not only were the chances of being sighted by passing ships nearly miniscule, but during the era, other captains were not obligated to rescue those stranded at sea. Often it was felt that survivors were actually pirates in disguise or carriers of ill luck that would befall any ship that was boarded. As a result of such customs, the decision of a captain to put to death one on board who was believed to be the creator of supernatural difficulties was not seriously questioned. The only explanation required for dismissal of most charges was that the master deemed the execution necessary for the survival of his ship.

Maryland's provincial court at Pautuxet was slightly more thorough in investigating the case of Elizabeth Richardson, executed aboard the *Sarah Artch,* a merchant ship belonging to Edward Prescott.

In 1659, John Washington of Westmoreland County, Virginia, great grandfather of President George Washington, complained to the Maryland court that Captain Prescott had committed a felony by hanging Elizabeth for witchcraft. On the basis of Washington's accusation, Prescott was arrested and released only after posting the considerable bond of 40,000 pounds of tobacco, a common means of exchange in the southern colonies.

After the trial date had been set for early October, Maryland's governor, Josias Fendall, wrote Washington, explaining that formal charges had been brought against the captain. The official also noted that if Washington wished to repeat his allegations, his presence would be required at the trial. "Witnesses examined in Virginia will be of no value here, in this case," Fendall wrote, "for they must be face to face with the party accused or they stand for nothing."

Fortunately for Captain Prescott, the hearing date was most inopportune for Washington. The Virginia planter answered by return post that a conflicting social engagement made the trip impossible. In requesting a postponement, Washington explained that during the period, "God willing, I intend to get my young son baptized, all the company and gossips being already invited."

The Maryland court, unwilling to waive Prescott's right to a speedy trial, refused to delay and convened the hearing without the principal accuser. Under questioning, Prescott claimed he had opposed the "turning off" of Elizabeth, but when his ship's master and crew threatened mutiny in retaliation, he withdrew the objection. After receiving Prescott's evidence, the court ordered that a final call be made for any witnesses who might shed further light on the matter. It was probably hoped that Washington would make a last minute appearance to press his claims of wrongdoing. However, no one stepped forward. Prescott stood unaccused and was released.

In one case, however, it was the threat of mutiny that brought about the hanging of Mary Lee on the ship *Charity of London,* captained by John Bosworth. The *Charity,* outward bound for Maryland colony in the spring of 1654, was confronted with a violent storm that pushed the vessel hundreds of miles off course. For two months the ship was pounded by the tempest. Mammoth waves shattered its timbers and the boat remained afloat only because of the efforts of the passengers and crew. Jesuit priest Francis Fitzherbert, one of the ship's company, described the scene by explaining: "Everyone in his turn sweated at the great pump in ceaseless labour day and night."

The effort proved futile and the situation became perilous. An attempt to abandon ship was thwarted by "huge, mountainous waves." Finally the panicked crew seized Mary Lee, a fragile and aged passenger suspected of creating the storm by magic.

Following a centuries-old tradition, Mary was stripped of her clothing and tied fast to the capstan. All night she stood bound on deck, facing into the storm. In the morning she confessed to being a witch. "They slay her, suspected of this very heinous sin," wrote Father Fitzherbert. "The corpse and whatever belonged to her, they cast into the sea."

The execution, however, did not end the devil-inspired torrent. "But the winds did not thus remit their violence or the sea its threatenings," the priest wrote. "To the troubles of the storm, sickness was added, which having spread to almost every person, carried off not a few."

The gale continued for three weeks, but at last the vessel managed to pass the Virginia Capes and anchor at St. Mary's. Soon after its arrival, Maryland's Royal Council called for depositions from two passengers who had knowledge of the events surrounding Mary's demise. On June 23, 1654, the colony's governor, secretary, and council members heard further and more detailed testimony from Henry Corbyn, a young merchant from London, and Francis Darly, identified simply as a "gentleman."

Both witnesses explained that Bosworth had attempted to save Mary several times. According to Corbyn, soon after the storm arose, the crew had begged the captain to try the woman. He refused. As the gale continued, complaints grew louder, until Bosworth proposed a compromise. Mary Lee would be abandoned at Bermuda. The crew seemed agreeable but, according to the London merchant, "cross winds prevented, and the ship grew daily more leaky, almost to desperation."

Bosworth, wary that the men would desert their posts, tried still a third approach. He suggested that Mary be tried after commanders of other ships in the small convoy could be taken aboard to serve as a jury. Once again the storm prevented a peaceful settlement, for foul weather made the transfers impossible.

At this point, the crew took matters into their own hands and extracted Mary's confession. Bosworth was asked to order an immediate execution, but again he would not consent to their demands. Unwilling to commit what might have been considered chargeable murder, but at the same time wishing to pacify his mutinous crew, the captain elected to relinquish control over the entire situation. Retreating to the roundhouse, Bosworth told his men that they were entirely responsible for the situation and should do more than what could be justified if later called to account. Gladly accepting the abdication of power, the crew hanged Mary Lee.

Francis Darly, who was with Bosworth during the hanging, testified that the captain had explained that he could not, under the laws of England, order Mary's execution. Darly further reported that when the skipper was told the deed was done, he, "speaking with trouble in a high voice, replyed he knew not of it. . . . "

The testimony of the two witnesses was found acceptable to the Maryland council, who lodged no charges against either the captain or his crew.

The sailors' decision to bind Mary to the capstan so that she would face into the storm may have been a seventeenth-century version of a custom described by Pliny. The Roman wrote that ancient mariners believed that a gale would subside if a woman was made to show herself *nuda corpore* to the winds. This ages-old superstition may also have been the basis for the Early American preference for shipsheads that portrayed partially disrobed woman.

In addition to the presence of suspected witch Mary Lee, the *Charity*'s passenger list included at least one other voyager whose presence signaled danger to the crew. This was Father Francis Fitzherbert, for during the colonial era, priests were considered particularly undesirable passengers. It was felt that Satan and his witches would direct their full wrath toward a black-robed man of God. A ship carrying such a marked target would naturally suffer from the devil's displeasure. To combat the danger and perhaps calm the complaints of superstitious crews, special rites of exorcism were devised for the use of priests at sea. Undesirable passengers such as Father Fitzherbert were called "kittle" cargo or "Jonahs." Suspicious travelers included not only priests, but also women, heretics, cross-eyed helmsmen, and people with black valises. Among the worst Jonahs were corpses; they supposedly slowed down a speedy ship and made it more vulnerable to ocean hazards.

The belief in the presence of witches at sea and the strength of their powers to control the elements was so firmly entrenched in Anglo-American concepts that only rarely did a voice speak out against the superstitions. One of the few cynics was Reginald Scot, who attempted to debunk the legend in his 1584 book, *The Discoverie of Witchcraft.* Scot wrote:

> I am also well assured that if all the old women in the world were witches; and all the priests, conjurers: we should have not a drop of rain, nor a blast of wind the more or the less for them. For the Lord hath bound the waters in the clouds . . . yea, it is God that raiseth the winds and stilleth them: and he saith to the rain and snow; be upon the earth, and it falleth. . . .

Despite protests such as Scot's, the common folk of England and the colonies did not seriously question the abilities of witches to sabotage voyages and create shipwrecks. Far too much proof of their wickedness was known to the public for the calamities at sea to be considered other than supernaturally inspired. King James I, leader of the Empire, claimed that in 1590 a witch had conjured a storm in order to capsize his boat on a voyage from Denmark to England. Such official proclamations were supported by the confessions of witches such as Scotland's Agnes Sampson, who claimed to have conjured up a boat-wrecking storm by throwing into the sea parts of a human corpse attached to a dead cat. Marion Pebbles, an enchanter in the Shetland Islands, was alleged to have performed magic by transmogrifying into a porpoise so that she might come close enough to doom a British boat.

Colonials so thoroughly accepted the superstitions connected to sea witches that settlers believed vessels were not safe even after they had put into port. In 1648, so-called proof of this theory was displayed when the wrath of a witch was directed against the *Welcome,* a ship that lay peacefully at anchor in Boston harbor.

Contemporary reports maintain that the incident was triggered by the execution of Margaret Jones, a convicted witch. After the hanging, Margaret's husband was so avoided by residents in the bay area that he was unable to make an adequate livelihood. In an effort to leave the scandal behind, Jones attempted to book passage to the West Indies on the *Welcome.* The widower, however, lacked sufficient funds to pay for the voyage and his request was denied. As Jones left the 300-ton vessel, then set in quiet water, the ship began to roll as if it would capsize at any moment. The pitching continued for eight hours. Desperate city officials issued a warrant for Jones' arrest, and only after his imprisonment did the boat again return to its steady mooring.

Four years earlier, Boston harbor had been the scene of another supernaturally inspired occurrence. On January 2, 1644, a vessel with five hands aboard was mysteriously blown up with all lost. Four bodies were recovered, but the fifth, a wizard supposedly skilled in necromancy, was never seen again. Sixteen days later, a series of dancing lights and disappearing fires was sighted over the wreck, while the voice of the supposed sorcerer cried out over the water.

Although colonial witches did not admit to creating shipwrecks, the possibility that enchantment lay behind the destruction of vessels lost at sea did not escape settlers. Salem's Abigail Hobbs was closely questioned as to her possible part in the "casting away" of various ships. A common belief in the bay area held that a powerful witch could sink ships without a trace by placing a saucer in a pail of water. The container was shaken vigorously, and when the saucer overturned the vessel would capsize and sink to the ocean floor.

Specter or phantom ships were also a large part of the mariners' witchlore. Several of the most common tales were recorded by John Josselyn in his 1672 *New-England's Rarities Discovered.* In commenting on the northeast provinces, Josselyn announced: "There be witches to many . . . that produce many strange apparitions if you will believe report." Among the stories told to Josselyn was that of a phantom shallop, crewed entirely by women, that sailed the New England waters. Like the *Flying Dutchman,* the ship never put into port and was seen only through mists at sea. Presumably, the women were a band of witches doomed to find no rest and condemned to search the waters for boats on which to prey.

Josselyn also recorded the tale of a famous New England specter ship that always carried a huge red horse standing by the mainmast. The vessel, observed while moored in a cove east of Boston, simply vanished one day without a trace. A final tale he recorded was a saga involving the experience of a mariner aboard a ship twenty leagues at sea. To the seaman's amazement, the threatening specter of a witch appeared before him. Immediately, the mariner "took up carpenter's broad axe and cleft her head with it." According to Josselyn's informant, a woman long suspected of witchcraft died at home of head injuries incurred at the same moment as the hatchet attack at sea.

CHAPTER IV

Tests and Counterspells

A LTHOUGH witchcraft was a crime expressly forbidden under the laws of many colonies, settlers often chose to ignore formal legal procedures and sought to establish the guilt or innocence of a suspect by more unorthodox means. Among the folk classes, witch tests or trials were considered more accurate and less complicated than traditional judicial remedies.

In some cases, the accused also preferred to be judged by these extra-legal methods. Although rooted in informal customs, details of trial by ordeal were as precisely regulated as those of common and statute law.

The efficacy of folk tests had been firmly established in England and continental Europe for many generations before the techniques were applied in America. The basic assumption underlying each trial was the theory that witches would react in predictable patterns when confronted with certain situations. The innocent, however, would not follow the same course.

For example, it was presumed that a witch could cry a maximum of three tears, and these from the left eye only. If more than three drops were shed, or if tears appeared from the right eye, the subject was deemed not guilty. To prohibit any undermining of the tear test's legitimacy, observers were cautioned to be watchful for any participant who might attempt to put spittle on her face or otherwise manufacture false tears.

In another trial, guilt was established if the hands of the accused showed no burns or scalds after being plunged into boiling water. An authentic disciple of the devil would remain unharmed in such a situation, protected by past exposure to the fires of hell, which hardened the body to all injuries from heat. A less frequently used ordeal involved the feeding of bread and wine to a suspect. If the items were consumed, the witch was freed. Like many other trials, this procedure was based in religious theory. Because both bread and wine were used in holy sacraments, these foods were believed to be poison to enchanters.

Not all colonials were enthusiastic about the widespread application of trial by ordeal. Increase Mather called them relics of the "dark times of paganism and popery," and suggested that many innocent citizens had been harmed as a result of their use.

Opposition from critics such as Mather was usually ignored, and the use of tests became an accepted method for ferreting out guilty defendants. On the frontier, where settlers were untrained in legal niceties, informal ordeals may have been the principal means by which justice was administered. In more populated areas, folk trials were often given legal sanction and incorporated as part of the legal process.

Although tests varied in substance, each was similar in form. A suspect was introduced to a contrived situation, witnessed by spectators, who noted the resulting response. The reaction was then compared to behavior patterns that were traditionally thought conclusive in proving guilt or innocence. The subject's fate was thus decided.

One of the most popular tests was that in which the accused was required to repeat without error the Lord's Prayer or some other biblical passage. While seemingly a simple feat, the recitation was deemed impossible for someone who cavorted with the devil. The basis of the prayer test was founded in continental Europe, where it was held that witches, accustomed to participating in the Black Sabbath ritual, where all prayers were repeated backwards, would be unable to reverse the words to the correct Christian order. Even though the sabbath did not play an important role in England or the colonies, the prayer test was considered useful in both areas.

One suspect who failed to pass the prayer ordeal was Goody Glover, the Irish woman apprehended in the possession case of the

Goodwin children. A major factor contributing to the woman's performance was that her interrogation was conducted in English, supposedly a foreign tongue for Goody, who spoke only Irish. In their
questioning, Boston's Puritan ministers tried to compensate for her
lack of linguistic understanding, but despite the efforts, the woman
was unable to repeat the Lord's Prayer without error. Cotton Mather
described the scene:

> It was found that tho clause after clause was most carefully repeated
> unto her, yet when she said it after them that prompted her, she
> could not possibly avoid making nonsense of it, with some ridicu-
> lous depravations.

Two drawbacks inherent in the administration of this trial may
have contributed to a high incidence of failure by participants. First,
the presence of a large mob of spectators undoubtedly tended to so
unnerve the suspect that errors would inadvertently be made. A second factor was the diversity of litany among the many religious sects
in the colonies. Differences in the wording of prayers or affirmations
was common and a participant who had spent many years repeating
one version of a prayer might well stumble in confusion when confronted with a new variation.

A suspect who successfully underwent a folk trial was usually
cleared from further legal prosecution, but it does not appear that one
reckoned innocent by ordeal was freed if already convicted in court.
Such a situation confronted George Burroughs, condemned by a
Salem court to die for witchcraft.

As he stood on the gallows awaiting the noose, Burroughs loudly
proclaimed his innocence and then stunned the large crowd by repeating the Lord's Prayer without hesitation or error. The spectators,
deeply impressed by the feat, called for Burroughs' pardon. However,
more legalistically minded officials overseeing the execution refused,
and the convicted man was hanged before the protesting spectators
could organize their opposition.

The water trial was probably the most heatedly attacked ordeal
used in America. Increase Mather described the examination as a
"diabolical invention" and stated:

> This superstitious experiment is commonly known by the name of
> The Vulgar Probation, because it was never appointed by any lawful

authority, but from the suggestion of the devil taken up by the rude rabble. . . .

In preparation for this trial, suspects were bound "hands and feet," a position in which the right thumb was tied to a toe on the left foot, the left thumb to a toe on the right foot. In this posture the accused was tossed into a river or pond, while crowds lined the banks to observe the outcome. It was presumed that an innocent person would sink to the bottom, while the guilty would float about on the surface, unable to submerge. This reaction was thought to occur because witches, being tainted and unclean by association with the devil, would be unable to immerse themselves in a pure medium such as water. To prevent accidental drowning of the innocent, a rope could be tied about a participant's waist, but in the excitement surrounding the spectacle, this precaution was not always remembered.

Several factors tended to give some categories of accused an advantage over others. The test grossly discriminated against fat colonials, whose excess body tissue provided buoyancy unshared by more slender settlers. Also at a disadvantage were males, who did not have the benefit of the many-layered skirts and bodices worn by women. In some cases, females may have been stripped to their shifts for the trial, but in no case were they tossed in without a significant weight of apparel.

A tandem ordeal by water was conducted on September 15, 1692, when Mercy Disborough and Elizabeth Clawson were "swum" near Fairfield, Connecticut. Both women "swam like a cork," according to report, and when one viewer attempted to push them below the waterline, the suspects bobbed back to the surface.

In her more formal court trial conducted one month later, Elizabeth was acquitted of witchcraft charges despite her failure to sink. Mercy, however, was found guilty. She was tried once more, probably in an effort to reverse the decision, but once more the jury brought in an unfavorable verdict. Mercy was sentenced to hang, but confusing legal maneuvering was begun. Results of the water trial were specifically discarded by an appeal judge and the defendant was ultimately pardoned.

Connecticut's William Ayers and his wife were also subject to the water trial. Evidently not satisfied with the outcome, the couple fled the area rather than risk a formal hearing in court. The settlers Ayers may have been the pair described by Increase Mather. According to Mather, a Connecticut man and woman subject to the ordeal swam "after the manner of a buoy, part under, part above the water." When a skeptical bystander protested that anyone so bound and cast into the water would "swim," he too was tied and tossed. The doubter immediately sank completely below the surface.

Accusations of witchcraft lodged against Maryland's Joan Michell were partially based on the concept of the water trial. In 1661, Joan was alleged to be an enchanter, primarily because of her ability to swim, an unusual accomplishment in Early America. Calmer minds prevailed and it was decided that her incriminating talent was "no cause for action" by legal authorities or sufficient proof for convening an organized water ordeal.

Grace Sherwood of Princess Anne County, Virginia, underwent the colonies' most confusing and famous water trial. The folk test was a last ditch effort by local authorities to resolve a tangle of legal difficulties that had consumed the area for months. The 1706 record of the Virginia enchanter was marked by repeated delays and indecision by the courts, Governor's Council, and local citizens. The reluctance to make a firm decision demonstrates the extreme caution with which institutions in the tidewater province proceeded in the area of supernatural crimes.

Grace Sherwood had long been suspected of possessing strange powers beyond the realm of ordinary mortals. One popular rumor suggested that she had immigrated to America not in a boat, but in a floating eggshell, an item with strong supernatural connotations. Despite the neighborhood gossip, Grace lived peacefully for many years in a rural area near the coast.

But by the late 1690s, tales of her unnatural charms had reached such an extreme level that Grace and her husband decided to halt further spread of the slander. In September of 1698, the couple sued Jane and John Gisburne for stating that Grace was a sorcerer who had bewitched their hogs to death and placed an evil spell on their cotton. After hearing the case, the jury rejected the Sherwoods' request for £100 sterling in damages and found instead for the Gisburnes.

At the same session, a similar action was brought against Anthony and Elizabeth Barnes. According to the court clerk, Grace claimed that Elizabeth had said: "Grace came to her one night and rid her and went out of the keyhole or crack in the door like a black cat . . . ." The statement was twice incriminating to Goody Sherwood. Not only was she charged with hagriding, but also with the ability to transfigure into animal shape and vanish through a keyhole, a well-known witch strategy. After four days of hearings, the jury found for Elizabeth and Anthony. The Sherwoods were ordered to pay the expenses of eight witnesses who had been called to testify.

If the court's findings against Grace had taken place in the witch-hunting areas of New England rather than in the casual atmosphere of Virginia, criminal trial and execution would have undoubtedly resulted. In the tidewater area, however, no attempt was made to investigate her guilt of witchcraft.

There were perhaps continued rumors concerning Grace in the period following the civil suits, but no mention of suspected sorcery appeared in court records until seven years later. In December of 1705, Grace, now a widow, sued Luke Hill and his wife, Elizabeth, for trespass and assault and battery. Grace complained that Mrs. Hill had "assaulted, bruised, maimed, and barbarously beaten" her. She requested £50 in recompense. While the exact cause of the dispute was not recorded, the jury found for the plaintiff and awarded twenty shillings damages. The Hills were ordered to pay all costs of the trial. One month later, Hill and his wife were back in court, this time as the instigators of a charge of witchcraft against their rival. Grace, who had been summoned to answer the allegations, failed to appear and the case was adjourned until the sheriff could "attach her body."

The attitude of the county court was casual, and officials seemed reluctant to press the matter. It was probably hoped that both Grace and the Hills could settle their differences without official intervention. A second reason for the lack of concerted action may have been that the local magistrates were uncertain as to exactly how the unusual charge of witchcraft should be prosecuted. Unlike the judicial bodies of the northeast, where allegations of sorcery constantly confronted officials, the Virginia magistrates were almost totally inexperienced in such cases.

Grace was present for an arraignment in February, but the county court's hesitation continued. Announcing that the situation had been a "long time debated," jurists returned a finding which pleased neither the accuser nor the accused. Luke and Elizabeth were ordered to pay court costs, but Grace was to be searched by a jury of matrons whose goal was to discover if any incriminating witches' teats or devil's marks were present on her body.

A group of local women led by Elizabeth Barnes, Grace's adversary in the 1698 slander trial, were impaneled to conduct the probe. On March 7, Elizabeth Barnes, as forewoman of the jury, reported: "We of ye jury have searched Grace Sherwood and have found two things like tits with several spots." Though armed with damaging evidence, the county court still refused to order criminal prosecution. The case dragged into its sixth month; on May 2, the sheriff of Princess Anne County was ordered to arrest Grace and search her house for "all images and such like things as may in any way strengthen the suspicion" against her. Evidently no damaging evidence was found, for in June, the court ordered that a new search be made of Grace's body. But the proceeding was becoming a nuisance in the area and the old jury of matrons refused any further part in the matter. Finally, on July 5, Grace and the court agreed that a water trial should be held to resolve the suspicion to which she had been subjected.

Foul weather thwarted the first swimming attempt. Solicitous officials cancelled the event, announcing that the climate was "very rainy and bad, so that possibly it might endanger her health." The ordeal was rescheduled for the following week and the sheriff was given several instructions to assure that the affair would be conducted in an agreeable manner. First, the lawman was directed to secure as many "ancient and knowing women as possible" to examine Grace at the scene for witches' marks. In addition, adequate precautions were to be taken so that the subject did not drown.

July 10, 1706, was not a happy day for Grace Sherwood. Tried in the usual manner, she swam "contrary to custom and the judgment of all the spectators." A further blow came when the matrons announced that their examination had proved Grace was not "like them nor no other woman that they knew of." She was committed to jail.

The prospect of a witchcraft conviction and subsequent hanging may have dampened the spirits of Luke Hill. After Grace was placed in jail, sentiment evidently turned against the prosecution. At some point, Grace was released from jail and court records are silent on any additional action which may have been taken.

An even more spectacular trial by water occurred in Mount Holly, New Jersey, during October of 1730, according to the *Pennsylvania Gazette*. There are strong indications, however, that the newspaper's account of the trial was actually a hoax fabricated by its editor Benjamin Franklin.

Franklin was America's greatest prankster during the eighteenth century and the wily colonial frequently made use of the literary hoax as a device to entertain and challenge the credulity of his readers. As late as the Revolutionary War, Franklin, as minister to France, churned out essays of dubious truth designed to spread propaganda unfavorable to England. In one hoax, the diplomat published a thorough account of an Indian massacre that had not taken place. Franklin's imagination was so vivid that the article even included a detailed listing of the number and types of scalps supposedly taken and packed in bales as a present for King George.

The *Gazette's* readers may have been so inured to Franklin's pranks that the water ordeal story was recognized as a farce or perhaps was considered a parody, for the humor was somewhat localized. But three months after the article appeared in the colonies, London-based *Gentleman's Magazine* reprinted the tale as a legitimate news item.

According to the *Gazette,* the incident included not only the water trial, but also a weighing test, which was assumed equally effective in proving the guilt or innocence of a witch. In this ordeal, the accused was weighed against a holy book such as a church Bible. If the participant outweighed the volume, innocence was proved. If the scales tipped in favor of the book, then the opposite conclusion was drawn. The rationale was that sorcerers who consorted with the devil or were sucked by a familiar lost all inner substance and were feather light. Such a clear resolution of guilt was not drawn in the 1730 episode:

> *Burlington, Oct. 12.* Saturday last at *Mount Holly,* about eight miles from this place, near 300 people were gathered together to see an experiment or two tried on some persons accused of witchcraft.
>
> It seems the accused had been charged with making their neighbors' sheep dance in an uncommon manner, and with causing hogs to speak and sing psalms, &c., to the great terror and amaze-

ment of the King's good and peaceable subjects in this province, and the accusers being very positive that if the accused were weighed in scales against a Bible, the Bible would prove too heavy for them; or that if they were bound and put into the river, they would swim. The said accused, desirous to make their innocence appear, voluntarily offered to undergo the said trials, if two of the most violent of their accusers would be tried with them. Accordingly, the time and place was agreed on, and advertised about the country. The accusers were one man and one woman; and the accused the same.

The parties being met, and the people got together, a grand consultation was held, before they proceeded to trial, in which it was agreed to use the scales first; and a committee of men was appointed to search the men, and a committee of women to search the women, to see if they had anything of weight about them, particularly pins.

After the scrutiny was over, a huge, great Bible belonging to the justice of the place was provided, and a lane through the populace was made from the justice's house to the scales, which were fixed on a gallows erected for that purpose opposite to the house, that the justice's wife, and the rest of the ladies, might see the trial without coming amongst the mob; and after the manner of *Moorfields,* a large ring was also made. Then came out of the house a grave tall man carrying the Holy Writ before the supposed wizard, &c. (as solemnly as the sword-bearer of *London* before the Lord Mayor). The wizard was first put in the scale, and over him was read a chapter out of the book of *Moses,* and then the Bible was put in the other scale (which being kept down before was immediately let go). But to the great surprise of the spectators, flesh and bones came down plump, and outweighed the great good Book by abundance. After the same manner, the others were served, and their lumps of mortality severally were too heavy for Moses and all the prophets and apostles.

This being over, the accusers and the rest of the mob, not satisfied with this experiment, would have the trial by water; accordingly a most solemn procession was made to the mill pond, where both accused and accusers being stripp'd (saving only to the women their shifts) were bound hand and foot, and severally placed in the water, lengthways, from the side of a barge or flat, having for security only a rope about the middle of each, which was held by some in the flat.

The accuser man, being thin and space, with some difficulty began to sink at last; but the rest, every one of them, swam very light upon the water. A sailor in the flat jump'd out upon the back of the man accused, thinking to drive him down to the bottom; but the person bound, without any help, came up some time before the other. The woman accuser, being told that she did not sink, would be duck'd a second time, when she swam again as light as before, upon which she declared that she believed the accused had bewitched her to make her so light, and that she would be duck'd again a hundred times, but she would duck the devil out of her. The accused man, being surprised at his own swimming, was not so confident of his innocence as before, but said: *If I am a witch, it is more than I know.* The more thinking part of the spectators were of opinion that any person so bound and plac'd in the water (unless they were mere skin and bones) would swim till their breath was gone, and their lungs fill'd with water. But it being the general belief of the populace that the women's shifts, and the garters with which they were bound, help'd to support them; it is said they are to be tried again the next warm weather, naked.

Another folk test fraught with excitement and suspense was the touch test. This procedure, also called the laying on of hands, the doctrine of fascination, or the bier right, presumed that the body of a person murdered by witchcraft would bleed, attempt to return to life, or show some other incriminating sign when touched by the hand of the enchanter who had cast the damaging spell. If the corpse remained unchanged, the death was not attributed to the toucher.

The corpse of Elizabeth Kelly of Hartford was subject to such a trial in the spring of 1662. During Elizabeth's brief and sudden illness, she had complained of being choked by Goodwife Ayres. Because of the accusation, Goody Ayres was forced to stroke the remains in full view of a mass of observers. Elizabeth's body was seen to "purge a little at the mouth" during the contact, but although foul play was indicated, the corpse was buried during the ensuing confusion.

After the interment, accusations continued to be lodged against the suspected witch. Complaints grew so strong that at last Guilford physician Bryan Rosseter was officially ordered to exhume the body for an examination.

Rosseter's findings tended to support the presumption that the death had not been routine. Included in the report were six particulars the doctor considered to be preternatural indications that unusual forces had attended the illness. For example, despite the burial, Elizabeth's body had remained pliable and not subject to rigor mortis. The corpse, which displayed a deep blue tint, was well preserved and secreted fresh blood when the grave was opened.

At Salem, a variation of the touch test was used on several young girls supposedly bewitched by magic. When the girls were touched by those thought to have cast the damaging spells, the affliction was instantly "cured." Presumably the evil had flowed from the patients back into the body of the witch as soon as personal contact was made.

The touch test was not limited solely to proving witchcraft, but could be used to investigate murder by any foul means. Virginia settlers seemed particularly intrigued with the technique. As early as 1655, William Custis of Northampton was required to stroke the face of dead Panell Rynurse. When the corpse showed no reaction, Rynurse's death was judged to have stemmed from natural causes.

The ritual of touch was not always forced upon a suspect, and in most areas the procedure was considered a natural right available to any accused of a crime. When viewed in this light, the operation was known as the "bier right," and traditionally could not be denied.

Demonic possession was slightly more difficult to prove by the touch test than was murder by witchcraft. If the victim temporarily recovered, as did the Salem girls, then guilt was indicated. But the opposite reaction did not necessarily prove innocence. Suspicion was also generated if the possessed ones continued in their seizures or became even more agitated when touched. This response suggested that the witch was transmitting even greater doses of magic through the hand.

Further complications in interpretation were caused by the belief that if an extremely good individual contacted the patient, additional fits might occur as the demons inside struggled to free themselves from the pure vibrations. Because of these ambiguities, the sole agreement on findings came if the possessed showed no reaction at all. Only then was the participant presumed innocent.

Perhaps the most conclusive folk test involved the searching of the body of a citizen for incriminating marks. For generations in England, detailed probings were conducted to discover the existence of either witches' teats or devil's marks. In America distinction between the two types of blemishes was not made. In most cases, witches were examined for any type of unusual body blemish that might have been supernaturally inspired. Their existence was universally accepted in formal courts as valid evidence of fact, for unlike most folk trial findings, the result of such a search was considered a highly reliable indicator.

Because of the semi-legal status accorded this custom, magistrates routinely appointed legally authorized juries to conduct body examinations. In communities where the probes were not connected with pending legal action, informally constituted groups of volunteers examined those suspected of being witches. Special precautions were taken to assure that searchers were as knowledgeable as possible in matters of human anatomy and disease, so that a normal body mark would not be mistaken for a supernatural sign. Traditionally, the oldest and most respected members of a settlement were selected for the task, because of their special qualifications and experience. In Grace Sherwood's case, for example, the court authorized that only "ancient and knowing women" should be impaneled. A jury convened in 1674 to check Mary Parsons was described as a group of "soberized, chaste women."

Neither a close personal relationship nor past animosities with the accused barred a citizen from membership on a committee of searchers. But seventeenth-century standards of morality did dictate that jury persons should be of the same sex as the suspect.

This restriction created certain problems, for colonial females were formally barred from holding positions of authority in legal areas. The only exceptions to this prohibition involved juries of matrons used in cases involving witchcraft, infanticide, and bastardy. These deviations were deemed acceptable because matrons were charged with determining only matters of fact, not the ultimate guilt or innocence of an individual.

If possible, a midwife was appointed to head a female jury. This amateur healer was expected to provide expert advice and guidance regarding any questions resulting from the search. Women were also free to consult with male physicians, but the inclusion of men into the actual examination of a female suspect was virtually unknown.

A concise definition of a devil's mark was never agreed upon. Most available descriptions were vague and differed widely. In most instances, searchers were left to their own experience to determine exactly what was supernatural in origin. Some jurists suggested that the blemishes were red or blue spots "like a flea bite," an encompassing trap in the colonies, where insect bites were probably suffered in great frequency by all settlers. Other witch-hunting experts simply called the marks "spots," which sometimes appeared in the form of an animal such as a rat, hare, or weasel. Any skin indentations were suspect, for these might be pronounced teethmarks of the devil or a familiar. Birthmarks or other extraordinary skin pigmentations were also incriminating because of their deviation from normal coloration.

Confusion also surrounded the witches' teats, known by some as "biggs" or "titts." Women suffering from polymastia, more than two breasts, or polythelia, multiple nipples, were automatically designated as possessing unnatural body features. Large warts, boils, wounds, infections, or protruding swellings could be considered proofs of guilt by searchers unfamiliar with the specific conditions.

Massachusetts' Thomas Brattle, who fought against the Salem prosecutions, recognized the dangers presented by the lack of firm criteria. Brattle noted: "And I wonder what person there is, whether man or woman, of whom it cannot be said but that, in some part of their body or other, there is a preternatural excrescence."

The form in which examinations were conducted varied from locality to locality, but generally, searches in America were not as sophisticated as those performed in England. For example, British custom dictated that the suspect's body be completely shaved before exploration was begun. This initial step was considered essential to prevent the devil from miniaturizing himself and hiding in the witch's hair. Another basis for the shaving was the belief that marks and teats were usually located in less accessible creases of the body.

John Bell, minister at Gladsmuir, suggested that the marks were usually located in "secret places, as among the hair of the head, or eyebrows, within the lips, under the armpits, and in the most secret parts of the body." Other "private" places where marks were rumored to occur were under the eyelids, on the shoulder blades, and on the posterior. The breasts and genitalia were particularly favored locations on female witches.

Body shaving was never adopted in the colonies and the concept may have been discarded during the earliest days of settlement for functional rather than philosophical reasons. In America, neither barbers nor shaving were considered essential in the daily lives of most pioneers.

If the suspect was already detained in prison, the search could be conducted in jail almost immediately after the procedure was authorized by the court. If an arrest had not been made, the jury might perform the examination at a convenient central location or in the house of the accused. Unlike the crowded sickrooms of possession victims, no spectators were admitted to a search. In order to retain strictest modesty, only the official committee and the suspect were allowed to be present.

If the probing revealed no incriminating teats, the individual was usually pronounced innocent and any court action being considered was dismissed, while a report detrimental to the charged was almost always considered proof of guilt. Positive reports were normally made in the form of affidavits to the clerk of the appropriate court. The descriptions contained in the findings were explicit in detail and left little doubt that something out of the ordinary had been uncovered. For example, four women appointed to conduct an examination of Elizabeth Clawson and Mercy Disborough swore that

... as to Goodwife Clawson forementioned, we found on her secret parts, just within ye lips of ye same, growing withinside somewhat as broad and reach without ye lips of ye same, about one inch and half long, like in shape to a dog's ear, which we apprehend to be unusual to women.

And as to Mercy, we find on Mercy, foresaid, on her secret parts, growing within ye lips of ye same, a loose piece of skin and when pulled, it is near an inch long, somewhat in form of ye finger of a glove flattened ... that loose skin we judge more than common to women.

Only rarely did the accused challenge the findings of a search. The acceptance was purely pragmatic, for most settlers, unlearned in matters of medicine, had no grounds by which to explain the existence of a body mark that others swore was supernaturally inspired.

Salem's Rebecca Nurse, however, did lodge strong objections to the results of her body search. Not only did Rebecca dispute the findings, but she also questioned the qualifications of the women who had been impaneled to conduct the probe. Her protest may have been justified, for of the nine females included on the jury, eight were illiterate and signed only their marks to the court affidavit.

Disagreement among members of the jury was not unknown either, and sometimes the confrontations were near violent. Arguments stemmed not only from the intimate relationships that some-times bound the searchers to the accused, but also from misinterpreta-tion of findings. Often jury members refused to commit themselves to any opinion or openly disagreed with the findings of the majority. A particularly critical fracas occurred after the execution of New Haven's Elizabeth Knapp, hanged as a witch in 1653. Precisely why the corpse of Mrs. Knapp was searched following the turning off was not recorded. The woman had been subjected to an examination prior to hanging and the posthumous repetition was not common practice. In this case, the latter search may have been made to satisfy the curiosity of spectators who wondered if witches' marks underwent changes after the death of the enchanter. A second possibility was that Goodwife Staples, a close confidante of the executed woman, was not satisfied with the result of the pre-death search and was attempting a final effort to clear the reputation of her friend.

Roger Ludlow, deputy governor of Massachusetts and Connecti-cut, was an observer of the post-execution incident. According to the official, Goody Staples was extremely distraught and insisted so fran-tically that a second search be conducted that she drew suspicion upon herself. The disruption grew so great that at last the corpse was taken down from the gallows and "tumbled" about by a group of women, who repeated the earlier examination.

Susan Lockwood stated that during the second search, Goody Staples repeatedly proclaimed there were no marks at all. When the teats earlier designated as devil signs were pointed out to the protester, she merely answered: "If these be teats, here are no more than I have myself, or any other woman, or you, if you would search your body."

Susan, as vehement in her own opinion as Goody Staples was in hers, answered she knew not the condition of others' bodies, but as for her own: "If any find such things about me, I deserve to be handled as [Mrs. Knapp] was."

The protester's unusual behavior, coupled with a purported gal-lows accusation by Mrs. Knapp, prompted Ludlow to charge that Goody Staples was also in league with the devil. An irate Thomas Staples promptly sued Ludlow for defaming his wife's good name. The jury agreed that Goody Staples had been unjustly damaged and awarded the complainant £10 in damages and £5 for his trouble in bringing the suit.

Ludlow returned to England after the unfavorable verdict and was later appointed Commissioner for Administration of Justice in Dublin. Goody Staples was only temporarily vindicated. Forty years later, she was once again accused of witchcraft and was brought to formal trial at Fairfield. Her end would be much happier than that of the executed Mrs. Knapp, however, for the jury returned a clear finding of not guilty.

In cases when disputes arose among the searches, two further tests could be made to clarify the findings. The first method was based on the medieval belief that a mortal's blood carried the soul of the individual. Thus it was thought that the witches' teats, from which the devil and familiars sucked blood, would be completely impervious to all sensation. To test this lack of feeling, the individual was blindfolded and long pins or needles were pushed into the suspected teats. If no reaction occurred when the sharp objects were injected two or three inches deep, then the mark was considered supernatural. If pain was felt in the area being pricked, then the blemish was considered normal.

The pin test required a delicate hand, so that the suspect would not realize when the procedure was being conducted and therefore react artificially. In Scotland, special "prickers" were formally educated in the subtleties of the technique and the profession became so popular that a special guild was formed to deal with pricking problems. Matthew Hopkins, England's official "Witch-Finder Generall," was the most important in the field. Hopkins, who traveled throughout the country at government expense, was responsible for the conviction of hundreds of witches; he was eventually unmasked as an irresponsible charlatan.

In most areas, prickers were paid not a flat fee for each test conducted, but received money only when a witch was discovered. Thus it was to a worker's financial advantage for suspects to be proved guilty rather than innocent. This incentive contributed to many abuses, such as the development of a retractable bodkin with a hollow shaft into which the pin would secretly retract when pressed against the skin. With no penetration, the subject would show no sign of pain and would therefore be deemed guilty. Professional prickers also used decal-like devil's marks, which were surreptitiously applied to a suspect and later "discovered" with much fanfare.

Increase Mather was aware of the prickers' tricks and warned his friends in New England to beware of those who might use "enchanted" pins in order to snare the innocent. Presumably those who resorted to such tactics were themselves messengers of Satan bent on framing godly Puritans.

Despite the abuses of the pricking test, the measure was considered highly reliable when administered correctly. The possibility was not considered that hysterical, though innocent suspects might self-anesthetize portions of their body and thus show characteristics of guilt. Aberfoill minister Robert Hink claimed to have seen clear evidence of the test's usefulness and wrote:

> A spot that I have seen, as a small mole, horny and brown coloured; through which mark, when a large pin was thrust (both in buttock, nose, and roof of the mouth), till it bowed and became crooked, the witches, both men and women, neither felt a pain nor did bleed, nor knew the precise time when this was doing to them (their eyes being covered).

Pricking was used in the colonies, but the activity was not a routine part of the searching examination. The technique was probably reserved only for instances when dissension occurred among the jurors. The practice was applied to Salem's George Jacobs, who was found to have unnatural teats on the right shoulder blade, right hip, and inside of the right cheek. Jacobs showed pain when a pin was run through one of the excrescences, but when the procedure was repeated on the other two teats, the jury discovered "he was not sensible of it."

A second method for checking the authenticity of teats was a test by stool. In this trial, the accused was bound to a seat in the middle of an empty room and left to sit alone for at least twenty-four hours. During this time the suspect's familiar would be forced to return for its daily feeding. Hidden observers watched the scene constantly for any signs that a witch's helper was returning. Not only were the spectators on the alert for larger familiars such as dogs or cats, but a careful lookout was kept for less obtrusive demons, which might appear in the shape of birds or mice. So that even the smallest demon would not slip through, the floors of the room were swept periodically for insects such as spiders, ants, or flies, which might be returning spirits in disguise. A tiny creature that escaped the net or could not be killed was deemed a familiar protected from harm by Satan.

In 1648, Margaret Jones of Charlestown was subject to a "watching," a common name for trial by stool. Records indicate that one of her imps did return and the spirit was clearly observed by a jailor. According to Governor Winthrop, the familiar, which took the guise of a young child, had earlier caused trouble in the area. The governor wrote:

> In the prison, in the clear daylight, there was seen in her arms, she sitting on the floor and her clothes up, etc., a little child, which ran from her into another room, and the officer following it, it was vanished. The like child was seen in two other places, to which she had relation; and one maid saw it, fell sick upon it, and was cured by the said Margaret, who used means to be employed to that end.

If such a comprehensive watching was not undertaken, similar results could be obtained through periodic inspections of the teats. Such a procedure was applied in the case of Bridget Bishop, on whose body a supernatural mark was discovered. Four hours after the original search, a reexamination revealed that the protuberance had disappeared. The change supposedly was evidence that Bridget had been sucked in the interim by her familiar.

Unlike the popular trials involving teats, water, or touch, the snow test was relatively unknown. One incidence of the procedure was known in Massachusetts, but the rationale was not recorded. The ordeal involved the burying of a suspect in deep snow. Presumably the chill would cool the witch's power and any victim bewitched by her spell would have temporary respite while the tormentor was occupied with survival.

In 1684, Mary Webster of Hadley was subjected to the snow trial by friends of Philip Smith, a well-known "hypochondriac person." Smith, a local judge and militia officer, was believed to be under Mary's evil hand and for some time had "languished and pined." As the patient's condition deteriorated and doctors proved unable to provide a medical explanation for the illness, the likelihood of witchcraft increased.

Concerned colleagues of Smith decided to take matters into their own hands. Mary was dragged from her house and hung up, according to observers, till she was "near dead." Finally, the group let her down, "rolled her some time in the snow, and at last buried her in it, and there left her." During the period in which Mary was being harassed, Smith was temporarily relieved from pain, but as soon as the woman worked free, the ailments returned.

The snow test not only assisted in the discovery of the identity of a witch, but was also useful as a counterspell. Counterspells varied in form, but all were intended to either ward off black magic, destroy the power of a charm, or turn evil magic back upon the instigator.

Certain items were judged to have special qualities in setting up impenetrable barriers through which evil could not pass. Bay plants and rue were among the most popular herbal charms, but inanimate objects could also be used. Horseshoes were considered powerful talismans which, when nailed near the entrance of a dwelling, prohibited the entrance of any person aligned with Satan. The placing of a horseshoe near a bedroom door was thought effective in eliminating nightmares or hagriding.

Horseshoes could also be used as a type of test to uncover witches. An individual who refused to pass beneath the charm was viewed with open suspicion. Conversely, a suspected enchanter could prove innocence by walking under the forbidden barrier.

Virginia's Hannah Neal of Northumberland County was secretly confronted by such a situation, and the results were surprising to her accuser. Hannah had been suspicioned by Edward Cole, a man with whom the Virginia woman had argued since their immigration passage from England. According to Cole, Hannah had prophesied that neither he nor his family would prosper in the new land. After the prediction, Cole's relatives and servants fell ill and many of his cattle died unexpectedly. When his wife succumbed to the sickness, Cole arranged a test to prove that his troubles were the result of curses set in motion by Hannah.

After nailing a horseshoe over his door, Cole sent for the suspect, supposedly that she might visit with his wife. To Cole's amazement, Hannah not only stepped unhesitatingly beneath the horseshoe, but she proceeded to pray most earnestly for the patient's recovery. Cole, no longer apprehensive, apologized for his earlier charges and admitted that the remarks were erroneous and "passionately spoken."

Like horseshoes, witches' doors were used to ward off the entrance of evildoers. These barriers were ordinary panels into which two crosses had been set. Despite the evident efficacy of this item, the use of religious symbols to combat witchcraft was never widely accepted in the colonies. Crosses, amulets, and medallions, which had long been a major part of the witchcult in Europe, were relied upon in the New World only by sailors and other citizens connected with the sea. This absence of religious insignia may have stemmed from the strong Puritan influence in New England, where the display of holy symbols was thought akin to heretical papism.

At no time did counterspells gain the popularity in America that they enjoyed in England. Throughout Britain, the practice of "unbinding" witches who used magic to break evil spells and cure supernaturally inspired disease was widely applied. Such charms were also helpful to a less kindly category of enchanters, who dealt in both black and white magic. These sorcerers supported themselves by casting evil spells in order to be paid by the victims for removing them.

One form of counterspell widely hailed in the colonies was that of urine boiling. This ritual probably developed from English charm bottles, containers which, when filled with pins and set before the fire, supposedly warded off destructive spells.

In 1692, a variation of urine boiling was conducted at Salem by Tibula, a Caribbean servant skilled in voodoo. The rite involved the baking of a spell-breaking cake, made from rye meal and the urine of bewitched victims. The dish was served to a dog identified as a witch familiar in the hope that the afflicted persons would be able to recover and name their tormentor.

Twelve years earlier, the test had been conducted in an attempt to snare Hampton's Rachel Fuller, suspected of bewitching a child of John Godfrey. Soon after members of the family placed a container of the child's urine before the fire, Rachel arrived unexpectedly, her face smeared with a thick layer of molasses. A witness commented that the sorcerer had applied the syrupy mass so vigorously that "she almost daubed up one of her eyes."

The spell had obviously been at least a partial success. Supposedly the boiling had so burned the guilty witch that she had been forced to treat the scalds with soothing molasses. In addition, the enchanter had answered the summons of the counterspell and had come to lift the curse that had befallen the Godfrey youth.

Rachel's reactions grew increasingly more incriminating. After bursting into the sickroom, she began a strange rite aimed at healing the victim. First, she took the sick child's hand in hers and then whirled about, clapping her own palms together several times. Next, Rachel spat into the fire and threw a collection of unidentified herbs into the flames. Finally, announcing that the youth would recover, the witch slapped herself three times and departed.

Rachel returned the following day with additional assistance. Perhaps fearing that some other enchanter might afflict the family with a spell for which she would be blamed, Rachel suggested that the Godfreys plant sweet bay under the threshold of their door. When the bushes were laid down, she carefully avoided using the entrance. The cure was satisfactory to all involved. Rachel was temporarily jailed, but released after posting a £100 bond to assure her good behavior.

The "urinary experiment" was not always a simple counterspell to prepare. One attempt conducted in Northampton was doomed to failure, supposedly because the afflicting witch was aware that the test was to be conducted.

In this instance, reported by Cotton Mather, the family of bewitched Mr. St——n, attempted to collect sufficient fluid for the ritual. The effort was prevented, however, by "a strange hole through the urinary passage shedding the water before they could receive it into the vessel." Without the aid of the cure, the patient died.

A coroner's jury, called to investigate the death, found a suspicious hole "quite through his yard," which had prevented the normal flow of urine. The inference was that the hole had been created by an enchanter anxious to foil the counterspell. In such cases, alternative means of countermagic could have been attempted. A bit of the hair of the victim might have been cut and placed in a pot of any boiling matter. At Salem, for example, one Roger Toothaker admitted that he had conducted such an effort. Toothaker claimed to have taken a "part" of a bewitched person to boil it. The following morning, the woman suspected of casting the afflicting charm was found dead.

A final means by which a black spell could be broken involved "scoring above the breath." This technique, long used in England, featured the slashing of a suspect above the nose or mouth. This scratching was never officially condoned, but was a popular folk remedy for unexplained illness. If the victim recovered after the scoring, the revival was credited to the idea that the bewitching familiars had left the body of the patient to suck the blood of the witch.

Belief in the scoring spell was particularly long-lived in America. As late as 1802, the practice was still being used. On that date, Nicholas Toncroy of Poughkeepsie was tried for assault on an elderly woman. Toncroy believed the female to be a witch and had slashed her three times across the forehead in an attempt to prevent her from using her powers to harm others.

Chapter V

Suspicious Characters

E ARLY Americans were not always impartial when confronted with the emotionally packed issue of supernatural magic. Certain citizens suspected of witchcraft were viewed not as innocent until otherwise proven guilty, but as inherently lying under a strong burden of guilt. These preconceived prejudices were not directed at provincials as individuals, but as members of particular groups who were considered closely tied to the devil rather than to God.

The most deeply ingrained bias knew no geographical bounds, but was common throughout all regions. This was the concept that women were naturally more likely to become witches than men. Males who were identified as possible sorcerers were usually connected by family ties to a female previously accused of delving in magic.

More than eighty percent of all citizens executed for witchcraft in the colonies were female. Excluding Salem, where the prosecutions involved a greater number of males than was customary, the figure rises to more than ninety percent. In non-capital cases, the percentage of female defendants is only slightly lower, and among accusers testifying against supposed witches, women outnumbered men by an estimated four to one. In the Old World, where prejudices were even stronger, the ratio of female to male executions has been estimated at from twenty to one to as high as a hundred to one.

The presumption that women were naturally attracted to witchcraft was a tenet firmly established in both the law and in religion. King James I enunciated the doctrine in his treatise *Demonologie* when he asked: "What can be the cause that there are twentie women given to that craft, where there is but one man?" James answered:

> The reason is easie, for, as that sex is frailer than man is, so is it easier to be entrapped in these gross snares of the Devil, as was ever well proved to be true, by the serpent's deceiving Eve at the beginning, which makes him the homelier with that sex sensitive.

King James' theory was one of "passive witchery," based on the idea that women were both physically and mentally weaker than men and thus susceptible to evil. In Europe, a similar but more menacing attitude was popular. This philosophy centered not on superficial physical differences between the sexes, but on the inner Satanic nature of women.

The continental dogma maintained that females were inherently wanton, morally corrupt, and possessed a proclivity to choose evil over godliness. The belief, directly traceable to the biblical portrait of Eve as the instigator of sin, also included strong sexual connotations, which described females as carnal seducers.

Even the Anglican Church, which did not emphasize the satanic nature of women, included sexual overtones in the theory of passive witchery. Among the most prominent and dreaded abilities of witches, at least according to male writers, were those of making men impotent or castrated by magical "theft." Women were also credited with the ability to cast "glamours," which made male sex organs disappear or become invisible. Cures for bewitched "privie members" were widely circulated. Although it was also believed that witches possessed the power to make women sterile and barren of milk, these problems were not extensively discussed. Significant attention was placed on incubus, while the corresponding act of succubus was given only minor attention as an infrequent occurrence. In the male-dominated seventeenth century, the prospect of women made all-powerful by the devil and thus subject to no masculine control was a frightening thought.

Religious attitudes were among the strongest supports maintaining the portrait of women as inheritors of evil. In the western world, where only men were allowed to serve as the clergymen of God, it was assumed that the opposite situation would exist in hell. In the nether-world, where all factors were the reverse of the heavenly realm, women would be selected as priestesses of the devil.

Strict Puritan dogma, which stressed the basic inferiority of women, reinforced old-world myths of feminine evil. In New England, where women could be arrested for "walking disorderly," the concept of females as natural Satanists was enlarged by basic and constant biblical references to the untrustworthiness of women.

English law, by designating females to a second-class station, also contributed to the deep-seated bias. Sir William Blackstone's dictum that "the husband and wife are one, and that is the husband" was the guiding factor of Anglo-American jurisprudence. Regulations barred females from voting; they could not hold property, sue in court, enter certain professions, receive higher education, or defend themselves against physical abuse by male relatives. Only in rare circumstances could females come before the court to gain redress from oppressive treatment from kinsmen.

Although colonials were subject to the same anti-feminine influences as residents in England, the practical conditions in the New World necessitated development of more gentle methods of treatment. As a result, the almost overwhelming presumption of guilt that confronted women accused of witchcraft in England and Europe was somewhat diminished in America.

From the days of earliest settlement at Jamestown, when "maids" were sold for wives, able-bodied women were highly valued. Unlike Europe, where females were often viewed as expendable, as unnecessary mouths to feed, women in the colonies were desperately needed to perform vital tasks in the home and field. With their help, life could be precariously maintained. Without it, survival was much less certain.

The influence of pietistic sects that openly advocated equality of women also limited the harshness traditionally accorded to the sex. Led by Quakers, these groups sought to establish equal justice for men and women. Their activities undoubtedly led to a diminishing of the importance of doctrines such as that proclaiming the satanic nature of females.

Despite the mitigating tendencies, strong remnants of European and English prejudices remained in America, but environmental factors made their acceptance less blind. Except in instances where mass hysteria created illogical reactions, strong proof was needed before a woman was either brought to court or condemned to death on a charge of witchcraft. Their value in building a new world was simply too great to be lightly sacrificed.

Although all women were deemed suspect, some were judged to be of greater danger than others. Perhaps the most menacing females were the aged. The suspicion in which the elderly were viewed did not lessen as a result of the colonial experience. Reginald Scot, in describing the "typical" witch, mirrored the general distrust of elderly women by announcing:

> The sort of such as are said to be witches are women which be commonly old, lame, bleare-eyed, pale, foul, and full of wrinkles; poor, sullen, superstitious, and papists; or such as know no religion.
> ... They are lean and deformed, showing melancholie in their faces, to the horror of all that see them. They are doting, scolds, mad, devilish, and not much differing from them that are thought to be possessed with spirits. . . .

Just as the young and middle-aged were valued for the contributions they could make to the colonial society and family, so were older women, no longer capable of caring for themselves, resented for their dependence upon others. The pioneer society had no room for the vagrant, the idle or aged, who could not assist in national building. Because of this scornful attitude, most widows, whatever their age, were urged to remarry immediately after the death of their mate. This move assured a continued private means of support, which would relieve the burden of maintenance from the public till. In addition, a remarried widow provided a single man with a household servant, so that he might be free for what was considered more vital tasks.

The physical qualities of old age helped to reinforce the connection between the elderly and witchcraft. Natural signs of aging, such as brownish spots, could be identified as devil's marks and protuberances seen as witches' teats.

Women who chose a single life, whatever their age, were subject to the same suspicions as were older females. Any unwed woman, living alone by choice or circumstance, was considered to be in an unnatural, ungodly state, far removed from the ideal situation sanctioned by the church. In a country where men outnumbered women by as much as six to one, a *femes sole,* woman without man, was viewed as near traitorous by the citizenry.

Most young girls were married by the age of fifteen, and if a reliable husband had not been found by eighteen, the single woman was termed a "superannuated maid." At age twenty she became a "stale maid," and by thirty gained the unflattering designation of a "thornback." Unmarried males met similar resentment. William Byrd, commenting on the situation in Virginia, announced: "An old maid or an old bachelor are as scarce among us and reckoned as ominous as a blazing star."

On the informal list of suspicious characters connected with witchcraft, healers and midwives were included just below aged and unmarried females.

A significant number of settlerwomen were involved in medical activities, for trained physicians were few in number. Doctors who did boast professional credentials were male and usually resided only in the most populated towns. For the great majority of rural and village-dwelling Americans, female folk healers provided the sole source of medical assistance.

The connection between healing and witchcraft was a long-standing one. Many of the cures distributed by healers had been handed down from mother to daughter for generations and were based on unwritten herbal concoctions. Much secrecy and professional jealousy was involved in the preparation of a woman's "physicks," and by custom, the whole bag of cures possessed by a folk doctor was called her "mysteries." The ancient connection between the supernatural and medical worlds is shown in the derivation of the word "witch." The term is believed to have stemmed from the medieval title *wicca,* which described a folk doctor who cured by mystical means.

Only a fine line separated legitimate cures from supernatural magic. In the seventeenth century, the origin of most disease was unknown and citizens attributed the majority of their ailments to the workings of illustrious providences. A healer whose secrets were effective against stubborn illness was considered particularly knowledgeable in the workings of supernatural influences.

While some of the herbal potions distributed by healers were useless, others contained medically efficacious ingredients such as foxglove, the source of digitalis. Hallucinogenics were not unknown additives and many components were highly potent and toxic in the extreme. The healer who by mistake miscalculated the amount of these dangerous herbs might contribute directly to the death of a patient. If any degree of ill will had existed between the doctor and her client previous to the error, the healer could well be charged in the death. But instead of being confronted with allegations of malpractice, the indictment would specify murder by witchcraft.

Several colonials who considered themselves to be witches may have openly practiced healing by magical acts rather than by the use of herbal remedies. Increase Mather condemned one Boston doctor who attempted to cure a severe toothache by giving to the patient a sealed letter that included "magical" characters and the words: *In nomine patris filu spiritus sancti.* The phrase, translated as "preserve thy servant such a one," was thought by Mather to be a common witch term.

A second record of supernatural healing was recorded as having taken place in Boston in the early 1680s. In this instance, a pagan healer applied a magical cure for the ague. The spell involved the printing of Greek words on pieces of bread, which were to be consumed by the patient in a prescribed order over a five-day period. The most important crust in the series was marked with the supernatural word *kalendant.*

Attempts to regulate self-trained doctors were made during the later colonial era, but these measures concentrated primarily on limiting the influence of obvious charlatans or setting maximum fees for services. Female healers were generally allowed to concoct their salves, nostrums, and ointments unrestrained by official intervention.

The lenient attitude toward amateur physicians was an indication of the seriousness with which illness was viewed. In the seventeenth century even the most trivial wound or sickness could result in death. Wide latitude was given to any seemingly responsible individual whose cures might be effective in saving lives.

Even the most prominent members of society were involved in the search for miraculous cures. Governor John Winthrop constantly conducted medical experiments, some of which included procedures that could have been interpreted as magically oriented. Winthrop was particularly proud of his concoction to cure ague. In describing the administration of his remedy, the official wrote:

I have of late tryed the following magnetical experiment with infallible success. Pare the patient's nayles when the fever is coming on; and put the parings into a little bag of fine linen or sarenet; and tye that about a live eel's neck, in a tub of water. The eel will dye and the patient will recover.

Winthrop's remedy, if proposed by a less respectable citizen, might have been seen as an attempt to use supernatural power, but because the inventor was beyond reproach, the eel cure was accepted as a valid solution. A second potion favored by the governor involved the use of a special black powder of toads. Toads and frogs figured prominently in traditional witch cures, and Winthrop's correspondence with London's Dr. Edward Stafford reinforced the belief in the animals as healing aids. Dr. Stafford's black powder was an all-purpose remedy that could be made only in the month of March. Not only was the medicine good for "ye plague, small pox, purple, all sorts of fevers," but the potion also helped to prevent or cure infections. When mixed with vinegar, it was a sure remedy for gangrene or the "bite of anie venomous beast."

The bodies of other animals were also thought to possess strange qualities of healing. The burned shell of a turtle, pounded into ashes and dissolved in wine and oil, was useful in curing sores of the feet. A pulverized turtle head, combined with egg whites, not only prevented baldness, but also eliminated hemorrhoids. Osprey beaks healed toothaches, and the oil of sea calf, "soile," healed cuts and brought women out of "mother fits."

An extremely popular medical theory of the seventeenth century was the doctrine of signatures. This school was based on the idea that plants were cures for whatever the flora resembled. God had supposedly marked each part of nature with an identifying symbol to guide humans to his miraculous healing aids. Thus, the plant eyebright, which featured a prominent spot resembling a pupil, was considered helpful in curing eye disease. Bugloss, a plant shaped like a serpent, was used for snakebite. Celandine, a herb filled with bright yellow juice, was administered for jaundice.

The supposed connection between disease and magic created major problems for successful practitioners. A healer who produced a potion that resulted in a cure for the stubborn and previously untreatable disease was liable to be charged with using supernatural charms.

In 1669 Goody Burt of Massachusetts was accused by a fellow physician of producing cures that could not be explained by natural causes. In effect, Goody had been so successful at her calling that the recoveries were attributed not to competency or luck, but to witchcraft.

More concrete accusations were made against Charlestown doctor Margaret Jones, the first person to be executed for witchery in Massachusetts. The prime evidence in Margaret's 1648 trial was that she had misused her medical knowledge and powers to bewitch others. In listing the charges against her, Winthrop wrote:

> June 4, 1648. At this court one Margaret Jones of Charlestown was indicted and found guilty of witchcraft, and hanged for it. The evidence against her was:-
>
> 1. That she was found to have a malignant touch, as many persons (men, women, and children) whom she stroked or touched with any affection or displeasure were taken with deafness, or vomiting, or other violent pains or sickness.
>
> 2. She was practicing physic, and her medicines being such things as (by her own confession) were harmless, as anise seed, liquors, etc., yet had extraordinary violent effect.
>
> 3. She would tell such as would not make use of her physic that they would never be healed: and accordingly their diseases and hurts continued, with relapse, against the ordinary course, and beyond the apprehension of all physicians and surgeons.
>
> 4. Some things which she foretold came to pass accordingly; other things she could tell of (as secret speeches, etc.) which she had no ordinary means to come to the knowledge of.
>
> 5. She had (upon search) an apparent teat in her secret parts as fresh as if it had been newly sucked, and after it had been scanned upon a forced search, that was withered and another began on the opposite side.

The allegation that Margaret possessed a malignant touch was not an extraordinary indictment. It had been long believed that extremely good or evil persons could pass their characteristic traits to any person who was physically contacted. English rulers were considered to have a powerful healing touch that was effective against most diseases. King Charles II is credited with having touched more than 100,000 sick subjects during his thirty-five-year reign. The concept of the Royal Touch was highly regarded in the colonies, where in 1687, a New Hampshire pauper petitioned the General Assembly for funds to make the journey to England so that he could be healed at the hands of the King.

Like medical healers, midwives were also considered closely aligned with the supernatural world and prone to the practice of witchcraft. The roots of this superstition were shrouded in the ages-old puzzlement concerning childbirth and the mysterious conditions that surrounded the beginning of life. Witches had long been depicted in illustrations holding broomsticks or pitchforks, symbols of fertility since the Middle Ages.

In Europe, midwives were not infrequently accused of stealing the caul, a membrane that covered the heads of infants in the womb. The caul was supposedly sold to witches, who prepared potions that brought good luck and provided protection from drowning. The bodies of unbaptized babies, procured by disreputable midwives, were considered a major ingredient in the ointment that enabled witches to soar through the air. City regulations in Würzburg, Bavaria, forbade midwives from taking the placenta from a delivery room, for the cords were used in the celebration of the black mass. In some areas, it was believed that midwives stole newborn infants for human sacrifices at sabbaths.

The overwhelming mistrust of midwives, which was prominent in Europe, was not carried over into the colonies. Although they were regarded with some suspicion, most midwives stood as highly valued members of American society. One reason for this increased tolerance was the importance accorded to childbirth. In the sparsely settled new land, infants were a cause for great joy. The festivities, however, were often marred by sorrow, for only three out of every ten babies lived to adulthood and the mortality rate for new mothers was extremely high. A midwife who could assure a safe delivery for both woman and child was highly praised and not easily sacrificed to baseless superstitions. The allegiances paid to these female surgeons was so great that it was not until the middle of the eighteenth century that male obstetricians began to make inroads into the midwives' traditional areas. Even at this late date, deliveries by male physicians were criticized in most areas as being immodest or immoral.

Midwives played important roles in the legal process as well as in health care. They served on juries of matrons called to investigate suspected cases of witchcraft, infanticide, and abortion. In bastardy actions, midwives were responsible for determining if a woman had indeed given birth, and in cases where convicted criminals sought to avoid punishment by "pleading their bellies," midwives determined if pregnancy did exist.

While successful midwives were usually free of suspicion of witchcraft because of their utilitarian value, those connected with a series of unusual or fatal births were not so fortunate. Just as the miscalculating healer was considered to be a potential murderer by magic, so the unsuccessful midwife was received with wariness.

Elizabeth Morse, tried in the 1680 poltergeist case involving her grandson, came under attack for the suspected use of magic in connection with her midwife practice. One of Elizabeth's accusers was Thomas Wells, who testified to strange circumstances that had taken place during the birth of his child. After Wells' wife had refused to call in Elizabeth to oversee the delivery, the pregnant woman was struck with great pain and suffered unproductive labor for many hours. When, as a last resort, Goody Wells agreed that Goody Morse should be summoned, the baby was easily born.

A vindictive midwife was also the subject of what was probably the first colonial investigation into witchcraft. In 1626, Virginian Goody Wright was accused of bewitching the spouse and child of Sargeant Booth. In a trial before the General Court, Booth testified that although he had arranged for Wright to "bring his wife to bed," Goody Booth had different ideas. The help of Goody Wright was vetoed by the prospective mother, because the midwife was left-handed, a trait that portended bad luck. Instead, a Goody Graue was asked to be present at the birth. According to Booth, Goody Wright was infuriated by the employment of a competitor. Court notations summarizing Booth's statements suggest that he believed the midwife took immediate steps to vent her revenge:

> The next day after his wife was delivered, the said goodwife *Wright* went away from his house very much discontented, in regard the other midwife had brought his wife to bed; shortly after this, this deponent's wife's breast grew dangerouslie sore of an imposture and was a month or five weeks before she was recovered. At which time this deponent himself fell sick, and continued the space of three weeks, and further sayeth that his child, after it was born, fell sick

and so continued the space of two months, and afterwards recovered, and so did continue well for the space of a month, and afterwards fell into extreme pain the space of five weeks and so departed.

The death of a newborn under unusual circumstance, although suspicious, did not usually result in the extreme reaction that occurred in cases of malformed infants. Two popular explanations for severe misshapenness were that the fetus had been enchanted in the womb by a vindictive witch or that the midwife had cast a spell during delivery to distort the infant. The concept that the tragedy may have been the result of incubus with a devil was not seriously considered.

Cotton Mather was one colonial who knew the sorrow of a deformed child. Mather's baby lived only a brief time after delivery, and the clergyman attributed his offspring's fate to the workings of a witch and her familiar. He wrote:

> I had great reason to suspect a witchcraft in this preternatural accident; because my wife, a few weeks before her deliverance, was affrighted with a horrible specter in our porch, which fright caused her bowels to turn within her; and the specters, which both before and after tormented a young woman in our neighborhood, brag'd of their giving my wife that fright, in hopes, they said, of doing mischief unto her infant. . . .

Because of Mather's high standing in the community, no thought was given to the fact that the birth might have been caused by impropriety on his wife's part, but not all mothers enjoyed such immunity. The delivery of a stillborn infant in the fall of 1637 resulted in allegations of witchcraft, deviltry, and heresy on the part of not only the mother, but the midwife and a bystander as well.

The incident began when the child was born to Mary Dyer, a close friend of Anne Hutchinson, the religious renegade of Boston. Witnesses to the delivery were Anne, a midwife named Jane Hawkins, and an unidentified woman who later proved "unable to keep counsel" concerning the event.

Only the four women present actually saw the child, which was immediately buried. Several days later, however, rumors began to circulate that the infant had not been a normal baby, but a supernatural "monster." Only after village elders pressed Anne for details did she admit that the birth had been other than routine. In excusing her silence on the matter, Anne claimed that she had originally intended to inform the authorities of the strange happening, but had been persuaded to remain silent by minister John Cotton.

Upon being informed of the admission, the governor called a meeting of church elders and local magistrates to investigate the affair. Winthrop recorded the results of the interrogation of midwife Hawkins:

> At first she confessed only that the head was defective and misplaced, but being told that Mrs. Hutchinson had revealed all, and that he intended to have it taken up and viewed, she made this report of it, VIZ. It was a woman child, stillborn, about two months before the just time, having life a few hours before. It came hiplings till she turned it. It was of ordinary bigness; it had a face, but no head, and the ears stood upon the shoulders, and were like an apes. It had no forehead, but over the eyes four horns, hard and sharp; two of them were above one inch long, the other two shorter. The eyes standing out and the mouth also, the nose hooked upward. All over the breast and back full of sharp pricks and scales, like a thornback. The naval and belly, with the distinction of sex, [were] where the back should be, and the back and hips before, where the belly should have been. Behind, between the shoulders, it had two mouths, and in each of them a piece of red flesh sticking out. It had arms and legs as other children, but instead of toes it had on each foot three claws, like a young fowl, with sharp talons.

Also called for questioning was Reverend John Cotton, the grandfather of Cotton Mather. Cotton admitted that he had counseled Anne Hutchinson to keep silent concerning the birth and claimed he had done so because he interpreted the event as a "providence of God." The minister explained that certain evidence had indicated that the malformed child was meant to be a sign or warning intended only for those present at the birth. Cotton reached this conclusion because although many women had been passing in and out of the delivery room, only four were in attendance at the actual time of birth. Thus he concluded that God intended knowledge of the incident should be "only [for] the instruction of the parents and such others to whom it was known." Cotton apologized publicly for his bad counsel, but maintained that if the tragedy had occurred in his family, he too would have wished the incident to remain private.

The governor and his council, not satisfied with the report of

Anne Hutchinson, Goodwife Hawkins, and Mr. Cotton, enlarged their investigation and exhumed the corpse of the infant. Women who had been attending, but who were not actually present at the birth of baby Dyer, were called as additional witnesses. The results of the new hearings supported the contention that supernatural factors and perhaps Satanism were involved. Winthrop continued his narration:

> The Governor, with the advice of some other of the magistrates and elders of Boston, caused the said monster to be taken up, and though it was much corrupted, yet most of these things were to be seen, as the horns and claws, the scales, etc. When it died in the mother's body (which was about two hours before birth), the bed whereon the mother lay did shake, and withall there was such a noisome savour, as most of the women were taken with extreme vomiting and purging, so as they were forced to depart; and others of them, their children were taken with convulsions (which they never had before nor after), and so were sent for home, so as by these occasions, it came to be concealed.

Strong proof of satanic presence was indicated by two factors in the new testimony. The shaking of the bed is consistent with the belief that demons struggle violently when confronted with their own demise. It did not seem unreasonable to conclude that such a battle would have taken place during the death throes of the "demon" infant. Similarly, the foul smell indicated that evil was lurking in the delivery room, for all devils were thought to emit an oppressive odor of hell and brimstone. Just as extremely good people were supposed to give off pleasing aromas, so evildoers were endowed with a noxious aura.

One result of the birth and follow-up attempt to conceal the event was the departure from the province of midwife Hawkins. Jane had been under suspicion for some time and after the mysterious delivery, her connection with the supernatural world was considered even more probable.

Anne Hutchinson, because of her close association with Jane Hawkins, was also suspected of witchcraft, but the issues arising out of the devil-inspired birth were overshadowed by a more severe charge of religious heresy. As a result of her free thought and actions, Anne had been occupied for some time in a confrontation that would make her one of the most important women in American history.

Anne immigrated to Massachusetts colony from England in 1634. Despite her lack of formal education, the woman almost immediately began questioning the accepted tenets of the Puritan hierarchy. Over increasing opposition from the established church, Anne held meetings in her home that centered around theological criticism of the Puritan clergy, which so firmly governed the colony.

In order to combat the abuses she believed were oppressing the people, Anne developed a new form of religion called antinomianism. Her creed was based on the concept of a more gentle God than that worshiped by John Cotton and John Winthrop. Her public pronouncements soon placed her in direct opposition to the teachings of the Boston clergy. The woman, together with her friends and religious colleagues Jane Hawkins and Mary Dyer, was publicly branded as a dangerous heretic.

The wide publicity given to the monster birth and the resulting insinuation of witchcraft may have been an attempt on the part of the establishment to discredit Anne and her followers. Implications of the birth were that deviates from accepted dogma were closely aligned with satanistic happenings. Cotton, who had advised Anne to remain silent, may have hoped that the story would eventually become public, and that her secrecy would be interpreted as an attempt to conceal a devil-inspired event.

News of the birth circulated far beyond the borders of Boston. On June 29, 1638, passengers aboard the ship carrying John Josselyn to America hailed two eastbound vessels off Cape Anne. When the passengers of the passing boats were asked for news from the colonies, two events were shouted across the water. According to Josselyn, one important happening was a violent earthquake. The other was "the birth of a monster at Boston, in the Massachusetts Bay, a mortality." Nearly a year after the delivery, the monster was again mentioned to Josselyn, this time on isolated Noddle's Island off the colonial coast.

Like Jane Hawkins, Anne Hutchinson was banished. In a celebrated event, the questioning woman was found guilty of seducing the clergy and was summarily excommunicated from the Puritan Church. When she was ordered out of Sunday services, Mary Dyer voluntarily rose to share Anne's humiliation.

Anne, accompanied by a small band of followers, settled in Rhode Island, where she helped to found the town of Portsmouth.

Her ministry continued to call and she moved again, this time to Long Island. Later she moved to an unsettled area near New Amsterdam, and it was here, in 1643, that Anne and all but one member of her family were massacred in an Indian raid. Back in Massachusetts, the clergy announced that the killings had been intended as a sign from God to show the just deserts received by heretics.

Mary Dyer and her husband William followed Anne into the wilderness. William became secretary of Rhode Island, while Mary, concerned more with spiritual rather than secular matters, converted to Quakerism. The act would later cost her her life.

Quakers, both male and female, were a final category of suspicious persons judged prone to the practice of witchcraft. In the eyes of most Puritans, the philosophies of the Friends were closely akin to the tenets of witchcraft. Both were considered instruments of the devil and were diametrically opposed to the true worship of God. Cotton Mather claimed that Satanism lay at the very heart of Quakerism, and suggested that the sect's members had been lured into the dogma by the devil himself. Mather announced:

> The stories recorded by my father (plainly enough) demonstrate that diabolical possession was the thing which did dispose and incline men unto Quakerism; their Quakerism was the proper effect of their possession. . . .

A 1681 disturbance instigated by several Quaker converts lent credence to the clergyman's theory. The incident centered around Thomas Case, a radical Friend accused of bewitching several other Quakers and luring them to a remote outpost at Southold, Long Island. Jonathan Dunen, one of "Case's Crew," as the splinter group was known, was not content to remain in the secluded area; he returned to Massachusetts to instigate a series of disruptions that brought both moral shock and rumors of witchcraft to Salem. The controversy reached a peak when Dunen supposedly possessed one Mary Ross. Mary's conduct was seen as confirmation that the devil was working through the Quaker sect. A 1742 work, signed Antienthusiasticus, described the events:

> One Jonathan Dunen drew away the wife of a man to Marshfield, to follow him, and one Mary Ross, falling into their company, presently was possessed with as frantic a demon as ever was heard

of. She burnt her clothes. She said she was Christ. She gave names
to the gang with her, as apostles, calling one Peter, another Thomas.
She declared that she would be dead for three days, and then rise
again, and accordingly she seemed then to die.

Dunen then gave out that they should see glorious things when she
rose again; but what she did was thus: Upon her order, Dunen
sacrificed a dog. The men and the two women then danced naked
together; for which, when the constable carried them to the magistrates, Ross uttered stupendous blasphemies, but Dunen lay for
dead an hour on the floor, saying when he came to himself, that
Mary Ross bid him, and he could not resist.

Long before the first Friends arrived in America, word of their
growing strength in England had reached Puritan ears. The news was
not well accepted, for the doctrines of the cult were interpreted as
being as great a danger as those of Anne Hutchinson and her An-
tinomians. Quakers strongly believed in the existence of an inner light
that glowed in each person as an extension of God. By following the
teachings of this light, individuals could determine what was the true
will of the divine being. Quakers also objected to the highly organized
structure of the traditional church; they believed in strict separation
of church and state and in the equality of women. Each of these creeds
was a radical departure from accepted Puritan teachings.

Massachusett's first confrontation with the so-called heretics
came in July of 1656, when Mary Fisher and Ann Austin arrived in
Boston from England to proselyte for their cause. This was not the
women's first attempt at missionary ministry. Mary had been earlier
apprehended while preaching at Cambridge University and together
with a fellow Friend had been ordered stripped and "whipped at the
market cross till the blood ran down their bodies." Ann Austin was
identified simply as a woman "strickened in years."

Despite their unthreatening appearance, the women were seized
as soon as their boat dropped anchor in Boston. Deputy Governor
Richard Bellingham, acting in the absence of Governor John Endicott, ordered the pair quarantined aboard ship while their possessions were ransacked for books containing "corrupt, heretical, and
blasphemous doctrines." Approximately a hundred such volumes
were found and ordered burned by the town's hangman. The Quakers
were then taken to jail and placed in a dark, secluded cell, isolated

from other detainees. In an attempt to halt the spread of contaminating Quaker heresies, a £5 fine was ordered levied on any citizen who attempted to converse with the women.

Matrons were called to search Mary and Ann for "tokens" of witchcraft and the examination was thorough indeed. Not only was a routine body search conducted, but the examiners made a careful probing between the women's toes and amongst their hair.

Bellingham's severe reaction to the seemingly innocent threat may have been partially motivated by his own self-interest. Only one month earlier, his sister-in-law Ann Hibbins had been hanged for practicing witchcraft. The deputy governor may have feared that any leniency on his part in dealing with the Quakers would indicate that he also was sympathetic to the devil.

The women were kept in solitary confinement for five weeks, but no incriminating marks had been found on their bodies and formal charges of witchcraft were not pressed. Bay colony officials decided instead on a non-violent means of handling the infiltrators. Ship's master Sewin Kempson was ordered to transport the prisoners "beyond the seas." Their Bibles would be confiscated to pay for their prison fees.

Two days after Mary and Ann were trundled out of Boston, eight additional Friends arrived in the port city. They too were seized and searched for witches' marks. After eleven weeks imprisonment, the group was deported back to England.

In an attempt to stem the growing number of incoming Quakers, fines of £100 were levied against any ship's captain who knowingly transported a heretic to Massachusetts. Despite the ban, the Friends continued to arrive. Most were immediately apprehended and ordered whipped, imprisoned, and banished. Any who returned after being officially exiled were sentenced to have one ear cut off. The penalty for returning in defiance a second time was the loss of the other ear. If the infraction was made thrice, the Quaker's tongue was bored through with a hot iron.

Soon the flood of immigrating Quakers became too great to be halted by the relatively mild means of banishment. In a desperate move, the Massachusetts saints enacted a series of harsh laws directed at controlling the dissidents. The statutes proclaimed the Quakers guilty of spreading "diabolical doctrines" designed to "overthrow the order established in church and commonwealth." "Mutiny, sedition, and rebellion" were also added to the list of possible charges.

Results of the laws were severe. Salem residents Lawrence and Cassandra Southwick, imprisoned for seven weeks for entertaining Quakers, became so impoverished by the costs of prison fees that they were unable to pay fines levied against them. In order to raise the money, the court ordered the Southwicks' two children sold into slavery "to any of the English nation at Virginia or Barbados." The attempt was unsuccessful, for no buyer could be found who would pay a fair price.

Whippings, brandings, and mutilations were added to the punishment suffered by apprehended Friends, but eventually these measures too proved ineffective. At last, Massachusetts officials authorized that the death sentence should be meted out to offending Quakers.

In 1659, Mary Dyer, mother of the Boston "monster," was seized in Boston, where she had journeyed in order to minister to several imprisoned Friends. She was sentenced to die, but the execution was commuted and instead she was banished. One month later, the woman was again apprehended within colonial borders and once more the court ordered her exiled. Mary would not be stopped and returned still again. This time, William Dyer feared that a reprieve would not be forthcoming. In a letter to Boston magistrates, William pleaded for his wife's life by announcing:

> Yourselves have been husbands of wife or wives, and so am I, yea
> to one most dearly beloved. Oh, do not you deprive me of her, but
> I pray you, give me her out again. Pity me—I beg it with tears.

The magistrates were not moved. Mary received the death sentence and in May of 1660 was hanged.

The Quaker executions were halted only through direct intervention by King Charles II, who forbade the persecution or putting to death of any citizen on the basis of religious belief. Puritan authorities, while ceasing the capital punishments, continued to inflict beatings, banishment, and brandings on Friends. The contention that Quakerism and witchcraft were inextricably connected also went undiminished. In October of 1662, Mary Tilton was exiled for "having like a sorceress gone from door to door to lure and seduce people, yea even young girls, to join the Quakers." Two years earlier, Oyster Bay's

Mary Wright had been sent to the General Court of Massachusetts for trial on witchcraft charges. Although she was acquitted on that count, Mary was found guilty of being a Quaker and was banished out of the Bay's jurisdiction.

As the reaction of the New England population and courts became more firmly entrenched against the Quakers, members of the persecuted sect began to adopt more militant methods. Increasingly, Friends were unwilling to moderate their ministrations. More extreme protests were undertaken against what was considered to be the corrupt moral atmosphere of the Puritans.

In July of 1677, Margaret Brewster and several other Quakers confronted a congregation gathered for worship at Boston's Old South Meeting. Before entering the church, Margaret took off her shoes, smeared her face with ashes, rumpled her hair, and clad herself only in a sackcloth. Amid great shrieking and howling from the Puritans, Margaret and her Friends stomped into the church shouting dire predictions of calamities they believed would come to pass if the saints did not mend their ways.

The local constable was called to quell the disturbance and the entire group was arrested. Margaret, however, escaped extreme punishment for her act. At a subsequent trial, the lawman was unable to positively identify her as the person he had apprehended. The confusion, he claimed, resulted from the fact that during the crime, Margaret had been disguised "in the shape of a devil." Instead of permanent injury, Margaret's punishment called for her to be whipped "up and down" the town at the cart's tail.

The public display of nudity also became a favorite tactic and one designed to symbolize the spiritual nakedness of Puritan settlers. Quaker Deborah Wilson was given thirty lashes for having walked through the streets of Salem without clothes, and colleague Lydia Wardwell of Newberry was ordered whipped in front of a local tavern for parading nude through a local meeting house.

CHAPTER VI

Climates of Witchcraft

DURING most of the colonial era, the circumstances surrounding witchcraft cases followed a simple pattern. A single individual would be charged with practicing magic by another settler or by a small group of neighbors. Usually the charge was triggered by an unexplainable calamity that had befallen the accuser soon after a disagreement with the suspected witch. A past history of similar coincidences might have created suspicions that were not then pressed because of lack of evidence.

After the accused was formally charged, the case proceeded through the courts much like any other case. Witnesses were called, testimony and cross examinations were conducted, and a verdict was reached. Depending upon the jury's finding, the defendant was either released or punished. Following the disposition of the case, years and perhaps decades might pass before witchcraft charges were once more lodged against an individual.

Occasionally this pattern of justice broke down and, for no seeming reason, entire communities became inflamed in large-scale witchhunts. During one such period, occurring in New England from 1647 to 1663, courts were swamped with scores of trials. An estimated five times as many colonials per capita were executed in this era than in England during the same years. A similar plague of accusations swept through Salem in 1692. During the town's six months of purges, more than twice as many citizens were arrested on witchcraft allegations than had been charged in all the colonies during the previous eighty-five years of European settlement. The trend toward periodic, multiple prosecutions was seen on a lesser scale in other provinces. Virginia, which had not been the scene of a trial involving witchcraft for sixteen years, saw six accusations settled in court from 1694 to 1698.

The climate surrounding plural sorcery cases changed not only traditional patterns of adjudication, but also altered relationships within the society. No longer was suspicion limited to a single individual who may have displayed eccentric behavior. Instead, the specter of witchcraft assumed a conspiratorial form in which friends, relatives, and even mere acquaintances of the suspect were investigated as possible collaborators in a larger plot. Accusations were no longer made by single, injured parties. Instead, large numbers of citizens, displaying symptoms of extreme mental instability, came forward to point accusing fingers. Charges and evidence assumed mystical and unrealistic characteristics. Defendants, instead of indignantly pleading not guilty, often confessed that they were indeed practitioners of the black arts; entire towns would take sides on the issue. Then, as suddenly as they had begun, the mass witch-hunts halted, and life returned to normal.

In the extreme, these periods of deviate social behavior are called manias. In less serious instances they are identified as delusions. But both terms describe periods in which traditional reactions are replaced by more radical methods of confrontation. William Graham Sumner, in his book *Folkways,* deals with the sociological implications of such conditions by writing:

> Manias and delusions are mental phenomena, but they are social. They are diseases of the mind, but they are epidemic. They are contagious, not as cholera is contagious, but contact with others is essential to them. They are mass phenomena.

Scholar Clyde Kluckholm was also intrigued with the patterns of witch-hunts. According to Kluckholm, persecution of "witches" serves an important function in assuring community survival in times of peril. Underlying this theory is the concept that witch-hunts provide a relatively non-disruptive and efficient means of dealing with anxieties and hostilities present in most non-developed or primitive settlements. Witches become scapegoats for problems that cannot be confronted directly. To do so might create dissension on a scale large enough to destroy the community's sense of common purpose. Although the accused individual might be sacrificed as a witch, complete destruction of the society is avoided.

The need for such safety valves was particularly important in frontier areas such as the American colonies during the seventeenth century. In this environment, community survival depended upon the cooperative workings of all settlers. Large-scale tensions, if brought into the open, might rent the consensus that protected the enclave from outside danger. Through a sorcery trial, angers and frustrations could be vented in a non-violent manner, leaving intact the common sense of purpose.

External factors played an important role in creating a climate conducive to the breeding of a witch mania, and threats beyond community control were particularly important factors. Disasters such as plagues, droughts, or wars created in the settlers strong feelings of impotence and the realization that they were largely incapable of controlling their own destiny. By turning inwardly upon a suspected witch, the community reassured itself that it was not completely powerless to direct the future. In the colonies, where witches were credited with powers to instigate natural calamities, the prosecuting of enchanters enabled settlers to rationalize that although they were powerless to control the forces of nature, the controllers could be regulated. With the urges of anger, hatred, and fear safely vented in the witch trial, the community was then able to return to normal operation.

An overwhelming burden of external pressures may have been the major factor in stimulating the Salem trials. For three years before the first accusations, the village had been subject to a series of stresses that reached their peak on the eve of the first direct charge. The threats to Salem came from many directions. In 1692, Indian raids were of considerable concern. Attacks by the red people had increased and several colonials had been slain in the town's environs. In preparation for a more concerted attack, Essex County officials had ordered scouts to be on continuous alert in case of a widescale invasion. From the sea came increasing dangers from pirate raids, and rumors of a possible war with France grew stronger each day. Great fires in 1690 and

1691 had leveled much of neighboring Boston, an important supply and distribution center for the town. A drought and corn blight had destroyed much of the harvest of 1691, creating increasing famine as winter continued. Heavy new taxes had been imposed on the colonists, who had also lost their liberal self-governing charter. All Salem, like other Massachusetts communities, anxiously awaited news from London concerning the new form of government, which most residents feared would bring strict control by England. The Salem church, center of moral strength in the settlement, was being wracked by internal feuding. A new, unpopular minister had been employed after a diligent search had failed to uncover a more capable candidate. Finally, influential Cotton Mather, preaching from his Boston pulpit, was haranguing Puritans in the colony to root out all evil so that the remarkable series of disasters might come to an end.

Internal pressures as well as external could produce a climate conducive to witchcraft accusations. In Puritan New England, where almost every facet of an individual's life was closely regulated by church dogma, the oppressive exercise of clerical power resulted in strong psychological upheavals. Forms of relaxation such as games, dancing, social gatherings, and physical recreation were all forbidden as evil practices. Repression of sexual activities, except for procreation, was stringent and open display of affection was frowned upon. Large segments of the community, especially women and children, were subject to harsh and relentless discipline.

In such a climate, the seeking out of witch scapegoats provided a significantly more effective means of dispelling intra-group tensions than would an aggressive attack upon the leaders themselves. As well as reducing citizen hostilities, the mass witch trials were a warning to the theocratic government that the power of the community to act independently could not be completely repressed.

A climate for witchcraft was also provided when new or disruptive elements entered into a formerly close-knit society. The disproportionate number of Quakers suspicioned in New England as witches may be explained by this factor. In communities frightened by the influx of new ideas, trials became an important means of keeping foreign elements under control and perpetuating the status quo.

While a favorable environment was necessary to set the scene for widespread witch-hunts, some degree of community hysteria was also needed to trigger the affair.

Periods of group hallucination, during which the behavior of vast numbers of people becomes drastically altered, are not unknown in western history. The Childrens' Crusades of the Middle Ages drew thousands of recruits into an irrational scheme created by adult enthusiasm. If the element of mass suggestion had been absent, the crusades might have been immediately rejected as impractical and potentially suicidal.

A more extreme example occured in the fourteenth century, when a dancing mania swept through the lowland countries of Europe. Beginning in July of 1374, peasants by the thousands took to the streets for mass revels and marathon dances, which resulted in thousands of deaths. The event is now believed to have begun in Aix-la-Chapelle, after a large number of citizens ingested bread containing the hallucinogenic ergot, which contains the chemical compound D-lysergic acid amide. Although the irrational behavior of the original core of dancers was organically induced, the thousands who later joined the revel did so because of mass hysteria.

To some degree, the colonies in Massachusetts and Connecticut were in a perpetual state of mania. The pressures of the unyielding Calvinists were not conducive to promoting a healthy mental state among settlers. The true believers of New England were compelled to spend many of their waking hours contemplating death, evil, and satanistic destruction. The remainder of their lives was filled with unceasing toil and constant danger of eradication. A preoccupation with witchcraft was a natural outgrowth of this morbid situation.

As early as 1651, a day of humiliation was ordered in the bay colony so that citizens might consider the degree to which devil-inspired witchcraft had become rooted. The Puritan concern with sorcery, however, was not unique to America. The most extensive periods of English witch-hunting took place between 1642 and 1660, an era which signaled the rise to ultimate power of Puritanism in Britain. Sir Walter Scott, in commenting on the relationship of Puritanism and magic, explained:

> It usually happened that wherever the Calvinist interest became predominant in Britain, a general persecution of sorcerers and witches seemed to take place of consequence. Fearing and hating sor-

cery more than other Protestants, connecting its ceremonies and usages with those of the detested Catholic Church, the Calvinists were more eager than other sects in searching after the traces of this crime, and, of course, unusually successful, as they might suppose, in making discoveries of guilt, and pursuing it to the expiation of the fagot. . . .

The factors that created more than three hundred cases of witchcraft in Puritan New England were obviously absent in areas such as New Netherland–New York, where only three trials were conducted. A similar lack was seen in Pennsylvania, the Jerseys, and New Sweden on the Delaware, where a compulsion with sorcery never developed.

New Netherland, controlled by the Dutch until taken under English rule in 1664, differed in many aspects from other new-world areas. Since it was founded as a trading province for commercial interests, the settlers of New Netherland had none of the religious zeal that marked the colonies founded by persecuted religious sects. With the help of the Dutch West India Company, Holland's colonial outpost was kept well supplied. At no time did the economic situation reach the desperate conditions frequently found in New England villages.

Although Lutheran in character, the New Netherland Dutch had intellectually outgrown the belief in a satanistic conspiracy of witchcraft. In this respect, American immigrants were merely mirroring the attitudes of their mother country, for while other European nations were hanging and burning great numbers of enchanters, not a single trial for witchcraft took place in Holland after 1610.

Because of the province's character, New Netherland became a sanctuary for citizens suspected of witchcraft in colonies to the east. Peter Stuyvesant, captain general of the government, approved of this situation and in 1662 personally intervened in a Connecticut trial in order to save suspected witch Judith Varlett. Judith, a distant relative of Stuyvesant by marriage, had been imprisoned in Hartford on suspicion of practicing magic. When news of the situation reached Stuyvesant, he sought to secure Judith's release. In an October 13 letter to the Connecticut governor and Court of Magistrates, he wrote:

> By this occasion, of my brother-in-law, being necessitated to make a second voyage for aid [of] his distressed sister Judith Varlett, imprisoned as we are informed, upon pretend accusation of witchery, we really believe and . . . we dare assure that she is innocent

of such a horrible crime, and wherefor I doubt not she will now, as formerly, find ye, your Honours' favour and aid for the innocent.

Stuyvesant's character reference and plea for pardon were effective and Judith was released from custody. After fleeing to New Netherland, she married the captain general's nephew, proof that accusations of witchcraft were not considered permanent blemishes, at least among the upper classes of the colony.

The climate of tolerance born in New Netherland spread to nearby areas in the Jerseys and Delaware, but even more influential in these territories were the philosophies of the Pennsylvania Quakers.

From the earliest days of settlement, William Penn welcomed all religious and political dissenters to his domain. The policy resulted in the growth of a liberal acceptance of differing opinions and behavior similar to the attitudes in New Netherland.

Among the first to arrive at Penn's province were German refugees, fleeing from regions where witchcraft accusations were an accepted part of society. The new Americans, however, were not catholic inquisitors, but members of splinter protestant groups. Because these sects had rejected the religious persecutions prevailing in their native land, a German witch hysteria did not take hold in colonial society. Swedes and Finns, who settled in Pennsylvania, though possessing a cultural heritage of witchcraft persecutions, did not immigrate in numbers significant enough to impose their superstitious beliefs upon the majority.

Several other factors helped to prevent the introduction of sorcery mania into the area. Like New Netherland, the eastern portion of Pennsylvania became a flourishing trade center, where widespread economic hardship was virtually unknown. Further pressure was removed by Penn's treaty with local Indian tribes, which assured peace until 1718. However, the most significant deterrent to the creation of a witchcraft climate was the teachings of the Pennsylvania Quakers, the group that held complete political power. America's Friends did not adopt all the teachings of George Fox, the sect's leader, who strongly believed in the existence of witches and felt he had been given special powers to detect evil enchanters. Instead, Pennsylvania members, influenced by a rising tide of intellectualism, shed almost all vestiges of superstition.

Quakers, both adult and children, received a continuing education aimed at living a peaceful and rational life. Through these methods, Philadelphia quickly outstripped Boston as the center of accomplishment in the literary, artistic, scientific, and education fields. The democratic organization of the faith also tended to eliminate persecution of deviate behavior. Because no formal class of clergy existed, it was impossible for witch-hunting demagogues to gain control over the population.

Only one case of sorcery marred the colony's unblemished record of tolerance. Pennsylvania's sole trial for witchcraft took place in February of 1684, when Margaret Matson, a Swedish woman from Delaware County, was tried before Governor William Penn. Most of the allegations involved circumstantial evidence to the effect that the defendant had bewitched animals such as livestock and geese. The most damaging assertion presented was that made by Henry Drystreet, who reported that some twenty years earlier he had been told that Margaret was a witch.

The defendant was released on a technicality when the jury found her "guilty of having the common fame of a witch, but not guilty in the manner and form as she stands indicted." In other words, the court ruled that most citizens truly believed that Margaret was a witch, but despite her accepted reputation, there was no proof that she actually was a sorcerer. Neither the indictment nor the law made "common fame" a crime.

During the eighteenth century, large numbers of immigrants from Germany and Holland brought scores of superstitions to the Pennsylvania colony. Hex signs and talismans shaped like stars, half moons, and circles appeared on barns and houses as protection against evil spirits and powwowing became an acceptable means of treating disease. But although the general level of superstition increased, a similar rise in a belief in witchcraft did not materialize. The failure was primarily due to increasing use of scientific methods to explain events that had previously been attributed to supernatural causes.

Maryland and Virginia did not have the guiding spirit of humanism found in Pennsylvania. But also absent from the two southern provinces was the theological rabidness that characterized New England. As a result, these colonies stood midway between the two extreme approaches to witchcraft that developed to the north.

A rugged and individualistic spirit of self-determination marked life in the tobacco colonies. The environment of self-reliance was fostered by the lack of a strong central government and the relatively minor role played in society by religion. Although Maryland had been founded as a haven for Catholic immigrants, the few priests in residence were English-trained and did not condone the witchcraft inquisitions that were so prevalent in Europe. A bill of religious tolerance further insured that overwhelming power would not be concentrated in the hands of any one denomination. In Virginia, the Church of England was the legally constituted faith, but residents were not religious protesters and were thus more tolerant of opinions that conflicted with established dogma. A flourishing economy made Maryland and Virginia perhaps the most affluent areas in America. Citizens were seldom prey to the frustrations of New Englanders, whose financial situation was often marginal.

While many factors tended to eliminate sorcery as a preoccupation, citizens of the tidewater area were nevertheless bound by traditional English witchlore. Charges of enchantment were not common, but allegations did occur.

In Virginia, almost all accusations were processed through civil courts as actions of slander. The sole case involving execution for sorcery was the ex post facto hearing designed to investigate the hanging on the high seas of Katherine Grady. Even fewer incidents of witchcraft were recorded in Maryland, but those accusations that did reach the courts were prosecuted vigorously. Of the five defendants formally charged with witchcraft in Lord Baltimore's colony, one bill was not presented, two defendants were acquitted, and two sentenced to hang. Convicted witch John Cowman was reprieved, but in 1685, Rebecca Fowler, found guilty of practicing "certain evil and diabolical arts," became the only colonial legally hanged for witchcraft outside of Puritan New England. The relatively high ratio of those sentenced to die to those tried does not indicate that Marylanders viewed the crime of witchcraft as a more heinous infraction than did other colonials. Instead, the seeming harshness, coupled with the small number of prosecuted cases, demonstrates that only those infractions in which there was "indisputable" proof of guilt were taken to court.

The lack of a settled population was a major factor limiting the number of sorcery cases in the southernmost areas of the Carolinas and Georgia. Until 1733, when James Oglethorpe and his band of Huguenot refugees settled near the mouth of the Savannah River, Georgia was inhabited only by adventurers, traders, and Indians. By the time the pioneer settlements were large enough to breed the frictions needed for the development of witchcraft accusations, the Age of Reason had made the concept of sorcery obsolete.

A somewhat similar situation existed in South Carolina. Although the colony's first Code of Laws, adopted in 1712, decreed death as the penalty for witchcraft, no formal cases appear to have been heard in the province. South Carolina's Chief Justice Nicholas Trott did compose an essay on the matter, which was forwarded to the General Sessions, but Trott's conclusions seem to have been intended as a philosophical guide rather than as a decision in a pending case. In his essay, the jurist announced:

> Now, though I am not at all inclined to believe every common, idle story of apparitions and witches . . . yet that there are such creatures as witches I make no doubt; neither do I think they can be denied without denying the truth of the Holy Scriptures or most grossly perverting them.

Trott's firm belief in witchcraft was probably not shared by the majority of South Carolinians, for the judge represented the law-and-order concept in its extreme. One of his most distinguishing actions while serving on the bench was to order the burning at the stake of a woman convicted of murdering her husband. Trott interpreted the crime not as homicide, but as petit treason. For a female to slay her male lord, he concluded, was an act that threatened the very structure upon which the state rested.

Only a single accusation of witchcraft appeared in North Carolina and that action did not result in an indictment. In 1697, the grand jury of Currituck Precinct in Albemarle County rejected a bill drawn against Susannah Evans. The accusation had suggested that Susannah, with the help of the devil, had afflicted with "mortal pains" the body of one Deborah Bourthier. Reportedly, Deborah "departed this life" as a result of the witch's spell.

The almost complete lack of witchcraft actions in the south was not due entirely to the lack of a settled population and the relatively late date of colonization. Sociological factors also tended to depress the level of charges. Many enclaves were inhabited by immigrants who had come from the same old-world villages and whose descendants had been intimate for generations. Close ties of friendship and marriage tended to discourage allegations that might lead to physical punishment. Such relationships were usually absent in the older colonies to the north.

CHAPTER VII

Accusations and Confessions

COLONIALS charged their neighbors with witchcraft for many different reasons. Some accusations were based on simple financial gain. Others were rooted in complex psychological impulses. All were dangerous.

Among the most obviously motivated were those allegations stemming from personal pique. Long-term feuds between the accused and accuser might lead to formal court trials involving witchcraft. Usually such charges, made in the heat of anger, were retracted by the contrite complainant or were dismissed by a magistrate familiar with the behind-the-scenes dispute.

Some allegations were actually a subtle form of blackmail. When the accuser achieved a desired end, the sorcery charges were dropped as erroneous. Personal greed was a similar, but less frequent factor. For one who coveted another's land or property, the customary confiscation of a convicted witch's estate offered a tempting method of securing those things an unobliging neighbor might refuse to sell. Personal rivalry in politics or other private affairs might also be the motivation behind the lodging of charges, as could the dissatisfaction of a marital partner.

Most cases involving obvious personal motives of retribution or gain were quickly rejected by grand jurors or local judges, who realistically recognized that less-than-honest causes might lie behind the seemingly helpful actions of a citizen.

A limited number of charges were made by settlers of dubious mental stability or by paranoids. Colonial law accepted the possibility that delusions of the mind could promote outlandish actions on the part of the eccentric, mentally ill, or mischievously inclined members of a community. For example, the instigators of the hagriding case against Colchester's Sarah Spencer were examined for possible mental illness and officially deemed "not insane." In the same category were religious fanatics, whose unstable processes might lead to the charging of less pious citizens with associating with the devil. These zealots may have believed themselves instruments of God designated to ferret out non-conformers who appeared to choose the evil life instead of godliness.

But neither personal pique nor mental instability was the basis for most accusations. Undoubtedly, most accusers, steeped from birth in an unquestioning belief in the supernatural, truly considered that their targets practiced black magic.

A combination of factors probably influenced Connecticut's Rebecca Greensmith, herself imprisoned for witchcraft, to cry out that her husband Nathaniel was a fellow conspirator. In providing a long list of evidence to support the charge, Rebecca explained that her accusations were made "out of love to my husband's soul." The charges may have been prompted not only by a desire to help Nathaniel reach salvation, but also by marital discord, mental instability, and a firm belief that he was indeed an enchanter. Whatever the reasons, Goodman Greensmith had just cause for failing to appreciate his wife's solicitous attention. As a result of her allegations, he was found guilty of witchcraft and hanged beside his wife on the gallows. Rebecca's accusations centered on five major proofs indicating Nathaniel was guilty. Although detailed by colonial standards, Rebecca's allegations are typical in substance to those customary in Early America. In court testimony given on January 8, 1662, she announced:

1. My husband on Friday night last, when I came to prison, told me that: "Now thou hast confessed against thyself. Let me alone and say nothing of me and I will be good unto thy children."

2. I do now testifie that formerly when my husband hath told me of his great travel and labour, I wondered at it, how he did it; this he did before I was married, and when I was married, I asked him

how he did it, and he answered he had help that I knew not of.

3. About three years ago, as I think it, my husband and I were in ye wood several miles from home, and we were looking for a sow that we lost, and I saw a creature, a red creature, following my husband, and when I came to him, I asked him what it was that was with him, and he told me it was a fox.

4. Another time, when he and I drove our hogs into ye woods beyond ye pound that was to keep young cattle, several miles off I went before ye hogs to call them, and looking back I saw two creatures like dogs, one a little blacker than ye other. They came after my husband pretty close to him, and one did seem to me to touch him. I asked him what they were; he told me he thought foxes. I was still afraid when I saw anything, because I heard so much of him before I married him.

5. I have seen logs that my husband hath brought home in his cart that I wondered at it that he could get them into ye cart, being a man of little body and weak to my apprehension, and ye logs were such that I thought two men such as he could not have done it.

In most cases, accusers complaining of injuries by witchcraft followed the same pattern of procedure that was used by victims of less spectacular crimes, such as robbery, assault, fraud, or attempted murder. The exceptions to this predictable behavior came in situations where complainants showed classic signs of hysteria. Instances in which this factor was involved led to activities far different from any other criminal prosecution. "Hysterical" accusations and the climate they promoted beared little resemblance to sorcery allegations brought in less emotional times. Instead of rational court hearings, in which the accuser and the accused related their stories before a discerning jury, trials involving the element of hysteria often took place in a carnival-like atmosphere filled with the shrieks and cries of both accusers and spectators. Often the complainants were present en masse and so overwhelmed the suspect with outbursts that little defense could be presented. Jurors and judges were usually swayed by the emotional environment. Pre-trial assumptions of guilt were commonly deduced, and usually little credence was given to explanations presented by the accused.

In many cases, large numbers of people supposedly afflicted by the defendants were present in the courtroom. These individuals would punctuate the trial with unexpected seizures, which could be alleviated only by the conviction and death of the bewitcher. Among the most common complaints of these sufferers were sensations of cutting, pricking, biting, squeezing of internal organs, and twisting of bones. Also popular were symptoms of hysteria such as temporary blindness, deafness, muteness, loss of appetite and memory, difficulty in swallowing, and a sense of strangulation. Stigmata, such as teeth marks, might also appear. All signs of bewitchment became most intense when the afflicted persons were in the presence of the suspected enchanter.

In most cases, the afflicted lodged the initial complaints against the defendants. Although others might step forward with corroborating evidence, the greatest reliance was placed on the testimony of those who personally were experiencing the pains of a witch's spell.

Afflictions could be limited to a single sufferer, but usually the condition spread quickly to others. The contagious nature of symptoms may have been the result of auto-suggestion or of mass hallucination created by an overwhelming atmosphere of panic or fear. A more remote possibility is that witchcraft accusations, like the dances at Aix-la-Chapelle, may have originated organically. A single accuser, subject to epilepsy or schizophrenia, may have unintentionally spread abnormal behavior to others.

The Freudian interpretation of hysteria stresses that the condition occurs when an individual's tensions become so great that they can no longer be eased by emotional or verbal release. In an attempt to lessen the frustrations and anxieties, physical symptoms are manifested. For centuries before the witchcraft delusions in America and Europe, hysteria had been recognized as a physical condition of mysterious origins. Traditionally it had been most often displayed in females. The term itself, derived from the Greek word *hystera,* or uterus, clearly suggests a sexual link.

In the colonies, incidence of hysterical accusations was limited almost entirely to women and young girls. Only rarely did adolescent boys show such behavior, and there were no significant instances of hysterical accusations by adult males.

Hysterical accusers also tended to belong to certain economic and social groups, with the disorder appearing most frequently among members of the yeoman class. The prescribed, inherited status that existed in England was only partially eliminated by the leveling nature of the colonial experience. An American "aristocracy," distinctly separated from the "middling" masses, was as firmly in control of the government as were the lords in Parliament. Citizens who reached this high level of financial or social achievement were rarely involved in hysterical accusations. Success seems to have been incompatible with the syndrome.

The prevalence of women and the poor among this type of accuser indicates that the allegations may have been a defense mechanism for less powerful elements in society. The poor, the young, and women had few means by which their grievances could be aired or their aims achieved. Barred from public councils, voiceless in forming community goals, and effectively helpless in the economic realm, these uninfluential settlers found a viable weapon in accusing the more privileged of witchcraft. Denied use of traditionally accepted channels of expression, those who had been assigned to passive roles in society were thus able to partially alleviate personal insecurity. By this method, accusers could temporarily break from their assigned social and physical roles and exert influence on the community.

In Puritan New England, such hysterical accusations may have been partially caused by guilt feelings. Those who saw their own repressed frustrations reflected in the unorthodox behavior of others might have subconsciously voiced their envy by lodging allegations of witchcraft. Bridget Bishop, accused by more individuals than any other witchcraft defendant, may have been a victim of such projection. Bridget, a woman of dubious moral character, flaunted most of the respected standards of Puritan society. Not only did she wear bright scarlet clothing, play the forbidden game of shovel board, and engage in frequent fist fights with her various husbands, but Bridget was also the successful mistress of two thriving taverns. When brought to court as an enchanter, Bridget faced a burden of allegations that were markedly vehement and vicious. Many centered not upon her supposed acts of witchcraft, but instead dealt with her unusual lifestyle.

Many of the factors present in hysterical accusations were also involved in cases where children were the chief accusers. The testimony of young people was particularly valued during the seventeenth century, when children were credited with possessing pure and uncorrupted thought. Unlike adults, adolescents were judged to be untainted by selfish or dubious motives. This idealistic concept was no doubt misplaced in many situations.

Offspring of colonial parents were inured from birth with a strong belief in the powers of the underworld. As products of an intellectually static society, young accusers served as mirrors of established beliefs, not as sources of the pure truth. Because of the validity considered inherent in their age, allegations lodged by children were doubly dangerous to a defendant. Children expressed inner fears and suspicions at the most basic level, untempered by mature judgments or realistic reservations. Youthful perceptions could easily result in misinterpretation of events that might be accepted as usual by more experienced adults.

Just as parental beliefs influenced childhood concepts, so did accusations by children confirm ideas held by their elders. Undoubtedly, many a settler who harbored suspicions of witchcraft against another hesitated to make a direct accusation because of lack of proof or fear of reprisal by a slander suit. But when an afflicted child named the suspect as a witch, the adult's unvoiced ideas were made more credible. It was not unusual for adult accusers to come forward with additional charges after allegations had been initiated by a child. In such cases, the young people may have been merely displaying adaptive behavior in an attempt to receive approval from their parents. Malice was not necessarily involved in the charge. Instead, the children were merely acting in a manner they considered to be acceptable in the adult world.

While the reports of young people were highly regarded by most, not all adults had confidence in the claims. Thomas Hutchinson, writing of the Salem trials, noted:

> A little attention must force conviction that the whole was a scheme of fraud and imposture, begun by young girls who at first, perhaps, thought of nothing more than being pitied and indulged, and continued by adult persons, who were afraid of being accused themselves. The one and the other, rather than confess their fraud, suffered the lives of so many innocents to be taken away.

Accounts of fraud were also leveled against Catreen Branch, young servant to Daniel Wescott. Catreen, known to be extremely devoted to her master, showed typical signs of possession and bewitchment. As a result of her accusations, three local women were brought before the court on witchcraft charges. But the approach taken by the Connecticut body was far different from the procedure at Salem, where judges unhesitatingly accepted as fact the claims of all afflicted persons. In this instance, the jurists, delved deeply into both Catreen's supposed affliction and her relationships with defendants Elizabeth Clawson, Mercy Disborough, and Goodwife Miller. The official cautiousness was based on a legitimate foundation, for one of their first discoveries was that a history of ill will had long existed between Catreen's beloved master and at least two of the accused women.

At least one resident suspected that Catreen had not been the sole instigator of the affair, but had been prompted in the hoax by Wescott. Abigail Cross testified that soon after Catreen began to display signs of bewitchment, Wescott had proposed a sporting wager. Under the plan, Abigail would bet her calf against Wescott's cow that he could not make Catreen perform a "trick" that no one else could do. When Abigail asked if Wescott could order the girl to appear bewitched, he answered with an unqualified yes.

Sarah Kecham also came forward with evidence tending to discredit the veracity of the accuser. Sarah claimed to have been present during a test administered to determine if the girl was actually beset by magic. The results of the experiment were questionable at best.

The idea of the trial was that if a naked sword was hanged over an afflicted person, the victim would laugh uproariously. The joy would be so uncontrollable that it would continue until the patient died from exhaustion. Sarah mannounced that when the sword was hung over Catreen, the girl indeed "laughed extremely." But when the weapon was suspended again, this time without the victim's knowledge, not even a giggle resulted.

Sarah Bates, a local healer called to minister to the afflicted one, also shed doubt on the truthfulness of the allegations. Sarah maintained that when she entered the sickroom, Catreen lay completely inert, as if in a deep coma. But when Sarah proposed that a bleeding should be undertaken, Catreen, who had seemed "senseless and speechless," instantly revived when the sharp instruments were brought out. Not only did the girl loudly protest against the bleeding but, according to Sarah, she was seen to laugh into a pillow when those in the room discussed the possibility that witchcraft was involved in the affliction. The cumulative doubts cast upon the reputation of Catreen proved telling to the jury. None of the three defendants was punished for the condition.

Colonial physician James Thacher reported a second case in which fraud was suspected to be the basis of witchcraft accusations. This incident took place in Littleton, Massachusetts, in 1720, when three sisters claimed to have been bewitched by a local woman. For eight months the girls insisted they were being tormented by painful pinching and other magical tortures. In one instance, when the accused witch was known to be suffering from a headache, the girls announced they had caused the condition by striking at an apparition that had been sent by the enchanter.

No trial was held and when the suspect died the girls recovered and the case faded from public view. But in 1728, interest was rekindled when the oldest accuser made a full retraction of the charges. She admitted that the entire episode had been manufactured in an attempt to gain attention. Because the sisters believed it was necessary to accuse someone, the elderly woman was chosen almost at random as a likely candidate.

Elizabeth Knapp, who accused several Groton residents and a local minister of bewitchment, found a less embarrassing way of extracting herself from possible punishment for fraud. When confronted with a doubting audience, Elizabeth explained that the devil had made her swear falsely.

More subtle motives for false accusations were involved in the 1658 witchcraft charge lodged in Easthampton, Long Island. In this case, Elizabeth Garlicke, a servant of Captain Lyon Gardiner, was accused by a fellow domestic of bewitching to death the accuser's child. The proceedings against Goody Garlicke were dismissed in court, evidently because of damaging evidence presented by Captain Gardiner. The officer announced that the accuser had actually starved her own child to death in order to obtain money for wet-nursing a foster child. To avoid punishment for the crime, she had chosen instead to accuse Mrs. Garlicke of causing the death by magic.

The reasons that prompted individuals to confess guilt of witchcraft were as complicated and varied as those motives that unlay the process of accusation. One of the most pragmatic was self-preservation.

In Early America, those found guilty of witchcraft could be temporarily reprieved from execution if they in turn confessed their guilt and implicated others in the act. As long as the accusations continued to pour forth, the accuser could not be "turned off," for the presence of the accuser was required at the court trials of the newly implicated individuals. Although it was in the best interests of a condemned witch to make as many accusations as possible, few settlers went to the extreme lengths that Essex County's William Barker did; he claimed that 307 active sorcerers were operating in his locale.

Margaret Jacobs had second thoughts concerning the use of confession and accusation as a method of personal survival. After the young woman had been "cried out upon" by a group of afflicted persons in Salem, she decided to name others as co-conspirators. Among those selected was former town minister George Burroughs and her own eighty-year-old grandfather. Margaret, however, did not charge her mother, who was also imprisoned on the grounds of sorcery.

Almost immediately after the allegations had been made, Margaret regretted the move. Burroughs and the elder Jacobs were sentenced to die, primarily on the evidence she had provided. In an attempt to reverse the convictions, she filed a petition of recant with the Superior Court. The document explained that the untruths had been made in a climate of fear, which had occurred when she was jailed and confronted by questioners. In describing the terror to which she succumbed, Margaret wrote:

> They told me if I would not confess, I should be put down into the dungeon and would be hanged, but if I would confess, I should have my life; the which did so affright me, with my own vile, wicked heart, to save my life made me make the confession I did, which confession, may it please the honoured court, is altogether false and untrue. The very first night after I had made my confession, I was in such horror of conscience that I could not sleep, for fear the Devil should carry me away for telling such horrid lies. I was, may it please the honoured court, sworn to my confession, as I understand since, but then, at that time, was ignorant of it, not knowing what

an oath did mean. The Lord, I hope . . . will forgive me my false forswearing myself.

What I said was altogether false against my grandfather and Mr. Burroughs, which I did to save my life and to have my liberty; but the Lord, charging it to my conscience, made me in so much horror, that I could not contain myself before I had denied my confession.

Despite the recanting, the charges stood against Jacobs and Burroughs. Both were executed and Margaret remained in prison. The remorse of the young girl grew stronger as the time for her own reckoning approached. In what she believed to be a final letter, Margaret bade farewell to her father and attempted to explain her earlier action to him:

From the Dungeon in Salem Prison
August 20, 1692

Honored Father:
After my humble duty remembered to you, hoping in the Lord of your good health as—blessed be God—I enjoy, though in abundance of affliction, being close confined here in a loathsome dungeon. The Lord look down in mercy upon me, not knowing how soon I shall be put to death by means of the afflicted persons, my grandfather having suffered already, and all his estate seized for the King.
The reason for my confinement is this. I, having through the magistrates' threatenings and my own vile and wretched heart, confessed several things contrary to my conscience and knowledge. . . . God knows how soon I will be put to death. Dear father, let me beg your prayers to the Lord on my behalf, and send us a joyful and happy meeting in heaven. My mother, poor woman, is very crazy, and remembers her kind love to you and to Uncle VIZ. D.A. So, leaving you to the protection of the Lord, I rest your dutiful daughter,

Margaret Jacobs

Margaret's hope for deliverance was satisfied, for just before she was to come before the court, a severe "impostume" or abscess developed on her head. The case was temporarily postponed, and by the time the wound had healed, the Salem hysteria had subsided.

Accusations among family members were not uncommon. Samuel Wardwell was hanged for witchcraft primarily because of the charges made by his wife and daughter. Abigail Faulkner was cried out upon by her own children, ten-year-old Dorothy and eight-year-old Abigail. Sarah Carrier accused her mother of being a procurer of witches who had baptized her as a devil's servant and promised her a black dog as a familiar.

Some of those who confessed to practicing black magic were undoubtedly "distempered persons," influenced by a hysterical climate of mass prosecution. But even in the most peaceable situations, when no sorcery trials were being considered, individuals occasionally voluntarily confessed their guilt and requested punishment. In these instances, magistrates scrutinized the impromptu admissions and the confessor was usually sent home unprosecuted but with an admonishment or fine.

In 1674, nearly two decades before the mass prosecutions, Salem's Christopher Browne approached the county court to admit that he had been "treating or discoursing with one whom he apprehended to be the devil . . . binding himself to be a servant to him." Browne was examined by officials who concluded that the tale was "seemingly inconsistent with truth." The court dismissed the settler with a warning and good counsel.

Hugh Crotia, who maintained that in 1688 he had signed a blood compact with Satan, also went unheeded by judicial authorities. Although Hugh insisted that he had been practicing "evil against every man" for five years, the grand jury refused to hand down an indictment. Upon payment of his prison fees, Hugh was released from custody.

James Fuller of Springfield was dealt with more harshly. In 1683, Fuller volunteered that he was a practicing witch, but when brought before the court to confirm the statement, he admitted he had lied. The judge sentenced the vacillating defendant to be whipped for deceit and fined for "wickedness and pernicious willful lying and continuance in it until now, putting the county to so great a charge."

Another distempered confessor was Ipswich's James Rowley, who, in 1652, claimed to have heard a supernatural voice asking what services were needed. The court refused to believe that the devil had been in contact with Rowley. The man was fined twenty shillings and ordered to be whipped for idle talk and telling a lie.

Legal provisions were made for examining those whose confessions seemed to be instigated by mental illness or obsession. Massachusetts statute recognized the possibility that "crazy, distracted persons," those with "deformed brains" or "hysterical vapors," could come forward with self-incriminating testimony. Witch-hunt critic Thomas Brattle warned judges against accepting confessions from those who contradicted themselves, for Brattle believed such discrepancies were "usual for any crazed, distempered person to do." The Salem judges, however, refused to accept Brattle's warning and maintained that contradictory statements by self-confessed witches tended to prove guilt. The jurists' rationale was that in order to prevent the confession, Satan would take away the memory of his follower and thus "impose on their brain." The contradictions in admissions of guilt were confirmation of this process.

Increase Mather was also leery of voluntary confessions and announced that false admissions might be made by those "distracted or under the power of phrenetic melancholy." The minister suggested that in cases where such mental unbalance was suspected, the jury should examine the confessor's neighbors to determine if the subject had displayed a past history of unnatural behavior.

Extreme mental instability was suspected by officials who observed confessed witch Goody Glover. The evening after the Boston woman had admitted her guilt, she was overheard in her cell "expostulating" with the devil. Despite the fact that Goody was alone in her cell, she carried on a detailed conversation for some time. The magistrates, already suspecting that she might be distempered, called for a thorough investigation into her total mental state. Cotton Mather wrote:

> The court appointed five or six physicians one evening to examine her very strictly, whether she were not craz'd in her intellectuals, and had not procured to herself by folly and madness the reputation of a witch. Diverse hours did they spend with her; and in all that while no discourse came from her, but what was pertinent and agreeable: particularly, when they asked her what she thought would become of her soul? She reply'd: "You ask me a very solemn question, and I cannot well tell what to say to it." She own'd herself a Roman Catholic; and could recite her Pater Noster in Latin very readily; but there was one clause or two alwaies too hard for her, whereof she said she could not repeat it if she might have all the

world. In the up-shot, the doctors returned her compos mentis and sentence of death was pass'd upon her.

Periods of hysteria caused even the most lucid individuals to become temporarily distempered and susceptible to soul-clearing confession. Six Andover women credited their admissions of guilt to the panic they experienced when confronted with accusations of witchcraft. According to the women's account, they were led blindfolded past several strangers said to be bewitched persons. As each passed, their hands were laid upon the victims, who reacted to the touch by crying out accusations of witchcraft. The women were immediately seized and imprisoned. Under intense questioning, each settlerwoman confessed guilt, but after sober reflection the group filed a petition to recant. Claiming they were "affrighted even out of our reason," the women announced:

> Our nearest and dearest relations, seeing us in that dreadful condition, and knowing our great danger, apprehending that there was no other way to save our lives, as the case was then circumstanced, but by our confessing ourselves to be such and such persons as the afflicted represented us to be, they, out of tender love and pity, persuaded us to confess what we did confess. And indeed that confession that it is said we made was no other than what was suggested to us by some gentlemen, they telling us that we were witches, and they knew it, and we knew it, and they knew that we knew it, which made us think it was so: and our understanding, our reason, our faculties almost gone, we were not capable of judging our condition: as also the hard measures they used with us rendered us incapable of making our defense, but said anything and everything which they desired, and most of what we said was but in effect a consenting to what they said. Some time after, when we were better composed, they telling us of what we had confessed, we did profess that we were innocent and ignorant of such things; and we hearing that Samuel Wardwell had renounced his confession, and quickly after condemned and executed, some of us were told that we were going after Wardwell.

| Mary Osgood | Deliverance Dane | Sarah Wilson |
| Mary Tiler | Abigail Barker | Hannah Tiler |

The pressures that compelled adults to confess worked even more persuasively on children. Numerous preadolescents who admitted their guilt were no doubt ignorant of the penalties that followed a self-incriminating statement, but their confessions were usually accepted without question by courts eager to gain convictions.

Child confessions were particularly prevalent at Salem. The village's seven-year-old Sarah Carrier freely admitted she had been practicing witchcraft since age six and announced that she preferred to afflict people by pinching them. Abigail Faulkner and her sister Dorothy made similar admissions. Perhaps the most vivid account was given by five-year-old Dorcas Good. Dorcas, who held the distinction of being the youngest confessed witch in America, maintained that her familiar was a tiny snake that sucked from a teat at the lowest joint of her forefinger. To support her claim, she displayed to the court a small red mark "about the bigness of a flea bite" on her hand. A group of afflicted girls verified Dorcas' confession by displaying stigmata in the form of tiny teeth marks supposedly left by the young witch.

A small number of confessors, realizing that conviction was quickly followed by execution, may have chosen to admit their guilt as a means of indirectly committing suicide. Laws governing self-murder were among the strongest in the colonies, and the penalties were often passed on to defendants in the form of corruption of the blood.

Not only were the estates of suicides confiscated, but the corpses of those who took their own lives were denied burial in Christian cemeteries. In several areas the law declared that the bodies should be interred at the intersection of two major roads, there to be driven over by passing traffic. mA final harsh judgment decreed that a stake should be driven through the highway grave. While witchcraft was considered an act equally heinous, the personal property of sorcerers was not always escheated and, more important, Christian burial was sometimes allowed for confessed enchanters.

Thomas Brattle presented still another motive for confession. The Massachusetts merchant claimed that innocent persons could be forced into confessing to witchcraft while they were possessed by the devil. According to Brattle's theory, Satan, seeing that his subject was unwilling to submit to servitude, used this device to destroy those who opposed his will.

An opposing view held that no witch could confess unless the approval of the devil was given. This two-edged sword incriminated both the confessed and those who pleaded not guilty. Defendants who admitted their guilt were viewed as Satan's servants who had been given permission from their master to acknowledge their deeds. Suspects who maintained their innocence were considered guilty but unable to confess because the devil would not permit it.

Perhaps the most logical group of confessed witches were those who actually practiced magic and thus believed themselves to be members of a secret society of evil. Settlers who actively performed black rites or cast spells probably composed only a small fraction of the total number of colonials who pleaded guilty. Because of the dreaded sentences meted out to convicted sorcerers, most of those who practiced magic undoubtedly chose not to confess their guilt in court.

It is impossible to estimate the number of citizens in the early colonies who considered themselves witches, but the powers supposedly possessed by enchanters were appealing to the unprivileged classes. Lone, defenseless, and aged women may have begun their sorcery as a means of fulfilling their dreams or in an attempt to find safety from environmental or societal threats.

Mental delusion was not necessary for a practicing witch to believe that her spells were effective. The sorcerer presumed, as did other settlers, that unexplained calamities following a curse were caused by magic. If the witch, in a moment of anger, had indeed cast a spell upon an enemy, any misfortune that later occurred to the victim might well be attributed to the supernatural charm rather than to accident.

Boston's Goody Glover admitted to practicing several forms of magic, but evidently she specialized in image spells. Goody had originally denied any connection with the supernatural, but she changed her plea to guilty after a court-ordered search uncovered direct evidence of sorcery. Mather reported:

> Order was given to search the old woman's house, from whence there were brought into the court several small images, or puppets, or babies, made of rags and stuff'd with goat's hair and other such ingredients. When these were produced, the vile woman acknowledged that her way to torment the objects of her malice was by wetting of her finger with spittle and stroking of those little images . . . one of the images being brought unto her, immediately she started up after an odd manner and took it into her hand; but she

had no sooner taken it, than one of the children fell into sad fits before the whole assembly. This the judges had their just apprehensions at; and carefully causing the repetition of the experiment, found again the same event of it.

Image magic was a form of witchcraft akin to the voodoo rituals of the Caribbean. In this technique, puppets or dolls representing the intended victim were "tortured" by burning or stabbing. The harm inflicted upon the puppet was supposedly transferred to the person represented by the doll. If the image was attacked in the heart area, the individual would die. When the doll was pierced in the head, the victim would go mad. If struck in the eye, the person being tortured would go blind.

Spells were most powerful if the image contained a relic of the victim, such as hair, skin, or nail cuttings, but charms could also be made workable if an item such as goat's hair was substituted. Goats, which possessed cloven hoofs and "devil's" horns, were believed to have an affinity with the supernatural world. An image using this animal's parts was considered a potent weapon indeed.

Goody Glover's use of saliva was indicative of another widely held superstition. For centuries, the common folk of western society had asserted that spittle possessed magical qualities. This tradition is still mirrored by people who simulate spitting upon their palms before undertaking a demanding task.

Although image magic was probably the most widely practiced form of magic in the colonies, it did not involve a trait common in European circles of sorcery. This was the use of live animals as puppets to represent intended victims. Like dolls, the animals would be tortured, and any pain inflicted upon them was thought transferred to the unfortunate subject.

In addition to Goody Glover, several other colonial women were connected with image magic. Dolls made from rags and hog bristles were reported found in Bridget Bishop's cellar, and at least three confessed witches admitted to preparing similar puppets.

Ann Foster claimed to have made two dolls representing the children of Andrew Allin. She announced that as a result of sticking pins into the images both children fell ill and one died. In a less successful effort, Ann attempted to choke to death several other enemies by squeezing images representing their bodies. Abigail Hobbs confessed that magical dolls were given to her by George Burroughs.

By following the wizard's instructions, she was able to cause at least one death by sticking pins and thorns into the images. Candy, a servant girl of one Mrs. Hawkes, announced that her mistress formed puppets out of "clouts" and rags, adding pieces of cheese and grass to complete the work. The images were then set on fire or soaked in pails of water, so that the human victims suffered death either by burning or drowning.

By the narrowest interpretation, all confessions of witchcraft in America were voluntary. Unlike Europe, where torture was widely used to extract admissions, physical pressure played an insignificant role in colonial justice. Although one critic maintained that at least fifty-five persons were tortured at Salem, the estimate is unsubstantiated and was probably based on false rumor.

Like England, the provinces rejected torture as a valid means of proving guilt. The basis of this stance was probably in common law rights long secured to citizens. In Europe, however, where no traditions protected the rights of the accused, any inquisitorial method was thought justified to bring the guilty to confession.

Torture became so frequent a method of justice in Germany that a special tariff was drawn up to guide the activities of lawmen in the Archbishopric of Cologne. The tariff, which included a price list of fifty-five different items, was an attempt to set price guidelines on torture. Included were procedures such as:

	Reichsthaler	Albus
29. For cutting out the tongue entirely, or part of it, and afterward for burning the mouth with a red-hot iron	5	0
30. For this procedure, the usual rope, tongs, and knife	2	0
31. For nailing to the gallows a cut-off tongue or a chopped-off hand	1	26
38. For putting in the pillory, branding, and whipping, including coals, rope, and rods, also the branding ointment	2	0
44. For the second degree of torture, including setting the limbs afterward, and for salve which is used	2	26

Traditional instruments of torture, such as the rack, thumb screws, or bone breakers, were forbidden in the provinces, but records do show that a "blade" was used in Andover. This device, however, was probably applied in conjunction with a witch test, rather than as a means to force confession.

Massachusetts law specifically authorized the use of torture only in capital cases to extract confessions mwhen it was "apparent there be other conspirators or confederates" involved with the defendant. If these requirements were met, then the law allowed the use of physical force, but forbade methods which were "barbarous and inhumane."

The tying of "neck to heels" was accepted as being within the framework of allowable procedures, but even this inducement was not widely used. Convicted witch John Procter believed that even a single operation of the tying was a base infringement on citizen rights and an injustice that should not be tolerated.

In a July 23, 1692, communication to ministers of Boston, Procter protested against the treatment, which he claimed had been applied to five prisoners involved in the Salem trials. Procter explained that as a result of the tying, the detainees had confessed their guilt and implicated others.

> Two of the five (Carrier's sons) are young men who would not confess anything till they tied them neck and heels till the blood was ready to come out of their noses. And 'tis credibly believed and reported this was the occasion of making them confess that (which) they never did, by reason they said one had been a witch a month and another five weeks, and that their mother had made them so, who has been confined here nine weeks.

> My son, William Procter, when he was examined, because he would not confess that he was guilty when he was innocent, they tied him neck and heels till the blood gushed out at his nose, and would have kept him so twenty-four hours if one more merciful than the rest had not taken pity on him and caused him to be unbound. These actions are very like the popish cruelties, and that will not serve their turn without our innocent blood.

Although physical torture was not a significant factor in the colonies, another form of persuasion was commonly accepted. This was the seventeenth-century version of brainwashing.

After an accused person had been jailed, "godly divines" or clerics were often sent to meet with the prisoner. For long periods of time the divines would berate the suspect, relating the horrors of hell that eternally confronted the unrepentant and painting glowing tales of the relief that came to those who freely confessed. Friends and relatives of the accused might also be called upon to aid in the process.

No relief from the constant pressure was allowed. In most cases, individuals were "walked" or kept moving about their cells so that sleep was impossible. In this manner, the interrogation continued for days, until exhaustion at last led to confession.

CHAPTER VIII

The Law and Trial
of Witchcraft

L ONG before the fledgling provinces began to enact statutes governing citizen behavior, witchcraft was legally forbidden in the
colonies. As liege subjects to the Crown, and in the absence of formal
colonial law, settlers were automatically subject to British statutes,
even though they did not dwell on the mother country's soil.

Witchcraft had originally been a misdemeanor under common
law, but during the Tudor period, stricter legislation began to be
enacted. In 1541, during the reign of Henry VIII, Parliament adopted
a statute that made conjuring, witchcraft, and sorcery illegal offenses.
Twenty years later, an Elizabethan measure specified that those found
guilty of practicing minor witchcraft or sorcery should be ordered to
stand in the pillory. For a repeated offense of a more serious charm,
the penalty was death. On the surface, both of these statutes appear
to have been framed in order to punish witches, but the intention was
actually much different. The regulations were probably aimed at halting the activities of sixteenth-century confidence men and women who
were preying on the populace in increasing numbers. These cheats, by
posing as active witches, extracted money from citizens in exchange
for promising to perform magical spells.

By the end of the sixteenth century, as influences from the European witch purges crept into Britain, a law decreeing death for those
who killed or maimed by magic had been adopted. Less harsh punish-

ment was allotted in instances when no harm resulted. At the turn of
the century, British attitudes toward witchcraft were still governed by
the principle of maleficium, the concept that sorcery in itself was not
an evil. The activity was to be regulated by the government only when
it resulted in harm to others. This traditional view changed, however,
with the ascension to the throne of King James I.

Elizabeth's successor had not been raised in England, but in
catholic Scotland, where witchcraft was considered a heresy against
the Church and a crime against the State. As a result of early indoctri-
nation, the new king became convinced that he had been marked for
attack by Satan. A series of coincidences gave some support to the
theory. Several plotters were apprehended who admitted they planned
to assassinate the monarch by magical poisoning. James' long term
rival, Francis Stewart, the Earl of Bothwell, based his revolutionary
activities on the advice of sorcerers and divines. To combat these
dangers, the king involved himself in a detailed study of witchcraft
and published a scholarly treatise on the horrors of the subject. Under
his aegis, a severe new law, striking down the philosophy of maleficium, was adopted by Parliament in 1604.

Basically, the act, which governed life in the colonies until specific
American codes were adopted, was divided into four parts. Section
one prescribed death for conjuration, for the use of or consultation
with spirits, or for exhumation of a dead body for use in sorcery. The
prohibition against exhumation was largely irrelevant in the provinces
for necromancy was never accepted as an important aspect of witchcraft.

A second section, based on the concept on maleficium and similar
to provisions in the Elizabethan statute, prescribed capital punishment for anyone practicing witchcraft that resulted in death. The
same penalty was applied under section three of the 1604 law concerning magic that only harmed someone. Under earlier measures, a witch
whose spells did not kill was reprieved for the first offense. The final
provision of the King James law made the practice of minor sorcery
and witchery punishable by death. This clause replaced the standing
custom of reprieve in the first instance and life imprisonment for the
second offense.

The 1604 law abolished the basic foundation by which witchcraft
had been viewed for centuries in England. No longer was the death

sentence imposed only for acts that proved fatal. Instead, the mere intent to cast a spell or converse with a spirit was deemed so evil as to warrant execution. The mixing of a love potion was considered equal in seriousness to the taking of a life. Thus the continental view of witchcraft as an evil in itself became the prevailing theory in Britain.

The exact degree to which English laws, like the King James statute, were applicable in the colonies was subject to disagreement. An extreme view held that English laws in every case overrode any statute framed by a provincial body. In the absence of a colonial law governing a specific crime, it was believed that British regulations of a general nature should be applied in every case. An opposite faction believed that provincial bodies were free to make their own unique codes, and that in the absence of specific legislation, the opinion of the judge could be accepted as legally binding. Even greater confusion was created by the general absence of case law precedents in America.

The charters and proprietary documents of individual colonies were usually silent on the matter of the total transplanting of English law and instead usually specified that provincial legislation should be "agreeable" to English traditions. The Maryland charter, for example, briefly noted that local law could not be "contrary or repugnant" to the statutes of Britain. In the charter of the Massachusetts bay colony, the wording was only slightly more informative. The document allowed the colony saints to "make, ordain, and establish all manner of wholesome orders, laws, statutes, and ordinances, directions, and instructions not contrary to the laws of this our realm of England. . . . "

The degree to which the laws of the mother country were applied in America varied among the jurisdictions. The Rhode Island Code of 1647, for example, was taken almost verbatim from Michael Dalton's *Countrey Justice,* a summary of English law. A similar situation occurred in Maryland, where criminal actions were judged almost totally by the regulations and court rulings of England.

In the other extreme, provinces such as Virginia and Massachusetts developed extensive codes based on old-world customs, but modified by colonial experience.

The growth of an indigenous American law was necessary for several reasons. Many of the actions occurring in the colonies were prompted by the pioneer environment and were unrelated to conditions in England. Colonial administration was a second factor. Unlike Britain, where a single monarch and Parliament governed with uniform justice throughout the land, the provinces were organized under a maze of different charters, proprietorships, and crown authorizations.

Despite the confusion, several colonial bodies moved aggressively to include witchcraft as a specifically prohibited act. The early attempts to frame native American codes were not as sophisticated in wording as the English standards, but the penalities were equal in severity.

The Plymouth Summary of Offenses, adopted in 1636 and probably the first formal set of regulations against witchcraft, was brief but harsh. The measure announced that those who made a compact or conferred with the devil by means of witchcraft or conjuration were "lyable to death." The 1641 Body of Liberties, adopted by the government of Massachusetts bay colony, was more encompassing. The document stated: "If any man or woman be a witch (that is hath or consulteth with a familiar spirit), they shall be put to death." The regulation also decreed strong punishment for those who simply met with sorcerers by specifying: "Consulters with witches [are] not to be tolerated, but either to be cut off by death or banishment or other suitable punishment."

By allowing execution of citizens who merely conversed with a witch, the Body of Liberties became the harshest provincial law dealing with witchcraft. The ramification of this clause was that those who attended a fortune-telling session could be punished as greatly as a practicing witch who murdered by magic.

In 1642, Maryland also made death the penalty for witchcraft, but in some cases allowed that those who had been convicted might be reprieved and branded on the hand. In the same year, New Haven colony adopted, verbatim, the provision of the 1641 Massachusetts law. In 1647, Rhode Island joined the list of colonies that made sorcery a capital offense when the General Court ruled: "Witchcraft is forbidden by this present assembly to be used in this colony; and the penalty imposed by the authority that we are subject to is felony of death." A formal statute decreeing the death penalty was not passed, however, until 1728.

At least two colonies elected not to frame original witchcraft statutes, but instead formally adopted the King James law of 1604. These actions, however, did not take place until witchcraft had ceased to be a real factor in society. In 1712, South Carolina included the English regulation in the provincial code, and in 1717, Pennsylvania took the same course. The English law was also in effect in Massachusetts when in 1684, the colony's charter was revoked and all crimes were made subject to British regulations.

A confusing situation occurred in Virginia, where certain sections of the 1604 law were accepted and others were ignored. To make the situation even more complicated, tidewater lawmakers adopted a provision that was openly contrary to the King James statute. Although witchcraft was made a capital felony in Virginia, a special category of petit sorcery was also recognized. This crime involved inoffensive acts of magic, such as divining or concocting love potions. The penalty for petit witchery was one year in jail and a public humiliation every three months, in which the prisoner was required to stand in the local pillory and make open confession of the crime.

Acts classified as petit witchcraft in Virginia were felonies under the King James law. The rejection by southern officials of the religious heresy concept indicates that although the mother country's view of sorcery had been at least legally altered, Virginia lawmakers still adhered to the concept of maleficium. There is no evidence, however, that any colonial was prosecuted under the petit provision of the province's regulation.

At least technically, all areas that failed to specifically deal with witchcraft as a crime fell under the jurisdiction of the British ruling. One exception was New York. When control passed from the Dutch, the colony became subject to a code of behavior known as the "Duke's Laws," a body of justice which made no mention of witchcraft per se. But instead of automatically applying the 1604 statute, officials chose to prosecute enchanters according to the nature of their charm. For example, in instances of death by witchcraft, the offender could be tried for murder. In thievery by magic, the witch would suffer the penalty prescribed for robbery. Bewitchment that resulted in physical harm would be considered assault or attempted murder.

In the colonies, as in Britain, death was not a sentence reserved for witchcraft offenders alone. During the seventeenth century, the perpetrators of scores of crimes were subject to the same fate. The 1650 Connecticut blue laws prescribed execution for fifteen offenses. In addition to witchcraft, the crimes considered worthy of turning off were blasphemy, willful murder, the worship of gods other than "Lord God," manslaughter through guile, bestiality, homosexuality, adultery with a married person, rape, kidnapping, perjury in a capital crime with intent to take a life, treason, insurrection, the "smiting" or cursing of a parent without extreme cause by a child above age sixteen, and "stubborn or rebellious" conduct by sons above age sixteen.

Colonists, while adopting many legal concepts of the Old World, did not accept one theory put forth in Britain. This was the somewhat tenuous suggestion that trials for witchcraft were illegal. The rationale was that witches worked their magic only because they had been endowed with special powers by the devil. Without his help, sorcerers were impotent. Thus, the devil should be tried for the deaths or harms that resulted from the practices of his followers.

Under this proposal, witches were viewed as accomplices of a greater criminal, and under common law, it was impossible to try accessories without also prosecuting the principal. Thus, until Satan could be summoned into court, his witch confederates could not be brought up.

Also rejected in the colonies was the Elizabethan notion that benefit of clergy might be extended to those convicted of minor witchery. Through this device, perpetrators of many capital crimes in England escaped the death penalty. Benefit of clergy was one of the most important facets of English law and a practice that served to mitigate the seemingly inhumane codes by which citizens were governed.

The tradition of "clergy" began in the twelfth century, when church personnel were exempt from trial and punishment in secular courts. In order to prove that one was subject only to ecclesiastical or canon law, clerics were required to read complicated sections of the Bible. Because literacy was primarily limited to members of the church community, the ability to read was thought conclusive evidence that a suspect was connected to the holy establishment.

Gradually, benefit of clergy was extended to non-secular personnel. Originally a tool by which a prisoner was released into the hands of the church courts, the custom became a lawful offense for any male who could read and had committed a crime covered by the policy. Instead of suffering criminal punishment, those receiving the reprieve were released from confinement.

Despite the fact that clergy had lost its direct connection to religion, women in England were prohibited from claiming the full benefit until 1692, and in the colonies, females were barred until 1732. The reasoning for this situation was that by no means could a female be considered a member of a religious order reserved only for males.

Scores of minor crimes, legally punishable by death, fell under the provisions of "calling for the book." Convicted persons were allowed to claim the defense only for the first offense, and to prevent abuses of the privilege, individuals were branded with a mark signifying that the claim had been made. If the individual was apprehended a second time, the brand alerted officals to the fact that the criminal had been once pardoned and must suffer the full extent of the law for the new act.

Benefit of clergy was used in the colonies, but to a lesser degree than in the mother country. Perhaps the widest acceptance of the concept came in Maryland, where "clergy" was acceptable in a wide range of cases, from burning haystacks to cutting out "another's tongue." For each of the crimes specified, the offender was freed if he could read "clerk-like in the judgment of the court." If successful in the recitation, the convict was subject only to the loss of a hand or to being branded with a hot iron.

Extension of clergy to convicted witches may have been denied for much the same reason that the tradition was withheld from women. Although the book no longer was connected with religion, colonial councils may have found it difficult to rationalize that a crime involving comradeship with the devil could remotely be pardoned under a custom originally granted only to priests of God.

Just as Americans adapted British laws to the specific needs of their area, so did the provincial court system reflect the unique characteristics of a pioneer society. Although minor differences in procedure or structure did occur among the colonies, an underlying principle of simplicity was present in each area. Concerted efforts were made to keep seats of justice as close to the people as possible and uncomplicated in operation. In this area, American justice was markedly different from English procedure.

Disorder at every level characterized the British legal system in the seventeenth century. Instead of courts of general jurisdiction authorized to hear many types of cases, more than a hundred bodies of specific authority were in operation. Among the most famous were the courts of common pleas, exchequer, equity, bishopric, chivalry, request, chancery, borough, manor, star chamber, king's bench, privy council, and high commission. Scores of lesser courts were organized to deal with obscure areas of the law. The Courts of Stanneries, for example, were concerned only with the complaints of tin mine workers in Cornwall and Devon. The multiplicity of courts created problems not only in jurisdiction but in administration of justice. Because each unit jealously guarded its prerogatives, a defendant convicted in one system might appeal to a rival court and gain an opposite verdict. Similar moves could be made on the part of the prosecution.

In order to eliminate the confusion that resulted in England, colonial lawmakers based American justice on courts of general jurisdiction.

The exact processes by which a suspect advanced from accusation to final verdict varied in the colonies. Not only were there differences between colonies, but the special conditions within a province resulted in variances. For example, the methods used in courts of large towns, such as Williamsburg, were unlike those applied in less cosmopolitan frontier settlements of the Shenandoah Valley. In the rural townships of Massachusetts, where trained legal authorities were unknown and law books were rare, the legal methods were far removed from the procedures used in Boston.

But despite structural and procedural differences, a unifying thread joined all colonial systems of justice and linked the American courts to those of the Old World. This was the basic concept of liberties granted to all British citizens for centuries. Because certain traditional and constitutional safeguards were thought the inherent right of every suspect, summary judgments or executions were completely alien. Included in these rights of the realm were provisions such as direct confrontation of accusers, examination of witnesses, fair and speedy trials, right of appeal, grand jury, oral testimony, writs, subpoenas, and trial by jury. Because each court in the provinces operated under the same philosophy, all witchcraft cases followed a similar pattern, regardless of geographical location.

First, a formal complaint was made by a citizen, who claimed to have witnessed or been a target of sorcery. Usually, this accusation was presented to a justice of the peace, county commissioner, or town magistrate, who was empowered to call a preliminary hearing to investigate the alleged crime.

If the magistrate concluded from the complaint that no immediate danger existed to the community, the suspect was allowed to remain free until the examination. In some instances, the jurist might order the accused to post a bond to assure attendance at the inquiry. If the magistrate determined that the suspect might flee or do harm if left at liberty, he could issue an arrest warrant ordering the local sheriff to detain the individual. These documents were simple affairs that listed the name of the citizen and the charge that had been lodged. One such order, issued at Salem, announced:

> To the Sheriff of the County of Essex or his deputie or Constable in Salem or Beverley:
>
> You are in their Magists. names hereby required to apprehend and forthwith bring before us: Ann Dalibar, the wife of Wm. Dalibar of Glocester, who stands charged this day with having committed sundry acts of witchcraft on the bodys of Mary Warren & Susannah Shelden to the hurt of their bodys, in order to her examination relating to the premises. Fail not. Salem, June the 6th, 1692.
>
> Bartho. Gedney
> P vs. John Hathorne   Justcs of ye peace
>   Jonathan Corwin

Because jails were unknown in most seventeenth-century settlements, prisoners were usually quartered in the sheriff's home and restrained from escaping by irons, ropes, or other physical bonds. The confinement was usually brief, for the magistrate's hearing was convened as soon as a suspect had been apprehended.

Most hearings were informal and open to the public. The goal was to judge not the guilt or innocence of the accused, but to determine if an incidence of witchcraft had taken place, and if there was reasonable proof that the crime had been committed by the detainee. In order to accomplish these ends, magistrates were vested with special powers.

Citizens could be subpoenaed to give oral evidence or written depositions pertinent to the case. This transcribed material might later serve as the basis for grand jury action. Non-oral statements, however, could be entered as evidence in higher courts only if the witness had died or was unavoidably absent. The accused was not always allowed to question witnesses at a preliminary hearing, and as a result, depositions did not meet the common law right of direct confrontation between the accused and those who testified against them. Witnesses might also be placed under personal bond to insure that they would be present for further hearings or had not testified to falsehoods.

In addition to taking sworn testimony and questioning witnesses, the local jurist could also collect physical evidence by ordering the homes of the accused to be searched for signs of magic. Another important power was the official's authority to impanel juries to examine the suspect's body for incriminating marks.

One of the most important functions of the preliminary hearings was the weeding out of unsubstantiated cases, which, if passed to a higher court, would be automatically dismissed as groundless. Courts at the grass roots level supposedly could most readily identify charges that were based not on fact but on personal motivation. This sifting technique was not always successful and some proceedings with little evidence did reach the trial stage. The witchcraft case of Elizabeth Garlicke of Easthampton was one such incident.

Elizabeth had been examined by local magistrates, who determined that the evidence against her was sufficient to call for a formal trial by the colony's General Court. The accused witch was sent to Hartford, where justices heard the case and dismissed all charges. The court congratulated the Easthampton magistrates for their "Christian care and prudence" in investigating the accusation, but inferred that the personal motives that prompted the case should have been determined at an earlier date. The Connecticut body wanted no further repetition of the feuding that had entrapped Elizabeth and announced to the local folk: "It is desirous and expected that you should carry neighbourly and peaceably without offense to Joseph Garlicke and his wife, and that they should do the like to you."

Difficulties in transportation and communications contributed to the popularity of the local courts as an initial forum for the airing of witchcraft charges. Witnesses, instead of having to travel many miles to the provincial capital, were able to attend the inquiry with a minimum loss of time and money. But in some cases, the closeness to the people was a liability that resulted in a loss of justice for the individual. Unlike colony-wide courts, local hearings were subject to the pressures of community emotions that might have been ineffective at higher judicial levels.

The examination of Captain John Alden, son of the *Mayflower*'s John Alden and Priscilla Mullins, demonstrated how local prejudices and panic could dictate the deliberations in a magistrate's court.

Alden, the seventy-year-old master of a sloop that carried supplies from Boston to remote frontier settlements, was summoned to the bay city on May 28, 1692, to answer charges of witchcraft. The hearing convened in a room thronged with curious spectators and in an atmosphere far from impartial.

Alden's accuser, when called forth to identify the man who had supposedly bewitched her, unhesitatingly designated not the captain, but an uninvolved bystander who happened onto the inquiry. An uproar ensued, but instead of dismissing the case, the local jurist allowed the woman to be told which colonial she was supposed to identify. During the disruption, the court was adjourned and somewhile later reconvened in the middle of a public street outside. Here the mob formed a ring surrounding Alden and his reported victim. Only then did the woman identify the sea captain as her tormentor by crying out: "There stands Alden, a bold fellow with his hat on, sells powder and shot to the Indians, lies with squaws and has papooses."

While the accusation seemed to concentrate on the suspect's morals rather than on his culpability to witchcraft, Alden was seized by town marshals and taken to a local meeting house for further questioning. The climate here was little improved. Alden's hands were tightly bound, supposedly so that he might not further bewitch his accuser. Despite the precaution, the woman, when brought into his presence, was struck with dreadful convulsions. In the face of such damaging evidence, the hearing was completed and Alden was carted away to Boston jail.

A finding unfavorable to the accused in magistrate's court did not determine the final fate of a suspected witch. Usually, the additional safeguard of a grand jury indictment stood between the accused and a court trial.

If the lower hearing determined that there was sufficient proof that a crime had been committed by a citizen, the judge's opinion and all evidence gathered during the inquiry were presented to a grand jury along with a drawn indictment. In some areas, grand jurors were selected from qualified spectators who happened to be in the courtroom or even passing by outside. In others, lists of potential jurors were kept by clerks, and individuals were called by name when an indictment was proposed.

Regardless of the method of impanelment, grand jurors in every jurisdiction had several common characteristics. All were male, free, and owned either land or property worth a significant amount. The actual number of jurors varied according to the jurisdiction or case, but the maximum figure was usually twenty-four.

Like the magistrates, the grand jury could call witnesses for sworn testimony and could question the defendant. Hearings were short and rarely lasted longer than a single day. If the jurors concluded the evidence was insufficient to sustain the charge of witchcraft, then the word "ignoramus" was written on the bill of indictment. This finding resulted in the immediate release of the suspect and the dismissal of charges.

Like the magistrate, grand jurors were called upon only to weigh the strength of a case, not to rule on the final guilt or innocence of an individual. However, one Maryland jury did chose to "acquit" a suspect. In 1665, after being ordered to consider the evidence against Elizabeth Bennett, accused of burglary, murder, and other felony "trespasses" by witchcraft, the grand jury found the bill not presentable and elected to clear Elizabeth "by proclamation." All charges were dropped, but it is unlikely that this vote of confidence legally prohibited the local commissioner from collecting additional evidence to support a new indictment.

If sufficient indications of guilt were shown, the grand jury might elect to return a "billa vera" or a true bill. Such a document was more complicated in wording than an arrest warrant. The 1692 true bill against Bridget Bishop reads:

Essex: ss
The jurors for our Sovereign Lord and Lady the King and Queen presents that Bridget Bishop, also Olliver, the wife of Edward Bishop of Salem, in the County of Essex sawyer, the nineteenth day of April in the fourth year of the reign of our Sovereign Lord and

Lady William and Mary, by the Grace of God of England, Scotland, France, and Ireland, King and Queen Defenders of the Faith, put and divers other days and times as well before as after, certain detestable arts called witchcrafts and sorceries: wickedly and feloniously hath used, practiced, and exercised at and within the Township of Salem, in the County of Essex, aforesaid, in upon and against one Abigail Williams of Salem Village in the County of Essex aforesaid singlewoman, by which said wicked arts ye said Abigail Williams, the nineteenth day of April aforesaid in the fourth year abovesaid, and divers other days and times as well before as after, was and is tortured, afflicted, pained, consumed, wasted, and tormented against the peace of our said Sovereign Lord and Lady, the King and Queen, and against the form of the statute in that case made and provided.

The issuance of an indictment enabled a colony's higher courts to instigate a criminal witchcraft trial. Although in some areas sorcery allegations could be conducted at lower levels of justice, the final disposition of a convicted sorcerer was usually considered within the jurisdiction of the highest court of the province.

In Maryland, county commissioners were authorized to investigate all cases of witchcraft, sorcery, enchantments, and magic, but magistrates were not allowed to order the taking of the life of any defendant. Witchcraft cases were thus resolved only by the provincial court. In Virginia, all cases involving the possible loss of life or limb by white defendants were triable only by the General Court, where the governor and his council acted as judges with a citizen jury. In New Netherland, Peter Stuyvesant allowed local courts to hear witchery cases, but announced that "in dark and dubious matters, especially in witchcrafts, the party aggrieved might appeal to the Governor and Council." Under British rule, the General Court of Assizes assumed jurisdiction. In Massachusetts, trials for life, limb, or banishment were heard by colony-wide courts and ultimately reconsidered by the governor and his private counselors.

In addition to hearings by the local magistrate, grand jury, and trial court, two other colonial bodies could be involved in the processing of witchcraft cases. These were coroner's juries and courts of Oyer and Terminer.

Coroner's juries supplemented magistrate's investigations and grand jury hearings in instances when death occurred by questionable means. Their primary function was to search the corpse for proof of foul play. Citizens on the juries could also call for the performance of an autopsy or postmortem examination, receive information bearing on the case, and make a final recommendation as to the cause of death.

Like medical practitioners of the era, coroner's juries were handicapped in their deliberations by the general lack of knowledge surrounding the nature and symptoms of disease. As a result of this ignorance, the findings were not always clinically precise or even valuable from a legal viewpoint. For example, one jury of matrons in Newberry reported in 1693:

> We judge according to our best lights and contents that the death
> of said Elizabeth was not by any violence or wrong done to her by
> any person or thing, but by some sudden stopping of her breath.

Despite significant drawbacks, several coroner's juries did bring in findings of death by witchcraft. During 1679, a jury in Northampton verified that John Stebbins had died in a manner "compatible" to murder by sorcery. According to the jury, Stebbins' corpse was found to have "several hundred small spots on the body as if made with small shot." When the spots were scraped, tiny holes leading into the body were revealed. Although the county court forwarded the jury's verdict to Governor Bradstreet, no action was taken to search out the responsible witch.

In 1684, a more incriminating case was made against Hadley's Mary Webster, the aged woman subjected to the snow test during the illness of Philip Smith. Several factors indicated that Smith's demise had been from supernatural causes. His illness had begun soon after an argument with Mary, and concrete signs of magic were seen in his sickroom. Pins were discovered about the bed, along with the unmistakable scent of musk. Mysterious scratching was heard and fires seemed to appear from no discernible source. Galley pots containing the victim's medicine were emptied though touched by no human hands.

The inexplicable signs of supernatural presence did not cease after Smith's painful death. According to reports, the evening after his demise, "a very credible person watching the corpse perceived the bed to move and stir more than once; but by no means could find out the cause of it." The following night, loud noises, resembling the dragging of chains, were heard in the room. Because of the many curious circumstances, a coroner's jury was called to view the corpse and determine if witchcraft had been involved. According to Mather:

> The jury that viewed the corpse found a swelling on one breast, which rendered it like a woman's. His privates were wounded or burned. On his back, besides bruises, there were several pricks, or holes, as if done with awls or pins.

Even more suspicious was the condition of the body, which appeared to be alive and showed no signs of rigor mortis or skin discoloration. Two days after the death, when Smith was taken from his bed, the corpse was still warm, even though it had lain in the cold New England winter. One observer noted that Smith "continued as lively as if he had been alive, his eyes closed as in slumber and his jaw not fallen down."

A final means by which witchcraft charges could be aired was through special courts of Oyer and Terminer, a title meaning to hear and declare. Unlike permanent judicial bodies, Oyer and Terminer courts were established on a temporary basis to deal with cases of unusual circumstances such as piracy or crimes by Indians. In addition, the courts could be set up as emergency tribunals to hear allegations that developed while permanent courts were in adjournment. As soon as the specific trial for which the court had been convened had been settled, the authorizing commission was dissolved.

Oyer and Terminer judges were appointed by the governor of a colony. Although the magistrate's hearing might be waived by the tribunals, grand jury indictment was considered necessary in most cases.

Regardless of the procedural method by which individuals accused of witchcraft were heard, one fact of colonial justice marked every aspect of the judicial process. Unlike English institutions, where his majesty's courts were filled with professional justices and barristers well learned in the intricacies of the law, provincials connected with the courts made little pretense of judicial expertise.

Local magistrates were usually untrained in legal matters and held their posts as temporary appointments while performing full-time occupations. Even at the highest levels, members of the General

Court were not chosen for judicial knowledge or experience. By tradition, governors and counselors were selected for their positions because of significant economic power, friends at London court, or the ability to purchase the post.

William Byrd II, who served on Virginia's General Court, recognized the extent of his unpreparedness and noted: "Indeed, I rest upon the absurdity of men judging over matters of law which they do not understand, which everybody knows is the case with most of us councillors."

Although a colony's attorney general was usually familiar with judicial processes, the greatest influences on American justice were not individuals, but books written by English authorities. Published judicial treatises were in constant use by judges who studied the volumes for precedents and procedural guidance. In almost every instance of civil or criminal controversy, the written opinions of British experts were consulted in order to determine a just settlement. In no area of the law were these references more sorely required than in cases involving witchcraft and magic.

Unlike routine criminal acts, where concrete evidence could be objectively received and weighed, witchcraft hearings usually involved subjective interpretations of supposed supernatural happenings. Dalton's *Countrey Justice* emphasized the dangers inherent in sorcery cases by warning:

> Now against these witches (being the most cruel, revengeful, and bloody of all the rest) the Justices of the Peace may not always expect direct evidence, seeing all their works are the works of darkness, and no witnesses present with them to accuse them. . . .

Because of the lack of eyewitnesses or tangible proof, the provincial courts seeking to detect and prosecute witches relied heavily upon criteria suggested in popular authorities such as Richard Bernard's *A Guide to Grand-Jury Men,* Joseph Keble's *An Assistance to the Justices of the Peace,* William Perkin's *Discourse on the Damned Art of Witchcraft,* and the collected opinions of Sir Mathew Hale.

Reference books usually included even the most grisly details concerning the workings of the supernatural, so that jurists would be fully informed on all "facts" that might be presented during a trial. Reginald Scot, in his *The Discoverie of Witchcraft,* was so sensitive to the expletives of some material that he inserted a warning to readers just before listing particularly immodest passages taken from other "experts." Scot advised:

> I must intreat you that are the readers hereof, whose chaste ears cannot well endure to hear of such abominable lecheries as are gathered out of the books of witchmongers . . . to turn over a few leaves, wherein (I saie) I have like a groom thrust their bawdie stuff.

Armed with legal guides and empowered by true bills of indictment, colonial jurists could proceed with the formal trial of an individual accused of witchcraft. The initial phases of a trial were routine in any criminal hearing and had been prescribed by centuries of English law.

Immediately after the court was convened, the defendant was brought forward to face the bench. The indictment was read to the prisoner and sometimes a less formal summary of charges was given. After the suspect had been made aware of the charges, the judge called for the entering of a plea. If the prisoner called out guilty, sentence was pronounced without delay. If a claim of not guilty was made, a jury was impaneled and the trial began.

Salem's Giles Corey refused to make the choice and instead elected to "stand mute." Failure to enter a plea was considered one of the most horrible crimes under law and an act akin to insurrection. Like treason, the move attacked the very foundation of government. By refusing to plead, the suspect paralyzed the judicial system. A trial could not be begun or punishment meted out. To avoid such obstruction of justice, prisoners who stood mute were automatically sentenced to a *peine fort et dure,* a penalty harsh and severe, which usually took the form of a pressing. This process involved the placing of heavy weights upon the body of the prisoner until the individual either consented to enter a plea or was crushed to death.

Giles Corey was the only colonial to undergo such a fate and may have done so in order to save his estate from confiscation by the Crown. As a major witness against his wife in an earlier witchcraft trial, Corey probably concluded that his chances of being found innocent were slim in view of the lynch mob mentality at Salem. By dying unconvicted, Corey may have hoped that his property would not be subject to the forfeiture that usually accompanied the execution of a witch.

After a plea was entered, a judge might address the jury concerning his opinions as to what acts constituted punishable witchcraft. Jurors might also be instructed on the degree of importance that should be attached to various types of evidence.

These preliminary opinions, based on English precedent and colonial witchlore, probably varied in style and content according to the jurisdiction in which the trial was being held. However, the procedures laid down by William Perkins, a Puritan jurist and theologian in the early 1600s, reflected the general ideas that governed colonial courts. Perkins' seventeen points for the discovery and conviction of witches, as recorded by Cotton Mather, revealed:

I.   There are presumptions, which do at least probably and conjecturally note one to be a witch. These give occasion to examine, ye they are no sufficient causes of conviction.

II.   If any man or woman be notoriously defamed for a witch, this yields a strong suspicion. Yet the judge ought carefully to look, that the report be made by men of honesty and credit.

III.   If a fellow-witch, or magician, give testimony of any person to be a witch; this indeed is not sufficient for condemnation; but it is a fit presumption to cause a straight examination.

IV.   If after cursing there follow death, or at least some mischief: for witches are wont to practice their mischievous facts by cursing and banning: this also is a sufficient matter of examination, tho not of conviction.

V.   If after enmity, quarreling, or threatening, a present mischief does follow: that also is a great presumption.

VI.   If the party suspected be the son or daughter, the man-servant or maid-servant, the familiar friend, near neighbor, or old companion, of a known and convicted witch; this may be likewise a presumption; for witchcraft is an art that may be learned, and conveyed from man to man.

VII.   Some add this for a presumption: if the party suspected be found to have the Devil's mark; for it is commonly thought, when the Devil makes his covenant with them, he alwaies leaves his mark behind them, whereby he knows them for his own:-a mark whereof no evident reason in nature can be given.

VIII.   Lastly, if the party examined be unconstant, or contrary to himself, in his deliberate answers, it argueth a guilty conscience, which stops the freedom of utterance. And yet there are causes of astonishment, which may befall the good, as well as the bad.

IX.   But then there is a conviction, discovering the witch, which must proceed from just and sufficient proofs, and not from bare presumptions.

X.   Scratching of the suspected party, and recovery thereupon, with several other such weak proofs; as also, the fleeting of the suspected party, thrown upon the water; these proofs are so far from being sufficient, that some of them are, after a sort, practices of witchcraft.

XI.   The testimony of some wizzard, tho offering to shew the witch's face in a glass: this, I grant, may be a good presumption, to cause a strait examination; but a sufficient proof of conviction it cannot be. If the Devil tell the grand jury, that the person in question is a witch, and offers withal to confirm the same by oath, should the inquest receive his oath or accusation to condemn the man? Assuredly no. And yet, that is as much as the testimony of another wizzard, who only by the Devil's help reveals the witch.

XII.   If a man, being dangerously sick, and like to dy, upon suspicion, will take it on his death, that such an one hath bewitched him, it is an allegation of the same nature, which may move the judge to examine the party, but it is of no moment for conviction.

XIII.   Among the sufficient means of conviction, the first is, the free and voluntary confession of the crime, made by the party suspected and accused, after examination. I say not, that a bare confession is sufficient, but a confession after due examination, taken upon pregnant presumptions. What needs now more witness or further inquiry?

XIV.   There is a second sufficient conviction, by the testimony of two witnesses, of good and honest report, avouching before the magistrate, upon their own knowledge, the two things: either that the party accused hath made a league with the Devil, or hath done some known practices of witchcraft. And, all arguments that do necessarily prove either of these, being brought by two sufficient witnesses, are of force fully to convince the party suspected.

XV.   If it can be proved, that the party suspected hath called upon the Devil, or desired his help, this is a pregnant proof of a league formerly made between them.

XVI.   If it can be proved, that the party hath entertained a familiar spirit, and had conference with it, in the likeness of some visible creatures; here is evidence of witchcraft.

XVII.   If the witness affirm upon oath, that the suspected person hath done any action or work which necessarily infers a covenant made, as, that he hath used enchantments, divined things before they come to pass, and that peremptorily, raised tempests, caused the form of a dead man to appear; it proveth sufficiently, that he or she is a witch.

Perkins' list of basic evidences of witchcraft did not include several other proofs considered by colonial courts to indicate guilt. Most of these presumptions involved traits of behavior believed to be common to witches. For example, workers of magic were thought prone to "cursing and bitter imprecations" and, therefore, inclined to fall easily into rages of anger. The refusal to confess was seen as an indication of stubbornness, a typical witch trait. Particularly suspicious was curiosity or "diligent inquiries" by a suspect into the condition of an afflicted person.

Evidence indicating that the defendant had a previous history of dealing in the black arts was damaging, and significant weight was placed upon testimony that showed a suspect had the common fame of being a witch. Such a reputation was not unusual, for in the colonies, a settler once implicated by either rumor or court action retained the stigma of suspect witchcraft throughout his life.

Acquittal of witchcraft charges did not permanently clear a defendant, and repeated prosecutions were not unique. Salisbury's Sussanah Martin was acquitted on sorcery charges in 1669, 1671, and 1673. Nearly two decades later, Sussanah, thrice cleared, was brought up again. This time the woman was found guilty and was executed. Bridget Bishop, hanged as a witch in 1692, had been freed of a similar charge in 1680, and Hampton's Eunice Cole was prosecuted at least three times over a twenty-five-year period.

One of the strangest cases in which the common fame of being a witch played a role was that of Windsor's Lydia Gilbert. Without the element of prior suspicion, the incident that triggered the Connecticut case would probably have been dismissed as an unfortunate, but natural occurrence.

The issue began in December of 1651, when Thomas Allyn was called before the Particular Court at Hartford to answer for the death of one Henry Stiles. Stiles had reportedly been shot in the back by Allyn during a military parade.

The jury rejected a finding of manslaughter and instead found Allyn guilty of "homicide by misadventure," a minor felony. The defendant was sentenced to pay a £20 fine and post a £10 bond for good behavior. In addition to the financial penalties, Allyn was forbidden to bear arms for one year.

Although the incident seemed explainable as a clear act of negligence, rumors began circulating that the death had been caused by supernatural means. Two years later, the case was reopened, and on March 24, 1654, Lydia Gilbert was charged with causing Stiles' demise by witchcraft. Suspicion had fallen upon the settlerwoman primarily because of her past reputation as a sorcerer, a fame reflected in her indictment, which noted: "Thou hast of late years, or still dost give entertainment to Sathat [Satan], the great enemy of God, and mankind, and by his help hast killed the body of Henry Styles, besides other witchcrafts. . . . "

It is not clear if Lydia was believed to have bewitched Allyn into shooting Stiles, or whether she was considered guilty of directly causing the death. Although Lydia was found guilty of witchcraft, there is no record that she was sentenced or suffered execution. The circumstances indicate that she was hanged, for Thomas Gilbert, in whose house she resided, moved immediately from the Windsor area. Documents from his new home in Hartford make no mention of Lydia's presence.

Although not as damaging as common fame, past indiscretions by a defendant could be introduced into court to prove a general reputation for shoddy dealings with the law. Several persons accused of witchcraft boasted a long list of acts against the public peace. Ten years before her first withcraft trial, Bridget Bishop had been brought to court for fighting with her husband Thomas Olliver. In 1687, an arrest warrant charging her with "feloniously taking away a piece of brass" from Thomas Stacey was issued. In 1678, she was found guilty of using foul language against her husband. As punishment, the pair was ordered to stand back to back in the public market on lecture day, with gags in their mouths and signs fastened to their foreheads describing their offense.

John Godfrey, tried but acquitted for witchcraft in 1666, had been earlier convicted for a series of felonies and misdemeanors, including stealing, swearing, drunkenness, and suborning witnesses. Nathaniel Greensmith had been convicted of stealing wheat, perjury, theft of a hoe, and battery. The personal record of Elizabeth Seager was marked by a long history of indictments for blasphemy and adultery.

When compared to British practices or modern trials, court activities in seventeenth-century America were informal affairs. Trials were not compartmentalized into initial presentations by the Crown followed by evidence from the defense. Instead, witnesses were summoned to the stand to relate their stories in narrative form. The citizens could be interrupted at any time by questions from the judge or jurors. The defendant was entitled to question the veracity of witnesses and make private inquiries as to possible errors of fact. Suspects might also interject their explanations or defense as the trial proceeded. The defendant might request the sheriff to bring in, by force if necessary, witnesses who might help in combating unfavorable testimony.

Capricious testimony could be challenged by either party in the dispute, and often punishment was meted out to witnesses who could not substantiate their statements. Chronic litigant William Mullener of New Haven was one citizen who fell afoul of the court in this manner. Mullener claimed that his pigs had been bewitched by William Meaker, who had supposedly cast the spell by cutting off their ears and throwing the items into a fire. Mullener's accusation was dismissed as groundless after Meaker brought a countersuit for defamation. As punishment for the wrongdoing, Mullener was ordered to either give bond for his future good behavior or to leave the colony.

Dinah Sylvester, who lodged a complaint of witchcraft against the wife of William Holmes in Plymouth colony, was also considered too flippant for the courts. When Dinah, who had sworn that Mrs. Holmes had transfigured into the shape of a bear, was asked: "What manner of tayle the bear had," she replied she did not know because the animal's rear was turned away from her. The court, who had intended to ask what story or "tale" the supposed witch had related, was not impressed with Dinah's levity. She was ordered to pay the cost of the prosecution and to be whipped. As an alternative to the beating, Dinah was allowed to make public apology to Mrs. Holmes.

Perjury by witnesses was punished severely, for lying was considered a serious sin in Early America. Under a 1642 Maryland law, those swearing falsely in court could be sentenced to lose their right hand. Eight years later the act was amended to provide for the loss of both ears and unlimited corporal punishment. Admitted perjurer John Goneere was ordered to stand in the pillory with his ears nailed to the backboard by three spikes. Upon release, the spikes were to be "slit out," and he to receive twenty lashes. Blanche Howell, found to have committed perjury, was also sentenced to loss of ears and the pillory. Immediately after the sentence was announced, the court adjourned so that the penalty could be carried out. The tribunal reconvened when the procedure had been finished.

Witnesses for both the defense and prosecution were reimbursed for expenses incurred in traveling to the court, and attending the trial. Legitimate costs included transportation and lodging and board, as well as incidental fees and losses from gainful employment. If convicted, these costs were borne by the defendant, but if the suspect was found innocent, the expenses were usually drawn out of the colony's treasury. In some cases of acquittal the judge was able to pass the charges along to the unfortunate accuser. If the case seemed to have been obviously groundless, the judge might be liable.

Virginia statutes were unusually vague regarding the payment of witnesses in witchcraft trials where no guilt was shown. In 1657 the Royal Council considered such a predicament in the case of Barbara Winbrow, who had been acquitted of sorcery charges. Unable to resolve the matter, the governor forwarded the question of who should pay to the House of Burgess.

Claims were not automatically approved as submitted, and to promote their accounts, citizens could file explanations concerning any unusual item. William Chandler, one of twenty-four witnesses asking compensation for attending the Boston witchcraft trial of Elizabeth Morse, noted on his claim: "I am aged, and came on foot, which is very hard for my aged body to bear, therefore, I hope this honored court will consider me for my pains and hard travel." For the two-day trip, Chandler asked costs of twelve shillings, sixpence, not an exorbitantly high figure.

As the witnesses proceeded through their testimony, no fact was considered too trivial for consideration. A minor occurrence, such as the spoiling of a pudding during a visit by a suspected witch, was considered equal in weight to an unexplained physical maiming. Both indicated that magic had been used. Hearsay evidence was also accepted with no corroborating support.

In addition to oral testimony, physical evidence that tended to prove either guilt or innocence was also admitted. Usually this material had been seized during a search of the defendant's house and could include puppets, books on witchcraft, or containers of evil-smelling potions or unknown substances.

Also of use to juries were petitions, submitted by friends or neighbors of the accused, that discussed the defendant's previous behavior. These affidavits were usually filed in an attempt to mitigate the severity of a sentence after a guilty verdict had been pronounced, but the documents could also be received as evidence to refute damaging testimony presented in court.

Ninety-three citizens signed such a petition in support of suspected witch Mary Bradbury. Included among those asking for the understanding of the court was Mary's husband of fifty years, who explained that she was old, "weak, and grieved under her affliction, [and] may not be able to speak much for herself, not being so free of speech as others might be." The inability to express oneself orally was particularly hazardous to the defendant. By custom and because lawyers were greatly mistrusted in the seventeenth century, the accused served as their own counsel and were responsible for presenting their defense and questioning all witnesses.

The good character of suspect Rebecca Nurse was also the subject of a petition. Two score neighbors announced in the document that Rebecca "hath brought up a great family of children and educated them well, so that there is in some of them [the] apparent savor of godliness." Twenty friends of John and Elizabeth Procter swore that the couple had "lived Christian life in their family and were ever ready to help such as stood in need of their help." Neither of the affidavits proved helpful to the defendants, for Rebecca Nurse, like John and Elizabeth Procter, was found guilty of witchcraft and sentenced to hang.

A final area of evidence available to juries was statements submitted by knowledgeable parties acting in an amicus curiae role. New England courts frequently asked that area clergymen give expert advice on ethical or moral aspects of criminal infractions. Although these opinions held no legal weight, the ideas undoubtedly influenced the thinking of both judges and juries. One such reaction, giving the opinion of a group of Connecticut ministers in the 1692 trials of Mercy Disborough and Elizabeth Clawson, dismissed as inadmissible much of the evidence that had been entered. The clergymen not only rejected results of a water ordeal and a search for teats, but suggested that the women's accuser was suffering from the "mother," the term used to indicate hysteria. The opinion, as submitted to the court announced:

As to the evidences left to our consideration respecting the two women suspected of witchcraft in Fairfield, we offer:

1. That we cannot but give our concurrence with the generality of divines that the endeavour of conviction of witchcraft by swimming is unlawful and sinful and therefore it cannot afford any evidence.

2. That the unusual excrescences found upon their bodies ought not to be allowed as evidence against them without the approbation of some able physicians.

3. Respecting the evidence of the afflicted maid, we find some things testified carrying a suspicion of her counterfeiting; others that plainly intimate her trouble from the mother, which, improved by craft and unusual effects affirmed of her and of those things that by some may be thought diabolical, or effects of witchcraft. . . .

4. As to the other strange accidents, as the dying of cattle, etc., we apprehend the applying of them to these women as matters of witchcraft to be upon very slender and uncertain grounds.

Hartford

October 17, 1692

Joseph Eliot

Timothy Woodridge

After all evidence and opinions had been received, the jury retired to consider its verdict. Deliberations rarely lasted longer than several hours, for speedy justice was a keystone of the colonial court system. A special incentive for quick reports was provided in Virginia, where it was required that jurors be secluded "without meat, drink, fire, or candle till they are agreed of their verdict." Such a stipulation undoubtedly resulted in lighting justice during the cold, dark winter months in the tidewater area. To protect the defendant against careless deliberations, jurors who brought in judgments contrary to the weight of evidence could be made liable to heavy penalties.

Hung juries were virtually unknown, but there is evidence that strong dissension often took place before a unanimous verdict was agreed upon. Elizabeth Seager, tried for witchcraft and adultery, was the subject of heated controversy according to the foreman of her jury. Although several citizens were "staggered" or undecided as to Elizabeth's guilt, she was "almost gone." Fortunately for the defendant, a hard-core group of jurors voting for acquittal managed to convert the others and Elizabeth was eventually found not guilty.

The prospect of a hung jury was presented in Mercy Disborough's trial. Evidence against the woman was slight, but all except a single juror voted to condemn. The seemingly inconsistent verdict was perhaps a reflection of panic spreading to the area from Salem. When the lone holdout refused to agree with the majority, the court was adjourned so that the opinion of a higher tribunal could be sought. The reply was unfavorable to Mercy and when the trial court reconvened, the defendant was found unanimously guilty. Mercy was sentenced to hang, but the execution was reprieved when the case was sent for review to the colony's Court of Assistants.

Fortunately for Mercy, the higher officials strongly opposed the prosecutions being conducted in neighboring Massachusetts. Fearing that an execution in their own area would result in "inextricable troubles," the Assistants announced: "Blood is a great thing and we cannot but open our mouths for the dumb in the cause of one appointed to die by such a verdict."

The Assistants, however, stopped short of pardoning Mercy on humanitarian or moral grounds. Instead, the condemned woman was released on a technical error in the composition of the jury. Near the end of the original trial, one juror had departed and was replaced by a new citizen. The action was ruled a breech of judicial procedure and due cause for overturning of the guilty finding. In stressing the importance of a fair trial, the Assistants wrote: "Tis the birthright of the King's subjects so, and no otherwise to be tryed and they must not be despoyled of it."

In most cases, the court accepted the findings of the jury by releasing the innocent and sentencing the guilty. But if the verdict differed significantly from the opinion of the trial judge, the jury could be sent back to reconsider its findings. Such a procedure was ordered in the case of Rebecca Nurse.

Although the jury unanimously found Rebecca not guilty, the chief judge remanded the body for further examination of the evidence, suggesting that the wrong opinion had been brought in. Thus prompted, the citizens returned with a verdict of guilty. In 1693, another Massachusetts jury proved less willing to submit to judicial arbitrariness. The body refused to convict Mary Watkins, a "distracted" servant girl who had confessed to practicing witchraft. When ordered to reconsider, the jury again found her not guilty.

CHAPTER IX

After the Verdict

CONVICTED witches were not sentenced to long periods of imprisonment as punishment for their crime. Incarceration for more
than a few months was rare in the early colonies, where prison facilities were usually considered a luxury.

In all but a handful of towns, prisoners who were ordered
confined until trial or execution were quartered temporarily in public
buildings, such as taverns, or in a constable's house. Both a lack of
need and an absence of community funds necessitated these makeshift
arrangements. In most areas, residents lived on marginal economic
levels, which allowed no provision for expenditures for a permanent
penal structure. An equally important factor was that America, unlike
England, had no extensive criminal class. Serious crimes were uncommon and jail facilities were not frequently required.

The penal situation in capitals was only slightly better than in
rural communities. For example, it was not until September of 1663,
more than thirty years after the original settlement of Maryland, that
the provincial assembly authorized construction of a prison at St.
Mary's. According to the legislature's report, the building was needed
because of "inconveniences" and "for want of places for the securing
[of] offenders." The body did not wish to finance an elaborate structure, and thus ordered that a "log house be built, twenty foot square."

Lack of money for building and maintenance was not the sole

factor limiting prison construction. The prevailing concepts of penology disregarded prolonged incarceration as a punishment for crime. Most considered imprisonment an unworkable penalty or deterrent and chose to rely on more economical or effective methods.

For "heinous" felons, quick execution eliminated the cost required for long-term jailing. Lesser felons were reprieved, an action compatible with the frontier nature of the American land, where each individual was considered of potential value in building the society. Reliance was placed on other non-capital punishments, such as mutilation, flogging, or temporary confinement in the stocks or pillory. Each of these solutions, allowed the criminal to remain free to work for the common good and make restitution to any injured party.

Peculiarities of the judicial system did result in the imprisonment of suspects for limited durations. Pre-trial detention could be for as long as three months, the maximum adjournment period of the quarterly courts. Post-trial incarceration was usually less extensive, for executions customarily took place within a fortnight of conviction. Bridget Bishop, for example, was charged, tried, and executed in eight days. In rare cases, detention after conviction could be for as long as a year if an appeal or request for pardon was pending.

Even the briefest periods of imprisonment were unpleasant, for although conditions in America's makeshift jails were far superior to the diseased-filled dungeons of England, the facilities were primitive. Males and females, both adults and children, were all crowded into common cells and supplied only with straw pallets for sleeping. Little distinction in treatment was made between convicted felons, the insane, and those awaiting trial. All shared the same accommodations. Fire was occasionally provided for both heat and light, but in socially advanced towns like Williamsburg, these amenities were made available only to those imprisoned for debt. Suspected or convicted felons were placed instead in semi-outdoor dungeons, which were partially exposed to the raw elements.

Only the cheapest gruel, incapable of sustaining life for extended periods of time, was served as food. The toll in disease and malnutrition was probably extremely high as a result of the substandard diet. As late as 1772, three prisoners died from starvation in Philadelphia, the most humanitarian and intellectually compassionate city in the colonies.

Friends and relatives of the jailed might be allowed to improve a prisoner's condition by providing blankets, lanterns, and nourishing food. Wealthy detainees were sometimes allowed to purchase additional articles from jailors, who made a personal profit on each transaction.

Medical attention for the aged or infirm was only rarely provided, and death from infectious disease was undoubtedly common. One victim was Rebecca Chamberlain, who died in Cambridge prison while awaiting trial on charges of witchcraft. In Andover, suspected sorcerer Ann Foster met a similar fate. Village citizens became so alarmed at the danger created by unhealthy conditions and lack of food that seven residents submitted a formal petition pleading for pre-trial release of women and children.

William Morse recognized that the substandard facilities of the Boston jail might seriously affect the health of his imprisoned wife. In a letter to local officials, the sorcerer's husband explained:

To the Honorable Governor and Council
now sitting in Boston, June 4th, 1680.

The petition of William Morse humbly showeth that whereas his dear wife was by the jury found guilty of witchcraft, and by the honorable Court condemned to dy: Yet, since God hath been pleased to move your Honors' hearts to grant her a reprieve until October next, your petitioner humbly prays that your Honors be pleased to show her so much pity as to grant her liberty in the daytime to walk in the prison yard, and to ye prison house, and that in the night she may have privilege of a chamber in the common gaol, and be freed from the dungeon, which is extreme close and hot in this season, and also liberty on the sabbath to go to Meeting; he and his children giving security for her safe imprisonment. So shall he be ever obliged to pray as in duty bound.

Wm. Moosse [sic]

The courts frowned on releasing suspected or convicted sorcerers for even brief periods. It was feared that once at home, the witches would cast new spells aimed at forcing their accusers into recanting their allegations. Instead of parole, suspects were securely restrained and watched so that rescue attempts by the devil could be foiled.

Children of incarcerated adults, if not cared for privately, were trundled off to prison with their parents. Minors jailed on direct charges of witchcraft received no special consideration. Among the supposedly dangerous witches of Salem, locked into cells were five-year-old Dorcas Good; Sarah Carrier and Abigail Faulkner, both age eight; ten-year-old Dorothy Faulkner; and eleven-year-old Abigail Johnson.

The results of imprisonment often left permanent scars on children who were forced to endure the harsh conditions of penal facilities. On September 13, 1710, William Good, in a petition to the Massachusetts court, detailed some of the damage that had been inflicted upon members of his family during the Salem persecutions. Good wrote:

1. My wife Sarah Good was in prison about four months and then executed.

2. A sucking child died in prison before the mother's execution.

3. A child of four or five years old was in prison seven or eight months, and being chained in the dungeon was so hardly used and terrified that she hath ever since been very chargeable, having little or no reason to govern herself. And I leave it unto the honorable Court to judge what damage I have sustained by such a destruction of my poor family, and so rest,

Your honor's humble servant
William Good

Salem, September 13, 1710

The chaining of Good's young daughter was the prescribed method of detainment for suspected witches. Leg iron, ropes, and other means of binding were accepted as necessary to insure that enchanters neither worked magic nor transmogrified in order to escape. Because it was believed that witches could slip through the smallest keyhole or crack in a door, thick double locks were customarily bolted onto the bonds.

Elizabeth Cary, wife of a Charlestown shipmaster, was confined in the usual manner, and the results were near fatal. Jonathan Cary had obtained his wife's release from Boston jail on a writ of habeas corpus and removed her to Cambridge prison, where he believed she would receive more gentle care. He soon discovered the situation had not improved and wrote:

Having been there one night, the jailor put irons on her legs (having received such a command): the weight of them was about eight pounds. These irons and her other afflictions soon brought her into convulsive fits, so that I thought she would have died that night. I sent to entreat that the irons might be taken off, but all entreaties were in vain.

Elizabeth's treatment might have been less harmful to a younger prisoner in healthy physical condition. But the Cambridge woman, like most suspected witches, had undergone an exhaustive examination by Salem magistrates. In describing the interrogation Jonathan noted:

She was forced to stand with her arms stretched out. I requested that I might hold one of her hands, but it was denied me; then she desired me to wipe the tears from her eyes and the sweat from her face, which I did. Then she desired that she might lean herself on me, saying she should faint. Justice Hathorne replied that she had strength enough to torment these persons and she should have strength enough to stand. . . .

Prisoners were not maintained at public expense, but were forced to pay for all food and any other expenses incurred during their detention. Incidental costs were not always voluntary purchases, but included anything deemed by the court to be necessary for the prisoner's maintenance. At Salem, male prisoners were charged five shillings for the use of the leg fetters by which they were kept bound. Women, presumed to be a greater danger, were more heavily secured. The average bill for a female's handcuffs and leg irons was seven shillings, sixpence.

Imprisonment costs varied among communities according to standards of maintenance, but a fee of three shillings a week was considered reasonable for one person's food and lodging. Basic charges may have occasionally been adjusted according to financial ability to pay. In March of 1663, Hartford jailor Daniel Garret was awarded six shillings a week for keeping both Nathaniel and Rebecca Greensmith. His fee for holding Mary Barnes for the same period was seven shillings, twice the amount paid for either of the Greensmiths.

Court charges, such as the salaries, food, and expenses incurred by magistrates, were added to the prison fees and could greatly inflate a citizen's tab. Maximilian Boush, who conducted the trial of Virginian Grace Sherwood, was granted five thousand pounds of tobacco for his trouble. Jailors' costs in transporting a prisoner to court and remaining during the trial were also chargeable to the prisoner. Fees were significant for defendants in areas distant from the colonial capital. Hannah Lee and Mary Marler, arrested in Charles County, Maryland, were billed 5,715 pounds of tobacco for the jailor's trouble in keeping them four months and escorting them to St. Mary's.

Charges for items such as subpoenas and warrants were usually waived if the accused was found innocent, but prison fees were always chargeable to a defendant. Even those acquitted were remanded in jail until full payment had been received. The more affluent suspect, if unable to produce immediate payment in sterling, might mortgage land or other property to the jailor, but for the poor, prison fees presented an unbreakable cycle of continued imprisonment and increasing charges that could not be paid.

Sarah Daston was cleared of witchcraft charges in 1693, but because she was unable to pay jail costs, Sarah remained in the lockup until she died. Boston's Mary Watkins found herself in a similar situation. After failing in an attempt to strangle herself, Mary volunteered to become an indentured servant to anyone who would settle her bill. A Virginian was found who accepted the bargain and Mary was sent south in bondage.

Jailors and sheriffs could legally garnish all property of delinquent prisoners in order to collect payment. Particularly active in this area were the lawmen in and around Salem. One aggressive official not only confiscated the entire estate of George Jacobs, but also claimed the wedding ring off the finger of the prisoner's wife.

Among the poorer classes, confiscation was usually inadequate to settle accumulated fees. Margaret Jacobs found herself penniless after the entailment of her own property and that of her grandfather and parents. When news of her predicament was made public, a generous stranger came forward with the funds needed to secure Margaret's release from jail.

Death did not limit the liability of a detainee. In order to remove from jail the body of Ann Foster, the enchanter's son was forced to pay £2 16s for prison fees. The corpse of witch Sarah Osburn, who also died in jail, was held until after settlement of a £1 3s 5d charge.

Prison fees played a key role in what appears to be the only

instance in which a defendant was sentenced to a long-term imprisonment as a penalty for practicing witchcraft. The results of the unusual
action proved disastrous not only for prisoner Eunice Cole, but also
for citizens residing in her home village of Hampton.

Eunice had been suspected of being a particularly foul and powerful witch for some time before her 1656 trial. Not only was she
credited with possessing an "invisible hand," which could drown
enemies at will, but she was also suspected of turning a local man into
an ape. Because of an overwhelming burden of proof, Eunice was
convicted of the witchcraft charge, but the court of Norfolk County
was hesitant to order execution. Instead, the officials ruled that Eunice
should be whipped and imprisoned for life or until released by the
court.

In the year immediately following the trial, all seemed quiet and
peaceful in Hampton, but in 1659, Eunice's aged husband submitted
a petition asking for her release. Cole maintained that Eunice's jailing
was placing a hardship on his finances. No longer could he afford to
hire laborers to farm his land, a chore which Eunice had evidently
performed before her trial. The court, perhaps fearing that Cole was
on the verge of becoming a public ward, ruled that the family's
property should be confiscated by the village of Hampton. The principal and income from the estate could be used to support Cole and pay
for Eunice's prison fees.

The confiscation, although unusual, was predicated on the seventeenth-century custom that all paupers within the borders of a town
were wards of the community and entitled to support by local citizens.
To avoid such a burden, the court had moved to assure that Cole's
funds would not be flitted away, and that maintenance of the couple
would not fall upon Hampton residents.

The plea for Eunice's release was rejected, but three years later
the enchanter entered a similar request. Eunice claimed that her
eighty-eight-year-old husband was desperately ill and needed treatment that only she could provide. Magistrates were not unsympa-
thetic to the situation. It was decreed that the woman could be sent
home if two conditions were met. First, all jail fees must be paid in
full. Second, Eunice must agree to leave the town within a month,
never to return. The provisions were not fulfilled. Cole died unaided
and Eunice remained in jail.

In 1665, after nearly a decade of imprisonment, Eunice again filed for parole. Again the court consented. Again she was unable to meet their conditions.

At some point, the convicted witch had become a public ward. Hampton records note that each year payment for her maintenance was forwarded to the jail keep. The charges were evidently a burden on the community, for in 1668, when insufficient sterling was available, £8 worth of hogshead staves were sent to jailor William Salter "for keeping Goodwife Cole this year."

After fifteen years in jail, Eunice was at last released and returned home destitute. To insure her survival, villagers were assigned to provide necessary food, clothing, and fuel. Each week a specific family assumed responsibility for producing the items and after seven days passed the chore along to a new clan. The arrangement was short-lived, for in October of 1672 Eunice was once more brought before the court on charges of witchcraft. This time she was not convicted and was released from jail, where she had been temporarily confined. Seven years later, another hearing was called. Although the evidence again proved insufficient for conviction, the Hampton judges ruled that they so firmly believed her guilty that she was to be imprisoned anyway. So that she would not escape, a lock was ordered placed on her leg.

At some unrecorded date, the Hampton witch was released for a third time and returned home. Here she lived alone and suspect for the remainder of her life. According to tradition, her corpse lay undiscovered for several days after the death. When she was at last found, her body was pushed into a hastily dug grave and a stake was driven through it.

Like all colonials imprisoned for crimes, suspected witches were unable to protect their property or possessions from damage by the public. The threat of vandalism and looting was a distinct problem to jailed enchanters, whose crimes were often considered infractions against the general public rather than harmful to a single complainant.

Connecticut's Katherine Harrison, tried in May of 1669, but bound over until the October session of the court, was a victim of extreme vindictiveness. When the magistrates reconvened for the fall hearing, Katherine submitted a petition for "due recompense" for the damages inflicted upon her property during a period including her jailing. The list of losses was gruesome indeed and included oxen, so "spoyled" by bruises that the animals were unusable, a cow whose back and two ribs had been broken, a wounded horse, a barnyard heifer and several pigs whose earmarks had been cut off and new ones cut in, a cow who suffered a broken jaw and a hole bored in her side, a three-year-old heifer stabbed to death, a milk cow wounded in the bag, a sow with one hind leg cut off and ears "lugged," and two year-old steers whose backs had been broken. Katherine also claimed that the vandals had driven horses through her cornfield and spoiled thirty poles of hops.

Loss of property on a grander scale was experienced by wealthy Philip English, who owned fourteen buildings and twenty-one ships. The damage, however, had not been inflicted by citizen looters, but was credited to Salem sheriff George Corwin. When English, who had fled the city to avoid trial for witchcraft, returned, he was near penniless. During his absence, Corwin had confiscated the escapee's wharves, warehouses, mansion, and £1,183 2s worth of personal property. English, claiming that his estate had been "seized, taken away, lost, and embezzled," sued the sheriff for damages, but the court absolved the lawman of all responsibility.

The merchant's attempts to recover the property did not cease. When Corwin died three years later, English seized the corpse for non-payment of a debt, and held the body until the lawman's executors paid a settlement of £60 3s . The presumption that Corwin had profiteered from the confiscation of English's estate proved false, for the sheriff's entire estate totaled only about £140.

Philip English and his wife had not originally intended to flee from trial. Instead, the couple had planned to remain in the bay colony, prove their innocence, and clear their reputations of witchcraft charges. But the couple, free on bail, grew increasingly more convinced that in the rabid atmosphere of Salem, trials were far from impartial affairs. The final decision to escape was triggered at a church service attended by the couple the day before their hearings were scheduled to begin. Appropriately, and probably not by accident, the Episcopalian minister's sermon was based on the biblical passage: "If they prosecute you in one city, flee to another." English and his wife heeded the religious sign and quickly sped off to New York. Both survived the witchcraft panic, but Mrs. English died prematurely in 1694, reportedly as a consequence of inadequate treatment in prison.

Flight to avoid trial or execution for witchcraft was a common tactic, but one reserved primarily for wealthy citizens who could financially afford to be uprooted. Because jails were often flimsy and temporary structures, escape was a simple procedure. Jailors, who received little pay from the courts, were primarily dependent upon income from prison fees and may have allowed their more affluent charges to flee upon payment of an adequate bribe. To discourage this practice, some provinces imposed severe penalties on prison keeps who, without suffering bodily harm, allowed any prisoner to escape.

Captain Jonathan Cary feared so strongly that his wife Elizabeth had been condemned before trial that he arranged for her escape from prison. The plan was successful, and the pair fled to Rhode Island. Apprehensive that the Salem persecutions might spread to the neighboring area, the Carys moved again in search of safety. This time to liberal New York.

In 1697, Winifred Benham and her daughter, once acquitted of witchcraft charges but subject to renewed allegations, left Hartford for New York, where further prosecution was avoided. James Walkley, accused of bewitching an eight-year-old child to death, also fled from Hartford rather than face witchcraft charges. In the same city, Elizabeth Seager, indicted thrice as an enchanter, chose the same course. Massachusetts' John Alden was also saved from possible execution by escaping from prison.

Dudley Bradstreet, son of a colonial governor, was perhaps the most famous colonial who picked life over reputation. As Andover's Justice of the Peace, Bradstreet had originally participated in the witchcraft hysteria of 1692 and had signed approximately thirty-five arrest warrants in one day of mass accusations. However, when Bradstreet became disillusioned and refused to approve further warrants, he was cried out upon by accusers who alleged that the justice and his wife had murdered nine persons by magic. Rather than face the charges, the pair chose exile.

Dudley's brother John also left Massachusetts under suspicion, but at least one death occurred as a result of his supposed magic. A dog, thought bewitched by John, was formally executed. This incident may be the only case in colonial history involving the punishment of a familiar, but the concept of putting to death animals or objects involved in a crime was widely accepted.

In 1642, teenaged Thomas Granger was condemned for bestiality with a mare, a cow, two goats, five sheep, two calves, and a turkey. Just before his execution, a group of animals was paraded passed Granger, who obligingly identified the guilty parties. According to Governor William Bradford, who witnessed the scene, the execution was terrible indeed. Bradford wrote:

> A very sad spectacle it was. For first the mare and then the cow and the rest of the lesser cattle were killed before his face, according to the law, Leviticus XX.15; and then he himself was executed. The cattle were all cast into a great and large pit that was digged of purpose for them, and no use made of any part of them.

Presumably, the goats, sheep, and turkey were spared.

An element of witchcraft was involved in a similar incident at New Haven in 1662. Here one Goodman Potter, considered a devoted saint, was convicted of bestialities. Potter, who had been a confirmed churchgoer in the community for twenty years, had shown no signs of his unusual fetish. Cotton Mather believed that the deception had been accomplished with the help of Satan and explained: "The unclean devil which had the possession of this monster had carried all his lusts with so much fury into this one channel of wickedness that there was no notice taken of his being wicked in any other."

On the gallows prior to Potter's hanging, a cow, two heifers, three sheep, and two sows were killed. When Potter's wife admitted she had seen the miscreant associating with a bitch some ten years earlier, citizens concluded that Potter had "conjured" her into remaining silent on the matter.

Benjamin Good, a Massachusetts settler found guilty of bestiality "instigated by the divill," was sentenced to die in 1673, but not until the offending mare was "knocked on the head," in his sight.

If escape was not a possible option, pardon usually stood as a last safeguard between those found guilty of witchcraft and the gallows. Complete pardons were extremely rare, possibly because of the great interest taken in sorcery trials by the public. Presumably, before the death sentence had been imposed, the highest officers in the colony had thoroughly evaluated all the facts in the case. Mitigating circumstances were difficult to uncover during the brief post-trial period. Officials who wished to prevent a hanging usually did not issue a public pardon, but instead authorized repeated temporary stays until publicity surrounding the case had abated.

A limited pardon was handed down in the 1674 case of Maryland's John Cowman, convicted of "witchcraft, conjuration, sorcery, or enchantment." Cowman was sentenced to hang, but the colony's House of General Assembly, calling him "so wretched and miserable an object," requested that he be reprieved. Charles Calvert, Lt. General of Maryland and chief justice of the provincial court, agreed, but ordered that the prisoner not be told of the action until the last moment. Calvert announced:

> The Lieutenant General . . . is willing upon the request of the Lower House that the condemned malefactor be reprieved and execution stayed, provided that the sheriff of St. Maries County carry him to the gallows, and that the rope being around his neck, it be there made known to him how much he is beholding to the Lower House of Assemblie for mediating and interceding in his behalf with the Lieutenant General, and that he remain at the city of St. Maries to be employed in such service as the governor and council shall think fit during the pleasure of the governor.

Conditional pardons may have been a popular means of punishment in early Maryland. Colonial records show that one unfortunate felon, sentenced to death for stealing, was pardoned on the provision that he agree to become the common hangman. The choice was not to be revealed to the prisoner until he was standing on the gallows with a rope around his neck.

The possibility of execution faced every citizen accused of witchcraft, for America, like other Christian nations, based its treatment of convicted enchanters on the biblical admonition: "Thou shalt not suffer a witch to live."

Throughout Europe, this instruction was used as the rationale for mass burnings and quarterings. French lawyer Jean Bodin applauded the penalties and explained: "Whatever punishment we can order against witches, by roasting and cooking them over a slow fire, is not really very much. . . . "

Burning was a prime method of death in British Scotland, where witches were dressed in sackcloth, hanged or garroted, and then burned in barrels. Like prison fees, "burning bills," were kept by jailors, who itemized each expense necessary for the execution. Typical costs included fees for buying and dressing the stake to which the prisoner would be tied, as well as for the peat needed to stoke the flames. One such bill, submitted for the November 19, 1639, turning off of William Coke and Alison Dick in Kirkcaldy showed expenditures for:

	£	s	p
For ten loads of coal to burn then, 5 marks @	3	6	8
For a tar barrel		14	
For tows [hangman's rope]		6	
For hurden to be jumps [shrouds]	3	10	
For making of them		8	
For one to go to Finmouth for the laird to sit upon their assize as judge		6	
For the executioner for his pains	8	14	
For his expenses here		16	4

Methods of witch disposal were even harsher in continental Europe than in Scotland. So that the process of dying might be as prolonged as possible, green wood was used to stoke the fires of those who had not cooperated in court. Witches were occasionally strangled before being put to the stake, but most found guilty, and all unconfessed enchanters, were burned alive.

The colonies, like most areas in England, rejected burning as a means of execution for witchcraft, and instead chose to eliminate sorcerers by hanging. Death by fire, however, was not unknown. In Maryland, during the seventeenth century, treason by a woman was legally punishable by burning at the stake. Men convicted for the same offense could be sentenced to be hanged, drawn, and quartered. If the convicted treasoner was a titled Lord or Lady, the method was beheading. In practice, burning was a new-world penalty usually reserved only for black members of society.

In 1666, a Negro woman who set fire to her master's house in

New York was condemned to death by burning, while in Orange County, Virginia, a slave named Eve was burned for poisoning her owner. During the eighteenth century, a black man and woman were burned for three deaths by poison in Charles Town, and in Kent County, Maryland, Esther Anderson met the same fate for murder. Esther's two male accomplices were hanged.

The pressing to death of eighty-year-old Giles Corey was not an exception to the hanging rule governing witchcraft executions, for Corey received the *peine fort et dure* because of failure to plead, not for conviction of witchcraft. Pressings were carried out under methods prescribed by ancient tradition. First, the prisoner was stretched prone, face upward, and tied by the arms and legs in a spread-eagle position. Next, a board or flat weight was placed over the trunk of the body and on this surface stones or iron pieces were piled until the offender was crushed. According to Blackstone, prisoners were to be given only three morsels of the "worst bread" during the first day and three draughts of "standing water" the next. After the liquid, nothing further was provided.

Giles Corey reportedly lasted two full days before he became unable to bear further pain. But instead of agreeing to enter a plea, Corey asked that his executioners pile additional weights on his body so that death would come more quickly. A somewhat grisly ballad commemorating the event relates:

> Giles Corey was a wizard strong,
> A stubborn wretch was he;
> And fit was he to hang on high
> Upon the locust tree.
>
> So when before the magistrates
> For trial he did come,
> He would no true confession make,
> But was completely dumb.
>
> "Giles Corey," saith the magistrate,
> "What hast thou here to plead,
> To these that now accuse thy soul,
> Of crimes and horrid deeds?"
>
> Giles Corey he said not a word,
> No single word spoke he,

"Giles Corey," saith the magistrate,
"We'll press it out of thee."
They got them then a heavy beam,
They laid it on his breast,
They loaded it with heavy stones,
And hard upon him pressed.

"More weight!" now said this wretched man;
"More weight!" again he cried;
And he did no confession make,
But wickedly he died.

Ironically, some eighteen years before, Corey had been suspected in the death of a man who had been "bruised" to death. The day after Corey's pressing, Judge Samuel Sewall wrote that the event had been completely forgotten by citizens in the village. However, it was brought back to memory in a strange and supernatural manner. Ann Putnam, one of the afflicted accusers, who had no knowledge of the event, was told of the former murder by Corey's apparition on the eve of the execution.

Executions were a major public spectacle and the procedures in turning off a felon were aimed at providing maximum exposure for those who wished to witness the event. Settlers came from miles around to attend hangings, and it was not unusual for a date of execution to be set to coincide with some planned observance, such as a harvest celebration or a government holiday. Witch Margaret Jones of Charlestown was ordered executed on Lecture Day, a time when large groups of rural citizens could be expected to visit Boston to hear the town's famous ministers preach on spiritual matters.

Inhabitants of all areas showed a curious interest in executions, but the Puritans seemed particularly intrigued. Their morbid fascination may have stemmed from the important role played by religion in the supposedly civil affair.

Before hangings took place, it was considered of utmost importance that convicted felons give a full, public confession and show proper contrition for committing their evil acts. Only then could an execution be considered by spectators to be a success. The burden of extricating admissions of guilt was placed on members of the clergy and a wide latitude was provided to assist them in the task.

On the morning of the hanging, clergymen closeted themselves with any prisoners who stubbornly maintained innocence. Alternately, the ministers threatened and cajoled the reluctant convicts in an attempt to establish a mental frame of repentance. Sometimes these sessions produced startling results. Goody Lake of Dorchester, scheduled to hang for witchcraft, steadfastly refused to admit her guilt, despite concerted efforts by a Braintree minister. But under pressure, the prisoner admitted that some years before she had "played the harlot, and being with child, used means to destroy the fruit of her body. . . . " Although she maintained her innocence of sorcery to the end, Goody Lake ultimately accepted the justness of the hanging as punishment for her earlier abortion.

If a prisoner did not repent in the privacy of the jail cell, the clergy retained two other chances to alter the situation. A prime opportunity came just before the trek to the gallows began, for at this time, prisoners were usually taken to a special church service. Here ministers spent several hours describing in gory detail the felon's crime and crying out against the sins of the perpetrator.

After the meeting, the prisoner was placed in an open cart and driven through streets thronged with citizens who had been unable to secure a satisfactory place in church. A greater mob waited at the place of execution.

Samuel Sewall, in describing a turning off that took place in June of 1704, wrote that in addition to a huge crowd surrounding the gallows, at least 150 boats and canoes filled with viewers bobbed on a nearby river. According to Sewall, when the hangman's rope was pulled taut, the spectators' single screech was so loud that it was heard by the judge's wife, who was working in an orchard a mile away.

Frequently, ministers unable to resist the temptation of addressing a large and captive audience delivered still another pre-death sermon while standing on the gallows with the condemned. Finally, the prisoner was allowed to make a last address. It was at this time that the felon ideally made a full confession and asked the forgiveness of any who might have been wronged. If the prisoner complied in the hoped for manner, the crowd was content, secure in the belief that once again a servant of the devil was about to meet a just end.

By removing all doubt as to guilt, the final confession also served to assure the populace that no error had been made by the judges and jury. Because incidents of witchcraft were rarely witnessed by observers, confession was particularly important in executions for sorcery. Equally important, the admission of guilt was believed to free the prisoner from the clutches of the devil. To die repentant of evil was considered essential for salvation.

Felons who did not accommodate the wishes of the mob and continued to maintain their innocence were described as dying poorly. Margaret Jones was soundly condemned by Governor Winthrop for her attitude at the Charlestown gallows:

> Her behavior at her trial was very intemperate, lying notoriously and railing upon the jury and witnesses, etc., and in the like distemper she died. The same day and hour she was executed, there was a very great tempest at Connecticut, which blew down many trees, etc.

Winthrop, angered at her demeanor, curtly added: "If the tempest was the wrath of God, it was visited upon the wrong people."

Supernatural signs such as the tempest in Connecticut were unsettling to those who believed that witches possessed the power to reach back from the grave and torment those who had punished them. A commonly accepted presumption was that long after the rope had been pulled tight, unconfessed witches presented a continuing threat to the community.

On her way to the gallows, Goody Glover flamed such beliefs by proclaiming that her death would not release the Goodwin children from their pains of possession. According to Cotton Mather, her prediction was true, for the children experienced torments "seven times hotter" than before.

An additional instance of posthumous revenge by an executed witch involved Sarah Good, hanged on July 14, 1692, at Salem. As Sarah stood on the gallows, she was harangued by local minister Nicholas Noyes for a final time. Tiring of the barrage of insults, Sarah announced to the clergyman: "I am no more a witch than you are a wizard, and if you take away my life, God will give you blood to drink." The threat was duly noted, and some twenty-five years later, when Noyes died of a cerebral hemorrhage, blood purging from his mouth, rumors immediately credited the death to the revenge of Goody Good. Nathaniel Hawthorne, a descendant of Salem magistrate John Hathorne, commemorated the event in his work *The House of the Seven Gables.*

The large number of executed but unconfessed witches proved unnerving to the people of Salem, who witnessed nineteen straight hangings at which each of the dying maintained his innocence. Particularly dismaying was the September twenty-second mass turning off of eight witches, most of whom had been respected churchgoers for decades. Not only did seven of the felons continue to maintain their innocence, but Samuel Wardwell, who had earlier confessed under pressure, recanted the document.

Only rarely were the corpses of hanged witches treated with common dignity. In some cases, such as Elizabeth Knapp's 1653 execution, the bodies were "tumbled" about by curious spectators. Ann Hibbins, hanged at Boston in 1656, recognized the possibility that her remains would be abused and took special pains to request that she be given decent burial. In a codicil to her will, Ann pleaded: "My desire is that all my overseers would be pleased to show so much respect unto my dead corpse as to cause it to be decently interred, and, if it may be, near my late husband." Ann's request to be buried near her husband was probably a plea that she be allowed Christian burial in a church cemetery. The perpetrators of many capital crimes were denied such a request, and in action involving witchcraft, the specter of religious heresy may have made the prohibition even more stictly enforced.

Robert Calef, in a somewhat disputed account of the August 19, 1692, hanging of George Burroughs, John Procter, John Willard, George Jacobs, and Martha Carrier, suggests that Salem citizens gave little attention to the bodies of the executed. In describing the treatment accorded to the corpse of Burroughs, Calef wrote:

> When he was cut down, he was dragged by the halter to a hole, or grave, between the rocks, about two feet deep, his shirt and breeches being pulled off, and an old pair of trousers of one executed put on his lower parts, he was so put in, together with Willard and Carrier, one of his hands and his chin, and a foot of one of them, being left uncovered.

Calef may have been implying that because of indifference or hatred, the prisoners' corpses were only partially buried. But the situation may have stemmed from an ancient belief that specific sections of dead bodies, if touched, were useful in curing diseases. The hand of a corpse, for example, was supposedly helpful in healing eczema, tumors, goiters, "the King's evil," and in erasing birthmarks. The tooth of a dead man was thought to cure impotency. The folk cures were presumed particularly effective if the deceased had been hanged or had met with a violent or unnatural death. The leaving uncovered of witches' bodily parts may have been done to enable local victims of disease to avail themselves of the potential cures.

Elizabeth Procter had been scheduled to hang alongside her husband and the four other convicted felons, but she escaped the ordeal by pleading her belly. Pregnant women in the colonies could be neither hanged nor flogged until after the birth of their child, for settlers believed that fetuses were innocent parties and could not be punished for the transgressions of the mother. If such a pregnancy was not externally obvious, a jury of matrons was appointed to determine if the woman was actually with child or was merely using a delaying tactic to avoid the court's sentence.

Executions of at least two other women were delayed as a result of pregnancy. In 1648, Mary Johnson, who admitted to having familiarity with the devil, was sentenced to hang. But the execution did not take place until after the birth of a son, born to her in prison. The child was bound out from infancy to age twenty-one to one Nathaniel Rescew, who promised to provide the baby with education and maintenance in exchange for £15 from Mary's estate and the child's services.

Salem's Abigail Faulkner also pleaded her belly and like Elizabeth Procter did not deliver her child until after the prosecutions had ended. Eventually both women were released from jail, but the new mothers found themselves in the curious position of being civiliter mortius, or "dead in the law." By virtue of being sentenced to die, both were considered non-persons, although they had escaped the rope. Neither could claim property that had been theirs before the death penalty had been imposed. Because neither Elizabeth nor Abigail was considered to exist, appeal for redress from the courts was impossible.

On May 27, 1696, Elizabeth made an attempt to seek official judicial recognition. In a petition to the General Court at Boston, Elizabeth protested her situation, explaining that before her husband had been executed, he had been persuaded to sign an illegal will that left her not a shilling. "It is evident," she noted, "somebody had contrived a will and brought it to him to sign, wherein his whole estate is disposed of, not having regard to a contract or writing made with me before marriage with him. . . . "

The circumstance behind the seemingly thoughtless will agreed to by John Procter may not have been rooted in deceit. Procter, perhaps believing that his wife would be hanged with him as scheduled, may have seen little point in recognizing her dower rights, despite a pre-marriage contract that had evidently reserved some funds for her sole use. Whatever the basis of the document, its application proved a severe handicap for the widow. The beneficiaries of Procter's will refused to give any financial assistance to Elizabeth.

"Those that claim my said husband's estate by that which they call a will, will not suffer me to have one penny of the estate . . . " she wrote to the court, "for they say that I am dead in the law. . . . "

The Massachusetts justices took a similar position. No action was taken on Elizabeth's plea for help.

CHAPTER X

Less Drastic Measures

DESPITE laws decreeing death as the penalty for witchcraft, execution was not always imposed by courts on enchanters. This approach was in great contrast with that of the Old World. In Britain, an estimated one out of every five persons accused of witchcraft was hanged. On the continent, the ratio was undoubtedly much lower. But in America, only one out of every twelve persons formally charged with witchery suffered death. Except during periods of hysteria, colonial courts were not marked by vindictiveness and an automatic assumption of guilt. Whenever feasible, alternative means of punishment were chosen as ways of dealing with supposed enchanters.

The physical characteristics of America and the unique attitudes of the settlers who chose to immigrate helped frame this more humane approach. In dealing with their problems, settlers frequently rejected traditional solutions for more pragmatic answers and ones more compatible to a society based not on institutions but on individuals. For centuries, England's middle and lower classes had been confined in narrowly assigned roles of depravation. Those who had fled the static society were not anxious to reestablish concepts that had made them prisoners of an uncontrollable system. Thus, in the New World, English standards of right and wrong were not always acceptable to the masses. Respect for legal authorities was often replaced by respect for the value of the individual. Forgiveness of error and the right to a second chance were deeply ingrained in America, where a large number of residents had arrived as convicted felons, debtors, and religious dissenters.

An additional factor contributing to judicial leniency was the compactness and intimacy of the colonial society. In day-to-day life, the interests of most settlers in a village were inextricably linked. Although this interdependence sometimes led to disagreement, the situation also contributed to less violent solutions of dispute. To condemn one's needed neighbor in a small pioneer settlement was far harder than to convict a stranger in crowded London.

In an effort to provide less than total punishment and, at the same time, provide sufficient warnings that witchcraft would not be tolerated, colonial courts applied several alternative means of punishment. One method was the posting of good behavior bonds.

Bonds were particularly effective in situations where members of a community demanded that action be taken against a suspect, yet the presiding magistrate did not wish to place the individual's life in danger by instigating a formal trial. Bonds were also popular in cases where evidence was insufficient for indictment or conviction, but where there was a strong suspicion of guilt. Such a case arose in the 1665 trial of Long Island's Ralph and Mary Hall.

Hall and his wife, indicted for practicing "some detestable and wicked arts, commonly called witchcraft and sorcery," were taken from their Seatalcott home for trial before the New York Court of Assizes. Hall was found not guilty, but the jury could not endorse such a clear acquittal of Mary. In describing their predicament, the jurors announced that they had found "some suspicions by the evidence of what the woman is charged with, but nothing considerable of value to take away her life."

As a result of the dilemma, the court decreed that the couple should be held in durance and Hall bound "body and goods" for his wife's appearance at the next sessions "and so on from sessions to sessions as long as they stay within this government." By requiring the bond, the court sought to assure disturbed citizens that Mary would not be tempted to continue her practice of magic. Under the directive, the suspect would be called to appear at each session of the court in order to face any accusations that might be lodged against her. Failure to present herself would mean the loss of her husband's entire fortune and imprisonment of them both.

Hall's bond was continued for three years, until August 21, 1668, when the requirement was withdrawn because of Mary's unblemished record of good behavior.

Banishment was a second non-violent means of dealing with supposed sorcerers, and a solution particularly compatible with the needs of the colonial environment. By exiling the offender, not only was a threat to the safety of a community removed, but the suspect was allowed to live and contribute to building the society.

In 1655, Nicholas Bayley and his wife, acquitted of witchcraft charges in New Haven, were confronted with the prospect of banishment. The Bayleys sported a long history of court appearances for numerous infractions, such as lying and making "filthy" speeches. Although the pair had been exonerated on sorcery accusations, the patience of many in the community was exhausted. The court, also tiring of the repeated disturbances, advised the couple to depart the colony for the benefit of all concerned.

Some colonials, perhaps realizing that acquittal did not always end suspicions of witchcraft, chose voluntary exile. Sawyer Hugh Parsons, found not guilty in Boston, elected to take such a step. After Parsons' wife, cleared of sorcery but executed for murder, had been turned off, the settler chose to remain in Boston rather than return to his Springfield home. When his possessions had been disposed of, Parsons left the port city for Narragansett in Rhode Island. From there he immigrated to Long Island and disappeared from public view.

Exile and good behavior bonds could be combined with other punishments. William Harding, of Northumberland County, Virginia, convicted on November 20, 1656, of "witchcraft sorcery," was sentenced to be "forever" banished from the county and was given a hundred strokes on his shoulders.

Multiple strokes by whipping or "scourging" was a common penalty for lesser felonies, such as theft or adultery. The beatings were usually administered by the local sheriff, who was remonstrated if the spectators or court officials believed that the lashes were being laid on too gently.

Plymouth's Mary Rosse was also ordered whipped, but her 1683 punishment did not stem directly from allegations of witchcraft. Mary was instead found guilty of exercising "inthewsiastickall" power over one Shingleterry. As punishment, Mary was ordered whipped and sent home to her mother. The somewhat puzzling offense probably involved the casting of a minor spell or hypnotic trance, but in this case, the victim was not considered entirely blameless. To assure that the incident did not occur once more, Shingleterry was also ordered flogged.

Not all of those suspected of practicing magic chose to docilely wait until rumors reached such a peak that criminal court action was necessary. Instead, many citizens, particularly in Maryland and Virginia, elected to bring their accusers into open court. The voluntary requesting of a hearing to weigh an unprosecuted accusation was known as "calling for a righting," and was eminently successful as a legal device. In no instance was any citizen who claimed the privilege convicted of witchcraft.

Mary Parsons was one of those who chose to take the offensive. In 1674, Mary discovered that Samuel Bartlett had begun taking secret depositions dealing with the suspicious death of his wife Mary Bartlett of Northampton. For eighteen years, a feud had existed between the two families. The difficulties probably stemmed from a 1656 slander suit in which Joseph Parsons had collected damages from one of Mrs. Bartlett's relatives who had called Mary Parsons a witch.

Goody Parsons, believing that the secret depositions accused her of causing Mrs. Bartlett's death by witchcraft, went before the court and demanded a full airing of the situation. In compliance with the request, Mary was formally indicted, tried, and found not guilty.

In 1661, Joan Michell filed a similar action with the court of Charles County, Maryland. Joan claimed that her good name was being taken away because of vicious rumors accusing her of witchcraft. According to the settlerwoman, the gossip had so inflamed the neighborhood that one local had attempted to stone her one Sunday as she made her way to church. Joan requested that the court investigate the charges and order a search of her body by "able women." If the rumors were found to be groundless, she would proceed with slander suits against the gossips.

Singled out by Joan as the prime rumormonger was Anglican minister Francis Doughty, a rector of questionable piety once described as being possessed by "many vices and especially to drinking." Doughty seemed to have made somewhat of a habit of accusing his parishioners of practicing magic. In 1657, while employed in a Virginia community, he had lodged witchcraft allegations against Barbara Winbrow, but as in the case of Joan Michell, the charges proved to be false. The minister may have been influenced by the same religious zeal that afflicted New England clergymen. After being forced out of his English vicarage for extreme Puritan leanings, Doughty settled for a time in Massachusetts before arriving in Virginia.

For Elizabeth Goodman, the technique of seizing the offensive was quite successful, at least in the first instance. In 1653, Elizabeth, long suspected of witchery, appeared before the Court of Redress at New Haven and demanded a hearing into accusations being made against her. As part of her request, Elizabeth asked that secret testimony previously gathered against her should be publicly read so that she might answer the slanderous charges. Elizabeth's request was granted and although the court found that she appeared very "suspicious," no action was taken against her.

But two years later, new allegations of sorcery were made, and in the fall of 1655, the Court of Magistrates was called to consider the situation. The most damaging evidence against Elizabeth was presented by tavern keeper William Hookes, who claimed that he had been severely damaged by her magical powers.

Hookes' tale began in the summer of 1655, when Elizabeth entered his establishment and ordered a mug of beer. When a previously drawn glass was set before her, she became irate and demanded that a fresh draught be drawn. Dissatisfied with the substandard service, Elizabeth left the tavern in anger, muttering threats.

Soon after the incident, Hookes discovered that his beer, which had been "good and fresh," had undergone a radical change. According to the keep, the brew was "hot, sour and ill-tasted, yea so hot as the barrel was warm without side, and when they opened it, the bung it steamed forth."

Hookes brewed five new batches of spirits and found each as spoiled and foul as the first. On this evidence of deviltry, a formal trial of witchcraft was called. Elizabeth, this time unable to explain the charges, found herself in a more critical situation than in the earlier righting and was required to "give securitie for her good behavior."

Some suspects did not choose to establish their innocence by calling for rightings in criminal court. A large number of alleged witches instead sued their accusers for slander in civil actions. This avenue provided several advantages for the supposed sorcerer. In slander or defamation suits, the suspected witch stood as the complainant, not as the defendant, who was required to explain possibly incriminating actions. If an individual did not win the civil judgment, the aftermath was not fatal. Instead of being punished for witchery, the unsuccessful complainant merely collected no damages. In order to be punished for witchcraft, new charges would have to be brought in criminal court.

Slander was second only to bastardy as the most common offense against women in the southern colonies, and the activity was a frequent charge against females in New England. Dockets at the local level were filled with actions relating to a wide variety of gossips, babblers, makebates, tale-tellers, scolds, and defamers, all charged with harming the reputations of supposedly honest citizens by spreading false tales.

Like English authorities, colonial magistrates imposed heavy fines on convicted gossips, but one punishment never decreed was the Brank or Scold's Bridle, which was used extensively in the mother country. This contraption resembled a heavy iron cage and was placed over the head of the offender. Attached to the front of the mask was a sharp spike that was inserted into the mouth. If the slanderer attempted to speak, the spike would pierce through his tongue, causing permanent damage.

Instead of the application of physical harm, provincial courts chose punishment aimed at bringing derision or humiliation upon slanderers. In Maine, women were gagged, while in New York and Massachusetts, cleft sticks were temporarily attached to the end of the gossip's tongue. Although operating on the same principle as the brank, the cleft stick, somewhat like a large clothespin, was intended to cause psychological, not physical punishment.

The ducking or "coucking" stool was one of the most popular penalties for women defamers and was widely used in the south. These devices ranged from simple armchairs attached to a pivoting board to elaborate "trebuckets" placed on tilting arms and permanently set on the bank of a river or pond. The slanderer, after being tied securely to the stool, was ducked repeatedly into the water in an effort to cool the heat of the gossiping tongue. To maximize the embarrassment, the slanderer was sometimes carted to the ducking place in a tumbrel, followed by a parade of hecklers. An extreme variation of ducking was developed in Virginia, where several women were sentenced to be tied and towed behind the stern of boats.

Public penitence was frequently ordered by magistrates dealing with slanderers. Churches were usually chosen for the site of the ceremony because of the large number of citizens who could be expected to be on hand to witness the criminal's mortification. On the Sunday designated for the penitence, the defamer, usually dressed in a white robe or sheet, was mounted on a stool amid the congregation. From this position, pardon was begged from any who had been wrongfully harmed by the deceitful gossip. The scenarios could be varied according to the nature of defamation. In 1646, a Northampton County slanderer was sentenced to stand at the door of the parish house with a gag in her mouth during the entire service. For more damaging rumors, slanderers were tied neck and heels together and placed near the church door to be scorned by all who passed.

Public apologies could also be made during court sessions, so that the humiliation became part of the community's public record. John Little, found guilty of slandering Maryland's Elizabeth Potts by claiming she had performed sexual intercourse with an Indian youth, was ordered to pay 500 pounds of tobacco as a fine and was instructed to stand in the door of the court for one hour with a sign in his hat saying he had "scandalized" the woman.

A convicted slanderer could also be sentenced to spend several hours confined in the community's stocks. During the incarceration, passersby were encouraged to pelt the prisoner with garbage or debris. The pillory, used in England as a punishment for minor acts of witchcraft, was also adopted in the colonies. However, not until the end of the seventeenth century was the pillory a legal sanction for sorcerers.

Like the stocks, the pillory consisted of two hinged boards placed on an elevated scaffold. For several hours at a time, a prisoner's head and hands were locked immobile through holes cut into the planks. While the stocks allowed the victim to perch on a thin rail, the prisoner of the pillory was forced to assume a half-crouched position.

Also called the "stretch-neck," the pillory was used for a wide range of offenses. Persons placed into the device often carried about their neck a sign that spelled out the infraction committed. To accommodate illiterate citizens, individualized touches could be added. One man, for example, convicted in New York for stealing vegetables, was pilloried with several cabbages balanced on his head.

Only the most vicious and repeated slanderers were branded with a hot iron. One colony resorting to such tactics was Maryland, where those convicted of seditious libel could be legally marked with the letters SL. These permanent designations, applied on the thumb or forehead, were used as a substitute punishment for long periods of incarceration; the practice may have been derived from the branding used in the benefit of clergy.

Although a wide range of punishments was available to justices dealing with slanderers, extreme penalties were not applied in actions involving false allegations of witchcraft. In Virginia, where the largest number of such defamation cases was presented, courts rejected harsh tactics such as branding and the pillory and chose to rely on more moderate sentences.

The courts' leniency indicates that in southern society accusations of witchcraft were not considered particularly serious defamations. The slanders may have been so common that they were regarded only as minor slurs that resulted in no permanent economic loss or social harm. The absence of severe penalities, however, did not deter many who were called witches from bringing suits against their accusers.

Even minor punishments served as deterrents, for in most cases, when the offending gossips were summoned into court, each refused to repeat the defamations and instead begged pardon for spreading the reports. A typical case, and perhaps the first colonial suit involving civil slander related to sorcery, was heard in the General Court of Virginia on April 13, 1641. The official record shows:

> Whereas it appeareth to the court by several depositions that Jane Rookens hath abused and scandalized the wife of George Barker by calling her a witch, which the said Rookens doth not remember, but denyeth in open court, and is sorry for the same offense with which the said [Barker] . . . was very well satisfied; the court hath therefore ordered that William Rookens, husband of the said Jane, forthwith

pay unto the said Barker, expenses and charges of court on this behalf sustained, otherwise execution.

The simple judgment against Jane Rookens was in extreme contrast to a slander settlement decreed by the same court less than six months earlier. In this trial, Francis Willis was charged with claiming that the governor, council, and House of Burgess had acted imbecilely and passed unjust laws. For these words, Willis was convicted of heinous slander and was sentenced to stand in the courtroom door with a sign about his neck indicating the crime. In addition, he was permanently barred from serving in the colony as a clerk or an attorney, fined £20 sterling, ordered to pay court costs of £8 sterling, and imprisoned at the governor's pleasure.

While magistrates never resorted to extreme sanctions against those who had harmed their neighbors with witchcraft allegations, punishments did become slightly more severe. On May 23, 1655, the commissioners of populous Lower Norfolk County issued a directive specifically increasing the liabilities of defamers who claimed to see witches among the citizenry. Acting in private session, the commissioners ruled:

Whereas divers dangerous & scandalous speeches have been raised by some persons concerning several women in this countie, terming them to be witches, whereby their reputations have been much impaired and their lives brought in question (for any doing the like offence), it is by this court ordered that what person so ever shall hereafter raise any such like scandal concerning any partie whatsoever, and shall not be able to prove the same, both upon oath, and by sufficient witness, such person so offending shall in the first place pay a thousand pounds of tobacco: and likewise be liable to further censure of the court.

The directive's language indicates that a minor witch hysteria may have been brewing. By announcing that the victims' lives were "brought in question," the commissioners emphasized that witchcraft was a capital felony and not to be taken lightly. The body underscored the seriousness of the situation by meeting in closed session, a rare move reserved usually for the most critical problems.

Unlike officials in New England, who allowed accusations to go unchecked until criminal cases were inevitable, the Lower Norfolk commissioners acted decisively to quell the potentially dangerous situation. Their order, in unmistakable terms, placed the burden of proof on the accusers rather than on the accused. The fine specified for the first offense was high, and in leaving open the penalty for repeated acts, the officials produced a psychological deterrent of even stronger weight.

The commissioners' action illustrates the philosophical differences toward witchcraft that separated the Virginia planter from the stern Puritan. Instead of publicizing a threat to society from witches, a common approach of New England officials, the southern courts warned instead of the more practical danger of witchmongers.

Quaker Ann Godby was probably one of the loose-tongued gossips whose tales prompted the commissioners' action. Concurrent with the proclamation, Ann was fined and put under a restraining order for claiming that several women were practicing magic. In 1659, she was recalled to the bar, this time on a charge of breaking the earlier injunction by slandering the wife of Nicholas Robinson. The court found Ann guilty of acting "contemptuously" and ordered that her husband, Thomas Godby, pay 300 pounds of tobacco in fines, court costs, and witness fees of twenty pounds of tobacco per day.

By ordering that Ann's husband stand liable for the fine, the Virginia court was merely enforcing the colonial and English belief that a wife had no legal entity except as a ward of her husband.

Because married women could hold no property, female offenders were theoretically unable under the law to pay a fine of even a single shilling. Related males were thus liable for any court settlements that resulted. Husbands who could or would not satisfy the fines levied upon their women might be whipped; or the females themselves might be subject to stronger punishments.

The situation in court settlements was further complicated by the limited colonial acceptance of the British philosophy that a husband was responsible not only for his wife's civil infractions, but for her criminal activities as well. Under common law, a man was considered punishable for any felony committed in his presence by his wife. It was assumed that the woman was under the total control of her husband and had been either coerced or permitted to perform the illegal act. This tradition may have been framed in an attempt to solve the obvious injustice that might occur if a couple were apprehended for jointly committing a felony. The husband, by claiming benefit of clergy, could be released unharmed, but the wife, unable to make a similar defense, would be liable for the death sentence.

In December of 1662, the Virginia House of Burgess enacted a measure designed to bring relief to husbands burdened with the numerous fines of their unrehabilitated wives. The law, although not calculated to increase domestic felicity, may have been instrumental in stemming the number of slander cases that confronted the court. The statute read:

> Whereas oftentimes many babbling women often slander and scandalize their neighbors, for which their poor hubands are often brought into chargeable and vexatious suites and cast in great damages: Be it therefore enacted by the authority aforesaid, that in actions of slander occasioned by the wife as aforesaid, after judgment passed for the damages, the women shall be punished by ducking; and if the slander be so enormous as to be adjudged at a greater damage than five hundred pounds of tobacco, then the woman to suffer a ducking for each five hundred pounds of tobacco adjudged against the husband if he refuses to pay the tobacco.

Slander suits by accused witches in Maryland were not as numerous as in neighboring Virginia, but the procedure was recognized as a useful, non-violent means of settling disputes. In October of 1654, Richard Manship complained against Peter Godson and his wife, claiming that they had called his wife a witch. As proof of the charge, Godson testified that she had asked him to jump over several straws, and that as a result of the charm he had gone lame the following day. Godson and his wife apologized for their error and paid court costs of warrants and subpoenas.

The same month that Godson was brought forward, the Maryland Assembly set a fine of 1000 pounds of tobacco on all who raised or published false news or reports that disturbed the public peace. The bill, probably prompted by the Manship case, decreed that those found guilty of "slandering, talebearing, or backbiting" should be censored to the satisfaction of the injured party and the commonwealth.

In at least one Maryland case, the slander suit was used as a method of redress by both the accused and the accusers. On January 15, 1702, Charles Killburn petitioned the Anne Arundel court to investigate the possibility that Katherine Prout was practicing witchcraft. Killburn claimed that while he was recovering from a debilitating illness, Katherine had announced that she wished he might "languish to death and never recover his health." Almost immediately, Killburn suffered an unexpected relapse.

The court found Killburn's evidence insufficient to proceed further on the witchcraft charges, but did not completely exonerate Katherine of blame. A fine of a hundred pounds of tobacco was levied because of her "misbehavior in her saucy language and abusing" of the court.

Katherine, an outspoken colonial, evidently continued in her "saucy" language, and two months later Killburn pressed a suit of slander. According to the settler, Katherine had publicly called him a "foresworn rogue," a common term for a perjurer. This time the justices were more severe with Katherine and ordered her to pay 1,101 pounds of tobacco in costs.

Still the matter was not settled. Katherine retaliated by suing Kate Quillin for reportedly calling her "Dame Ye." The complainant maintained that this reversal of the common term of address, "Ye Dame," was meant to infer that she was a witch and was accustomed to things being repeated backwards as in the black mass. Goody Quillin retorted by accusing Katherine of stealing molasses and New England capons, a slang term for mackerel. The court supported Katherine, and ordered Kate to pay £3 sterling in damages for the implication of witchcraft.

CHAPTER XI

Salem

THE winter of 1691–1692 began like any other in Danvers, now called Salem. With the harvesting completed and shipping curtailed by the advent of cold weather, the town's citizens retired to their homes to spend the drab winter months preparing for the coming of a new planting season.

But underneath the calm surface, Salem, like other settlements in the colony, was experiencing critical difficulties.

The loss of the area's liberal charter had set a pall of uncertainty over residents. Indian attacks were on the increase. A smallpox epidemic had swept through the community. A boundary dispute was dividing locals into opposing groups, and the town's new minister, Reverend Samuel Parris, was proving to be a foul-tempered, disagreeable man and was disliked by many in his flock.

Seething beneath the external events, however, was a bigger threat. Before the year was out, Salem and adjacent communities would be rent by a division in the greatest witch-hunt to occur in the colonies. Twenty citizens would be executed. Fifty others would confess to practicing sorcery and 150 settlers would be jailed awaiting trial. Accusations would be outstanding against 200 others. But this largest and most violent outbreak of colonial witch hysteria would be the last.

The roots of the witchcraft prosecutions began innocently

enough. In order to pass their idle hours, a group of young women and adolescent girls decided to meet periodically at the house of Reverend Parris. Although social gatherings were frowned upon in Puritan Salem, the "circle," as the group became known, appeared harmless. Conducted in the shadow of the meeting house, the group included Parris' nine-year-old daughter Betty and his eleven-year-old niece Abigail Williams.

Joining the minister's kin was a mixed assortment of young females who represented all levels of the village's social and economic ladders. Sarah Churchill, Mary Warren, and Mercy Lewis, each about twenty years of age, were servants in local households. Teenagers Mary Walcott, Elizabeth Booth, Susannah Sheldon, and Elizabeth Hubbard came from relatively secure families. Twelve-year-old Ann Putnam was perhaps the most distinctive member. Long a sickly child, Ann boasted a quick mind, but one obsessed with the gloomy aspects of Puritan theology. Her mother, Ann, was a neurotic woman who also became interested in the circle's activities.

Reverend Parris was initially unconnected with the group, but later the clergyman would become intrinsically involved as a catalyst, transforming adolescent fantasies into seemingly legitimate accusations.

Samuel Parris did not enjoy the respect and power granted to most Puritan ministers in New England villages. Unlike his fellow clergymen, who were viewed as pillars of wisdom and reservoirs of sound advice, Parris was publicly opposed by a large segment of the Salem meeting. Lack of theological training may have contributed to the situation, for Parris, a Harvard College dropout, had spent most of his adult life as an unsuccessful merchant in the West Indies trade. The Salem post was his first office, and one that held little appeal for more qualified men of God.

Residents of the village meeting were well known for their chronic infighting. Two earlier ministers had left the town in disgust. Parris' demands for an increased salary and a land grant served to set off new arguments among the congregation. The minister's requests were reluctantly granted only after long squabbling and over the objections of Rebecca Nurse, a powerful force in the settlement. Against this background of dissension and discord, the young girls instigated their social circle.

The meetings probably began innocently enough, but soon a more ominous note appeared. Attention shifted to the study of mysticism and the occult. The change may have been suggested by Parris' West Indian slave, a woman named Tibula. Under her able instruction, the girls quickly became immersed in the study of spiritualism, witchcraft, and magic, topics not unknown in Salem. Books on the supernatural had been circulating for some time, and Dorcas Hoar of nearby Beverly had been famous for divining fortunes for at least twenty years. Although investigation of the supernatural was seemingly inconsistent in a community where religion was so firmly based upon the pursuit of godliness, Puritanism was undoubtedly an important impetus to the activity. A fear and dread of the unknown world was instilled in every true believer, and for those touched by adolescent curiosity, the desire to learn the secrets of such an important dominion was perhaps irresistible.

Study of the supernatural proved insufficient for the appetites of the Salem girls. At some point during the winter of 1691–1692, the circle moved into the active practice of rites and incantations. Their spells were simple in form and derived from Caribbean voodoo rituals, which were familiar to Tibula. For example, one experiment at divining was conducted with the use of eggs and glass to simulate a crystal ball. The charm was not sinister in purpose, but was aimed at predicting the occupation of one member's future husband.

Ann Putnam emerged as the leader of the clan, and all signs of the unholy investigations were carefully hidden from outsiders. Even the youngest members no doubt realized that strong disapproval and punishment would result if word of the practices leaked to adults in the community.

Despite the precautions, an event occurred in February that resulted in total exposure. Without warning, Betty Parris and Abigail Williams were taken seriously ill with violent seizures similar to the symptoms of demonic possession. The afflictions instantly became a major source of conversation among villagers, who lavished sympathy and attention on the patients. As news of their condition spread, several other circle members became afflicted. Excitement rose even higher.

In an attempt to discover the origin of the mysterious ailment, local physician William Griggs was summoned to conduct a medical examination. When word of the doctor's findings reached the public, the mood changed radically from curiosity to fear. The physician, uncle of Elizabeth Hubbard, was unable to discover a natural explanation for the illnesses. As a result, he pronounced that the condition of the two girls was being caused by the "evil eye," cast by means of witchcraft.

For centuries throughout the world, the evil eye had been among the most dreaded of all magical spells. Through its use, it was believed that witches could do harm to others merely by a glance. The crippled, aged, incurably ill, and spinsters were credited with possessing an affinity for the evil eye, for persons in these categories were considered weak and thus susceptible to satanic motivation.

Because their innate beauty contrasted so greatly with the ugliness of a witch, women and children were considered special targets of the charm. In the Near East, careful pains were taken to disguise the attractiveness of such persons, so the jealousy of passing enchanters would not be aroused. Women donned heavy veils and painted black marks on their faces. Children of the wealthiest families were dressed in rags and smeared with dirt.

The residents of Salem did not adopt the extreme precautions frequently taken in other societies, but belief in the power of the evil eye was apparent in the bay colony. Word of Dr. Griggs' diagnosis spread quickly through the news-starved village, and although settlers gave constant attention to the victims, no improvement was noted. Within several days, the remaining members of the circle had also become bewitched.

During less trying times, or in a less superstitious environment, their illnesses might have disappeared had residents ignored the complaints or examined the symptoms with cynical thoroughness. But in Salem the climate was not one of clinical evaluation. Reverend Parris, spurred into action by his dependents' ailments, sought to rouse the village against the dangerous witches who he believed were operating in the area.

Suspicion centered upon Tibula and her husband John Indian, a half-black, half-Carib native of Barbados. After brief inquiries, Tibula was arrested and questioned as to guilt. Instead of denying all knowledge of the afflictions, the slave woman readily confessed that she indeed had bewitched the girls. In what may have been an effort to gain temporary reprieve, she added that four other enchanters had assisted in the crime. The conspirators, according to Tibula, dressed in black hoods and met frequently with the devil. Satan had not been content to appear in a single form, but had assumed a multiplicity of shapes, such as that of a swine, a black dog, a black rat, and a red rat.

The confessed witch claimed to be ignorant of the identities of two of the confederates, but she did name Salem's Sarah Good and Sarah Osburn as the remaining miscreants. To villagers, the accusations seemed plausible. Both of the women were held in low esteem and fitted neatly into the preconceived concept of what a witch should be. Pipe-smoking Sarah Good was a destitute settler who disturbed the neighborhood by tramping from door to door begging for food. Sarah Osburn was a partial invalid who was well known for erratic behavior and a "depressed" mind.

Confirmation of Tibula's accusations appeared almost immediately. With loud shrieks and cries, the afflicted girls announced that they indeed were being tormented by the named women. Osburn's husband supported the possibility that his wife was a caster of spells. Not only did he announce that she had a supernatural teat, but he stated that her devilish nature had been clearly revealed through her "bad carriage to him." On February 29, warrants were issued for the arrest of the two women, and public examinations held the day after their apprehension seemed to confirm their guilt. After repeating her accusations against Good and Osburn, Tibula revealed that several other names had been listed in the devil's book, which she had been shown. Unfortunately, she could not remember a single one.

While local magistrates Jonathan Corwin and John Hathorne committed the supposed witches to Boston jail, the condition of the afflicted girls showed no change. According to Reverend Parris, Ann Putnam's mother, and several other conservatives in the village, the reason for the continued affliction was that the witches unidentified by Tibula were still at large. Notice spread that the situation was much more dangerous than had at first been realized. Apparently, a consortium of witches was conspiring to destroy Salem. The unidentified charmers should be rooted out and destroyed if the threat was to be averted. The task would be difficult, for the devil's agents might be lurking in any house, disguised as respected members of the community.

Some voices did attempt to halt the spreading mania, but those who did protest the rabble-rousing of Reverend Parris and his young comrades found themselves under suspicion. West Peabody's Martha Corey openly questioned the motives of the girls and doubted the legitimacy of their accusations. On March 11, Ann Putnam claimed to have seen a vision of Martha and alleged that the woman was one of her tormentors. A warrant was promptly issued and Martha became the fourth suspected witch to be jailed.

Rebecca Nurse, the seventy-one-year-old matron who had strongly opposed Parris' appointment, voiced her opposition to the proceedings by boycotting the meeting. In late March, this most respected woman in the community was arrested and charged not only with afflicting the girls, but with the murder of several children who had died previously. Rebecca's sister Sarah Cloyse attempted to quell the disturbances by walking out of the church services in protest. Her gesture was unsuccessful and she was promptly charged as a witch. The arrest of Mary Esty, sister of Rebecca and Sarah, soon followed. Eventually, anyone absent from Sunday services was suspicioned, for word was spread that the non-attendees were not at home, but were meeting with the devil.

The afflicted girls continued to respond enthusiastically to the call for a thorough witch-hunt, and began to see sorcerers at every turn. Elderly and poor inhabitants were increasingly eyed as suspicious characters, and the issuance of arrest warrants took on an assembly-line appearance. Giles Corey joined his wife Martha in jail. Tavern-owner Bridget Bishop was charged along with her son and daughter-in-law. Deliverance and William Hobbs were imprisoned together with their daughter Abigail, who cheerfully admitted her guilt. The local jails were soon filled to overflowing and facilities in nearby settlements began receiving the newly accused.

As the allegations became more volatile, two of the original offenders were forgotten. Sarah Osburn died in jail before she could be brought to trial. Tibula, after proclaiming that Rebecca Nurse and Martha Corey were two of her unknown confederates, was quietly sold to a Virginia settler in payment for jail fees. Sarah Good, who probably had borne a child in prison, silently awaited her hearing.

While the circle members continued to be the main accusers, others like sixteen-year-old John Doritch joined the group of supposedly "behagged" persons. Eventually fifty other settlers would claim to be afflicted by various sorcery spells. The sudden rush to be numbered among the bewitched may have been a calculated move by residents who concluded that the most effective way in which to avoid being cried out upon was to join those crying out.

Some accusers were undoubtedly influenced by the oppressive atmosphere of hysteria. Tales of horror related by afflicted persons became increasingly more ghastly and mystical. Abigail Williams announced that she had been "grievously pinched" and her bowels "almost pulled out." Deliverance Hobbs claimed that she had been whipped with iron rods by Bridget Bishop. Another victim maintained that "several gallons of corruption" poured forth when his bewitched and infected foot was lanced.

Allegations also flowed forth from jailed suspects who sought temporary reprieve by accusing others. Elaborate explanations were not considered necessary to support either a confession or an accusation. The examination of Richard Carrier indicates that a simple affirmative answer to an incriminating question was sufficient to condemn a defender and others who might be implicated. Carrier's July 22nd interrogation was brief, but damaging. Under intense questioning, the accused witch not only admitted his own guilt, but lodged accusations against his brother and nine other settlers:

Q. Have you been in ye devil's snare?
A. Yes.

Q. Is your brother Andrew ensnared by ye devil's snare?
A. Yes.

Q. How long has your brother been a witch?
A. Near a month.

Q. How long have you been a witch?
A. Not long.

Q. Have you joined in afflicting ye afflicted persons?
A. Yes.

Q. You helped to hurt Timo [thy] Swan, did you?
A. Yes.

Q. How long have you been a witch?
A. About five weeks.

Q. Who was in company when you counanted with ye devil?
A. Mrs. Bradbury.

Q. Did she help you afflict?

A. Yes.

Q. What was ye occasion Mrs. Bradbury would have to afflict Timo. Swan?

A. Because her husband and Timo. Swan fell out about a scyth, I think.

Q. Did they not fall out about thatching of a barn, too?

A. No, not as I know of.

Q. Who was at the village meeting when you was there?

A. Goodwife How. Goodwife Nurse. G. Wildes, Procter and his wife, Mrs. Bradbury and Corey's wife.

Q. Was any of Boston there?

A. No.

Q. How many was there in all?

A. A dozen I think.

Q. Was Jno. Willard there?

A. I think he was.

Q. What kind of man is Jno. Willard? A young man or an old man?

A. He is not an old man. He had black hair.

Q. What meeting was this meeting? Was this that, that was near Ingersals?

A. Yes. I think.

Q. What did they do then?

A. The[y] eat and drank wine.

Q. Was there a minister there?

A. No. Not as I know of.

Q. From whence had you your wine?

A. From Salem I think was.

Q. Goodwife Olliver there?

A. Yes, I knew her.

Entire families were imprisoned on the weakest of charges. Martha and Thomas Carrier were incarcerated along with their children Andrew, Richard, and Sarah. John Procter, his wife Elizabeth, and their three offspring were also apprehended for practicing witchcraft.

Procter had drawn suspicion upon himself because of his firm defense of his accused wife and his lack of respect for the circle members' accusations. His arrest proved a great shock to accuser

Mary Warren, a servant in his household who was known to be extremely dedicated to her master. According to report, Mary withdrew from the band of accusers following Procter's apprehension. But when she began questioning the validity of the witch-hunt, she was cried out upon by her former colleagues. For some time, Mary held out against those who pressured her to recant her doubts. Eventually, however, she succumbed, and rejoined the pack by charging that Procter was indeed part of Salem's witch corps. A similar period of doubt was said to have been experienced by Sarah Churchill following the arrest of her employer, George Jacobs. Unwisely, the elderly Jacobs had supposedly referred to the accusers as "witch bitches." Apprehended in addition to Jacobs were his granddaughter and daughter-in-law. Jacobs' son was able to flee before a warrant in his name could be served.

As spring came to Salem, all criticism of the witch-hunt halted. Disapproving voices were probably stilled out of fear, for the power of the afflicted girls had become overwhelming. The victims had grown so bold that charges were no longer limited to the poor and helpless, but centered upon the most affluent members of the community.

Only one of those accused and brought in for questioning was spared by the chargers. When Nehemiah Abbott, a settler supposedly nearly a hundred years old, was brought forth, the circle unanimously agreed that he was blameless. The case of Boston's Samuel Willard was somewhat more complex. Willard, minister of the city's prestigious Old South Church, had spoken out strongly against the rising hysteria. Reportedly, he too was denounced by the young girls, but presiding magistrates, unable to accept the pronouncement, concluded that the clergyman had been confused with one John Willard, who was already in custody.

Panic spread from Salem to nearby villages such as Beverly, Lynn, Reading, West Peabody, Amesbury, Billerica, Marblehead, Boston, and Charlestown. A major outbreak occurred in Andover following the contracting of a strange illness by the wife of Joseph Ballard. Ballard, suspecting the condition had been magically inspired, requested that witch-hunters from Salem be sent to seek out the village's dangerous sorcerers. Ann Putnam and Mary Walcott answered the call. During one afternoon, most of Andover's residents were paraded past the girls, who pointed out from among the strangers two score who were supposedly guilty of practicing magic. A similar confrontation at Glouster was less productive. Only four locals were imprisoned as a result of the confrontation.

As jails in the areas surrounding Salem were filled to capacity, new detainees were sent to Boston, where the prosecutions were being watched with some satisfaction by Cotton Mather and several of his fellow ministers. The crowded prison conditions were being created not only by the radical increase in the number of allegations, but also by administrative difficulties in processing the supposed felons.

The charter revocation had in effect abolished the colony's sitting courts, leaving no means by which the accused could be tried. In order to resolve the situation, the Governor's Council on May 27th appointed a special Court of Oyer and Terminer to handle the hundreds of witchcraft cases pending in Essex, Suffolk, and Middlesex counties.

Seven jurists were named to the bench. From Boston came four members, including Samuel Sewall, who would become the most famous of the court appointees. Nathaniel Saltonstall was selected from Haverhill, and from Salem came Bartholomew Gedney. Deputy Governor William Stoughton of Dorchester was appointed as presiding judge. Salem magistrates Corwin and Hathorne were not selected to sit in judgment, but were designated to assist in conducting examinations of the suspects.

Each of the justices boasted previous experience on the Court of Assistants, but none had been formally trained in the law. In an attempt to prepare themselves for the trials, the officials assembled a library of books relating to witchcraft and the supernatural. As a further aid, a request was sent out from the court asking members of the area's clergy to draw up a document explaining the clerical position on the issue of sorcery and suggesting procedures that should be followed in the actual trials. Such requests by civil authorities had been commonly used in Massachusetts. The practice, however, would end with the 1692 opinion.

Cotton Mather, charged with preparing the requested document, soon produced a paper entitled "The Return of Several Ministers," a body of thought that supposedly represented the views of many prominent clergymen. The philosophies contained in the "Return" were not favorable to those who were awaiting trial.

The minister strongly emphasized that all afflicted persons de-
served support and assistance from the courts. The guilty should be
decisively and harshly punished for their crimes. In what appeared to
be a counciliatory attitude toward the accused, the document suggested that extreme care be taken in the conduct of the trials; however,
the proposal was not intended to be a protection of the rights of the
individual. Instead, the step was considered necessary in case the devil
attempted to disrupt the hearings and distort the workings of justice.
To eliminate this possibility, unnecessary noises and distractions were
to be kept to a minimum.

In the most important section of the "Return," the clergyman
dealt with the controversial issue of spectral evidence. The debate over
the acceptance of this type of proof was central in framing the rules
under which the witch trials would be held. It would prove a decisive
factor in the ultimate outcome of the hearings.

Spectral evidence was a term used to describe the supernatural
phenomena thought to occur when a vision or "specter" of an accused
witch appeared to a witness. In most cases, the apparition either
confessed to being a sorcerer or performed acts of magic witnessed by
the person to whom the specter appeared.

One faction of citizens believed that the sighting of a specter
should be accepted as conclusive proof that the person so represented
was indeed a witch. This view was based on the theory that only those
who had signed a compact with the devil possessed the power to
appear in spectral form. The ability to take on such a shape was
interpreted as a type of transmogrification used by enchanters to
perform their evil deeds. Thus, while a witch might be safely locked
in prison, its specter could be sent to torment an afflicted person
located many miles away. Any alibi was thus invalid. Any confession
made by the specter would be as acceptable in court as one made by
the witch under usual circumstances.

A second group held that all spectral evidence should be ruled
inadmissible. These critics charged that the devil possessed the power
to assume the shape of innocent persons, and that most specters were
actually demons. By this transmogrification, crimes could be committed for which the godly would be blamed.

The "Return" agreed that the devil could take on the form of an
innocent suspect, but maintained that this happened only in extraordi-

nary circumstances. In most cases, the clergyman announced, specters appearing to afflicted persons were indeed human witches and their presence should be admissible as proof of guilt. So, while Mather and his colleagues stopped short of total commitment to spectral evidence, the effect of their position was to reinforce the power of the group calling for acceptance of the visions as proof in court.

Supported by the "Return," judges of the Court of Oyer and Terminer ruled that all types of spectral evidence might be admitted and should be considered valid. The move opened the record to reams of accusations that oftentimes bordered on fantasy, but were given full legal sanction. Testimony presented by Susannah Sheldon was typical of the claims classified as spectral in nature. Susannah described one experience involving numerous apparitions that mysteriously appeared to her one night, and, in the process, she helped to condemn Mary English, Giles and Martha Corey, and Bridget Olliver Bishop:

> On the fourth day at night, came Goody Olliver and Mrs. English and Goodman Corey and a black man with a hi-crowned hat, with books in their hands. Goody Olliver bade me touch her book. I would not. I did not know her name. She told me her name was Goody Olliver and bid me touch her book. Now I bid her tell me how long she had been a witch. She told me she had been a witch about twentie years. Then there came a stretched snake creeping over her shoulder and crept into her bosom. Mrs. English had a yellow bird in her bosom and Goodman Corey had two turcles hang to his coat and he opened his bosom and put his turcles to his breast and gave them suck. Then Goodman Corey and Goody Olliver knelt down before the black man and went to prayer, and then the black man told me Goody Olliver had been a witch twentie years and a half. Then they all set to biting me and so went away. . . . Goodman Corey gave me a blow on the ear and almost choked me. . . . Goodwife Corey presented me a book. I refused it and asked her where she lived. She told me she lived in Offton prison. Then she pulled out her breast and the black man gave her a thing like a black pig. It had no hairs on it and she put it to her breast and gave it suck and when it had sucked one breast she put it to the other and gave it suck there. Then she gave it to the black man. Then they went to pray to the black man. Then Goody Olliver told me she had killed four women, two of them were Foster's wives and John Traske's wife and did not name the other. . . .

Spectral evidence also included tales concerning the visits of ghosts to accusers. In most cases, witnesses claimed that the apparitions had returned from the dead to charge that they had been murdered by suspected witches. Elizabeth Booth said that the spirit of Hugh Joanes had appeared to announce that he had been murdered by Elizabeth Procter. According to Joanes' ghost, Elizabeth had taken the drastic step because "he had a poght of cider of hers which he had not paid her for." Ann Putnam related a similar tale. Ann's visitors were two women in shrouds or "winding sheets," who claimed to be the deceased wives of George Burroughs. Ann's mother also played hostess to specters from the underworld. Her spirits were six children who said they had been murdered by Rebecca Nurse. Mercy Lewis announced that she had been visited by a more kindly specter, who took her to a "glorious place," where all was bright and clean. Attending them was a "great multitude in white glittering robes who sang songs and psalms."

Although the judges did follow the advice of the Boston clergy concerning the matter of spectral evidence, the ministers' admonition that a decorous courtroom should be maintained was not accepted. From the beginning, the Salem trials were conducted in a near circus atmosphere. The afflicted girls, who received choice seats from which to harass their presumed tormentors, constantly disrupted the hearings with a cacophony of shrieks and cries. Defendants were unmitigatingly bullied, and witnesses who attempted to give evidence tending to prove innocence were openly attacked.

Among the most damaging activities of the accusers was the practice of the so-called doctrine of fascination. Under this concept, which was similar to the evil eye, a witch could presumably inflict torment upon enemies in an unobtrusive manner. Any action taken by sorcerers would be similarly applied to the victims of their wrath. For example, when defendant Martha Corey bit her lip in anger on the stand, the afflicted girls howled that they were being bitten.

An equally important factor in creating a burden of guilt was the prejudicial attitude of the examiners and justices. Questions put to Bridget Bishop by Salem magistrates John Hathorne and Jonathan Corwin clearly indicated that the woman's guilt was beyond dispute. Even the personal comments interjected into the official record by court clerk Ezekiel Cheever were aimed at incriminating the defendant:

(Bridget Bishop, being now coming in to be examined relating to her accusation of suspicion of sundry acts of witchcrafts, the afflicted persons are now dreadfully afflicted by her as they do say.)

Q. Bishop, what do you say? You here stand charged with sundry acts of witchcraft, by you done or committed upon the bodys of Mercy Lewis and Ann Putnam and others.

A. I am innocent. I know nothing of it. I have done no witchcraft.

Mr. Hathorne: Look upon this woman and see if this be the woman that have been hurting you. (Mercy Lewis and Ann Putnam and others do now charge her to her face with hurting of them.)

Q. What do you say now you see them charge you to your face?

A. I never did hurt them in my life. I did never see these persons before. I am as innocent as the child unborn.

Q. Is not your coat cut?
(Bishop answers no, but her garment being looked upon, they find it cut or torn two ways. Jonathan Walcoate saith that the sword that he struck at Goody Bishop with was not naked but was within the scabbard so that the rent may very probablie be the very same that Mary Walcoate did tell that she had in her coat by Jonathan's striking at her appearance.

The afflicted persons charge her with having hurt them many ways and by tempting them to sign the devil's book at which charge she seemed to be very angry and shaking her head at them saying it was false. They are all greatly tormented, as I conceive, by the shaking of her head.)

Q. Goody Bishop, what contact have you made with the devil?

A. I have made no contact with the devil. I never saw him in my life. Ann Putnam sayeth that she calls the devil her god.

Q. What say you to all this that you are charged with? Can you not find it in your heart to tell the truth?

A. I do tell the truth. I never hurt these persons in my life. I never saw them before.

Mercy Lewis: Oh Goody Bishop! Did you not come to our house the last night and did you not tell me that your master made you tell more than you were willing to tell?

Q. Tell us the truth in this matter. How comes these persons to be thus tormented and to charge you with doing?

A. I am not come here to say I am a witch, to take away my life.

Q. Who is it that doth it, if you do not? They say it is your likeness that comes and torments them and tempts them to write in the book. What book is that you tempt them with?

A. I know nothing of it. I am innocent.

Q. Do you not see how they are tormented? You are acting witchcraft before us. What do you say to this? Why have you not a heart to confess the truth?

A. I am innocent. I know nothing of it. I am no witch. I know not what a witch is.

Q. Have you not given consent that some evil spirit should do this in your likeness?

A. No, I am innocent of being a witch. I know no man, woman, or child here.

Marshall Herrick: How came you into my bed chamber one morning then, and asked me whether I had any curtains to sell? (She is by some of the afflicted persons charged with murder.)

Q. What do you say to these murders you are charged with?

A. I am innocent. I know nothing of it.

(Now she lifts up her eyes and they are greatly tormented.)

Q. What do you say to these things here, horrible acts of witchcraft?

A. I know nothing of it. I do not know whether there be any witches or no.

Q. Have you not heard that some have confessed?

A. No, I did not. (Two men told her to her face that they had told her. Here she is taken in a plain lie. Now she is going away; they are dreadfully afflicted. Five afflicted persons do charge this woman to be the very woman that hurts them.)

(This is a true account of what I have taken down at her examina-

tion according to the best understanding and observation. I have
also in her examination taken notice that all her actions have great
influence upon the afflicted persons and that [they] have been tormented by her.)

Ezekiel Cheever

Because of the antics of the accusers, and the attitudes of the
jurists, John Procter became convinced that he would not receive
impartial justice before the court. In an attempt to remedy the situation, Procter requested that the Boston clergy intervene and halt the
riotous proceedings. Procter announced that the Salem citizenry was
"enraged and incensed" toward the defendants, who were in effect
condemned before entering the courtroom. Procter's request for aid
in halting the proceedings went unanswered by the ministers.

Much of the evidence against Procter, as with most of the other
defendants, was circumstantial in nature and would have been dismissed as insufficient if spectral proof had been ruled inadmissible.
Perhaps the most damaging proof against the colonial was the testimony of Joseph Bayley, who claimed that once, as he was riding near
Procter's house, he was stuck on the breast with a great pain and made
mute. He recovered after passing Procter's dwelling, but on the return
trip the extraordinary blow came once again as he neared the residence. The coincidental attack was impressive to the jury. Procter was
quickly found guilty and sentenced to hang.

Circumstantial evidence also helped to condemn John Willard.
Willard was a former deputy constable who supported the witch trials
in the beginning. However, the excesses in the courtroom made him
increasingly less enthusiastic. As Willard began to voice his doubts,
a cousin fell ill without apparent cause. Two circle members examining the sick relative announced that the ailment was created by spells
that Willard had cast. Evidence mounted as Mrs. Ann Putnam volunteered that the ghosts of twelve deceased settlers had revealed to her
that they were murdered by the constable. Willard fled Salem, but was
arrested while seeking refuge in Lancaster. Like John Procter, Willard
was confronted with both spectral and circumstantial evidence. Witness Samuel Wilkins testified that once, as he was riding to Marblehead, he was attacked by a strange, unseen force:

Just as I came to Forest River Bridge, I was immediately seized with
a violent weight on my back and I saw a black hat and was immedi-

ately pulled off my horse or mare and almost pulled into the river, but holding fast, and last I got up again. . . .

One hour later, Wilkins saw Willard approaching on the road. Because Willard was clothed in a dark coat and hat similar to those present in the attack, Willard was assumed to have been the instigator of the attempted drowning. He, too, was condemned to be executed.

In cases where no direct proof, however circumstantial, could be given to link the accused to acts of witchcraft, inferences of guilt could be made from even the most trivial personality trait. Such factors influenced the trial of the Reverend George Burroughs, a short man of small build who possessed supposedly supernatural strength.

Burroughs, a non-ordained minister who had left his Salem parish to settle in Maine, was not unfamiliar with the accusers of the village. According to reports, his leave-taking had been marred by a bitter dispute with John Putnam, uncle of the chief accuser. The argument centered on Burroughs' relationship with his ailing wife, a woman who Putnam believed to be much mistreated by the clergyman. After Mrs. Burroughs' untimely demise, Putnam not only alleged that Burroughs' activities had contributed to the death, but also claimed the minister had reneged on several debts. The issue was settled in Burroughs' favor and created considerable criticism of Putnam.

Witnesses at the Burroughs trial claimed that the minister exhibited numerous traits of preternatural gifts. Not only was he credited with carrying whole barrels of molasses or cider for great distances, but it was also maintained that he could run at speeds faster than that of a horse. It was firmly asserted that the minister could lift from the ground a seven-foot-long rifle, by merely sticking his forefinger into the muzzle and raising his arm. Other witnesses testified that Burroughs possessed the uncanny ability to repeat conversations at which he had not been present. Most damaging of all, the clergyman was identified by several self-confessed witches as Satan's personal representative at Salem's sabbaths. The meetings, it was reported, were personally organized and presided over by sorcerer Burroughs. Like Procter and Willard, Burroughs was condemned.

Not all of the accused remained to hear the evidence presented against them. Edward Bishop and Sarah, his wife, fled the area and were followed by Philip and Mary English, Nathaniel and Elizabeth

Cary, John Alden, and Dudley and John Bradstreet. Mary Bradbury, who stood trial and was condemned, also managed to escape. Flight was made particularly easy for wealthy colonials, who were allowed to post their estates as bonds and thus remain at liberty during the period between hearing and trial. But for the poor, opportunities to flee were less convenient. The sure road to the gallows began with the issuance of an arrest warrant, and little chance was provided to halt the journey before its conclusion.

Bridget Bishop was the first Salem witch to suffer hanging. On June 10, the controversial woman was taken to Gallows Hill and executed by Sheriff George Corwin. More than a month passed before the site was the scene of another turning off. On July 19, Rebecca Nurse, Sarah Good, Elizabeth Howe, Sarah Wildes, and Susannah Martin were hanged en masse.

The trials continued throughout the summer, and justice in the crowded courtroom grew increasingly more swift. On August 19, John Proctor, John Willard, George Burroughs, Martha Carrier, and George Jacobs mounted the scaffold for another large scale spectacle. By September 17, an additional sixteen witches had been sentenced to be executed. Eight of the felons were hung simultaneously on September 22. Included in the group was Martha Corey, whose husband Giles had been pressed to death in an open field less than a week earlier, and Mary Esty, sister of Rebecca Nurse. Completing the company were Ann Pudeater, Wilmot Redd, Samuel Wardwell, Alice Parker, Mary Parker, and Margaret Scott.

The remaining condemned witches had avoided the gallows by three methods. Mary Bradbury had escaped. Abigail Faulkner and Elizabeth Procter had pleaded their bellies. Abigail Hobbs, Mary Lacy, Ann Foster, Dorcas Hoar, and Rebecca Eames had confessed and had been granted temporary reprieves.

As September drew to a close twenty residents of the Salem area, seven men and thirteen women, had lost their lives because of the circle's accusations. While several of the executed were young or middle-aged, at least half of the victims could be classified as elderly. George Jacobs and Giles Corey were over eighty. Martha Corey, Rebecca Nurse, and Ann Pudeater were in their seventies. Margaret Scott, Mary Esty, Wilmot Redd, Susannah Martin, and Bridget Bishop were also considered aged by colonial standards.

Similarly, although some of the hanged witches had indeed exhibited suspicious or unseeming behavior during extended periods of their lives, the majority had been highly respected members of their community for decades. The hangings, by presenting visible evidence of the results of the prosecutions, may have contributed to the sense of uneasiness that began to develop, for following the September 22nd executions, a rumble of public opposition began to be felt.

One of the first to openly oppose the prosecutions was Robert Pike of Salisbury. In an impassioned letter to the justices, Pike attacked the credibility of the afflicted girls and questioned the validity of admitting spectral evidence. This was not the first show of bravery by Pike. Some four decades earlier he had been one of the few colonists to protest the harsh treatment of Quakers in Massachusetts. As a result of his attempt to halt the religious persecutions, Pike had been disenfranchised and disgraced.

John Foster, a member of the Governor's Council, joined Pike in opposing the trials, and influential John Hale of Beverly spoke out when his own wife was accused of sorcery. In Andover, organized opposition surfaced. Twenty-four residents of the village signed a petition calling for an end to the trials and suggesting that the afflicted girls were actually "distempered persons." The document also implied that the accusers were under the power of the devil and were a danger to the community. The message suggested: "We know no one who can think himself safe if the accusations of children and others who are under diabolical influence shall be received against persons of good fame."

Other dissidents chose more direct methods of protest. Joseph Putnam, uncle of accuser Ann Putnam, openly wore a bared sword and announced that if any member of his immediate family were accused, he would kill whomever had cried out. Judge Nathaniel Saltonstall resigned from the court, disgusted with the manner in which the trials were being conducted. While Saltonstall made no public protest, he privately called the accusers "blind, nonsensical girls." A major blow to pro-trial forces came when an unidentified suspect in Boston filed a £1,000 libel suit against his Andover accuser. Immediately all allegations ceased in that area.

As the pendulum of public opinion began to swing against the prosecutions, confessed witches in large numbers began to recant their earlier admissions. Relatives of the imprisoned demanded the immediate release of their loved ones.

Opposing voices also began to be heard outside of Massachusetts. On October 11, a group of New York clergymen, replying to an inquiry by Deputy Governor Joseph Dudley, denounced every unorthodox category of evidence being admitted in the Salem court. The clergymen suggested that only in isolated instances could those who had appeared virtuous during their lives suddenly become workers of the devil. All spectral evidence was rejected as invalid and the afflicted girls were called a greater threat to the community than the accused witches.

Two weeks after the New York opinion had been received, the Connecticut Court of Assistants also voiced their disagreement with Massachusetts' procedures. In reprieving a death sentence against a convicted enchanter, the Assistants announced:

> As for the common things of spectral evidence, ill events after quarrels or threats, tits, water trials, and the like, with suspicious words, they are all discarded . . . and the miserable toil they are in the Bay for adhering to these last-mentioned litigious things is warning enough.

In late November, in response to the growing outcry and infuriated that his own wife had been accused, Governor Sir William Phips dissolved the Court of Oyer and Terminer. The official ordered that a new special session of the Superior Court be convened to hear the remaining witchcraft cases. The upcoming proceedings would not automatically take place in Salem, but instead would be in the home village of the accused. New jurors would be chosen from a panel representing not only Puritan believers, as had been the case in the earlier trials, but all qualified citizens.

On December 14, a new law governing witchcraft was adopted in the colony. The act specified the penalty of death only for those convicted of casting charms that killed or hurt humans, or for sorcerers who conjured up the dead. Lesser forms of magic, such as the use of witchcraft to find stolen property, to harm livestock, or to provoke "unlawful love" would be punished by imprisonment and the pillory.

When the new court convened in January of 1693, all spectral evidence was ruled inadmissible. As a result, thirty of the fifty-six pending indictments were found ignoramus. Of the remaining twenty-six billa vera, all but three defendants were dismissed or acquitted. The three citizens found guilty of witchcraft had confessed their guilt. Two were considered mentally defective.

Phips refused to sign death warrants for the three convicted in 1693 and for five others who had been condemned at Salem but not executed. Although eight graves had been dug, the governor ordered that all punishment be delayed until instructions could be received from Queen Anne.

Chief Justice Stoughton, infuriated with the delay, resigned from the court, criticising Phips for the new direction in which witchcraft was being viewed. Phips, in turn, accused Stoughton of fiscal misman-agement in seizing "the estates, goods, and chattel of the executed" without due process.

The disagreement between these two powerful figures reflected the diverse nature of colonial society. Unlike aristocratic Stoughton, Phips had begun life on a sheep farm in Maine as one of twenty-six children borne by the same mother. The governor had risen to promi-nence partially as a result of marrying Samuel Sewall's wealthy moth-er-in-law. His peerage stemmed from his discovery of a hidden Carib-bean treasure, which enriched not only his fortune, but the royal coffers of the Crown.

Charges of financial misconduct would soon face Phips. In the fall of 1694, the governor was recalled to England to answer for incompetency. The inquiry would not take place, for several weeks after their arrival in London, Phips died. Stoughton was made tempo-rary governor and ruled the colony until 1698.

Even Increase Mather, who had returned from England in the midst of the prosecutions, voiced disapproval of the oppressive cli-mate in the bay colony. In his pamphlet *Cases of Conscience Concern-ing Evil Spirits,* Mather announced:

> It is an awful thing which the Lord has done to convince some amongst us of their error: This then I declare and testifie, that to take away the life of anyone merely because a specter or devil in a bewitched or possessed person does accuse them, will bring the guilt of innocent blood on the land, where such a thing shall be done.

Like the majority of those who criticized the Salem court actions, Increase Mather did not doubt the realness or evil of witchcraft and magic. Few complaints were based on the idea that witches were superstitious impossibilities. Instead, the opposition stemmed from abhorrence at the unjust manner in which the guilt of the accused had been determined.

In order to accommodate both citizen belief in witchcraft and opposition to trials, a popular rationalization grew to explain the entire Salem affair. Under this theory, the accusers, judges, and jurors were credited with acting not out of malice but under the instigation of the devil. Through the trials, it was suggested, Satan had hoped to destroy the Puritan settlements with discord. To further this end, the devil had made it appear that witches were operating in the area.

This explanation satisfied most residents of Massachusetts, and in April, a directive from Queen Anne effectively ended any further prosecutions. Although the ruler did not order that the trials be suspended, she did warn that due care should be taken to assure that further inquiries should not be marred by abuses of power or oppression of citizen rights. In the April 15th correspondence to Governor Phips, the Queen announced:

Trusty and Well-beloved, We Greet You Well.

It having been represented unto Us that a most horrible witchcraft or possession of Devils hath invested several towns in Our Province of Massachusetts Bay under your government, and that divers persons have been convicted of witchcraft, some whereof have confessed their guilt, but that others being of a known and good reputation, these proceedings had caused a great dissatisfaction among our good subjects, for which reason you had put a stop thereunto until Our Pleasure should be known concerning the same. We therefore approving of your care and circumspection herein have thought fit to signify Our Will and Pleasure, as We do hereby will and require you to give all necessary directions that in all proceedings against persons accused for witchcraft or being possessed by the Devil, the greatest moderation and all due circumspection be used, so far as the same may be without impediment to the ordinary course of justice within Our said Province. And so We bid you very heartily farewell. Given at Our Court at Whitehall the 15th day of April, 1693, in the fifth year of Our Reign.

By Her Majesty's Command

In response to the Queen's directive, Phips cleared the jails of all accused witches who remained imprisoned. In addition, the governor issued a general pardon, which permitted all those who had fled the colony to return home.

The complete cessation of hearings was opposed by a small but vocal group of radicals who claimed the activities would prove of assistance to Satan. Increase Mather was so incensed that he ordered burned in Harvard Yard a pamphlet entitled *More Wonders of the Invisible World.* Robert Calef, author of the work, had been highly critical of the Salem trials and the part played in them by Cotton Mather. The burning came a century after Sir Reginald Scot's anti-witchcraft book had been burned in England by the public executioner.

Because the prevailing attitude placed almost total blame for the hysteria on the devil, neither the magistrates nor the judges were condemned for their part in the affair. Most were viewed as innocent parties, and in 1693, every judge who had sat on the Salem court was elected to the Governor's Council, the highest offices of honor in the colony.

Reverend Samuel Parris did not escape so lightly. Even before the Queen's missive had arrived, dissatisfied parishioners were attempting to have the clergyman dismissed from his post. Parris was directly charged with "teaching such dangerous errors, and preaching such scandalous immoralities, as ought to discharge any man, though ever so gifted otherwise, from the work of the ministry." Parris refused to resign and gathered about him a conservative group of loyalists. The stage was thus set for a long and bitter battle within the Salem congregation. In a petition calling for dismissal, the dissident group suggested: "Mr. Parris hath been the beginner and procurer of the sorest afflictions; not to this village only, but this whole country, that ever befall them." The dispute lasted for four years and was ended only with Parris' departure after a financial settlement was imposed by the Court of Common Pleas for Arbitration.

The philosophy that only the devil and Reverend Parris should be blamed for the Salem prosecutions faded as time passed. A general feeling of repentance began to grow in the colony. The remorse, however, was not stirred by conscience, but by a series of disastrous occurrences that began soon after the halting of the trials. In accordance with the Puritan belief in supernatural signs, Massachusetts leaders interpreted the area's poor fortunes and the outbreak of war with France, as the wrath of God sent to punish the area for their erroneous behavior during the 1692 hysteria. An official declaration based on this interpretation announced that despite repeated prayers and supplications, "the anger of God is not yet turned away," then continued:

> God is pleased still to go on in diminishing our substance, cutting short our harvest, blasting our most promising undertakings, in more ways than one unsettling us, and by his more immediate hand snatching away many out of our embraces by sudden and violent deaths even at this time when the sword is devouring so many both at home and abroad. . . .

In an attempt to appease God and thus improve the deteriorating situation, officials ordered that a formal day of prayer and fasting should be held on January 14, 1697. All servile labor was forbidden and citizens were directed to spend the entire period in prayers of penitence for the sins committed at Salem.

Samuel Sewall did not need the official reminder, because for many months the judge's soul had been filled with remorse. Sewall believed that he had been singled out by God for special vengeance; and the trail of sorrow that marked the jurist was terrible indeed. In the years following the Salem affair, two of Sewall's fourteen children died. The deaths continued until only three of his offspring remained.

Sewall saw the tragedies as direct evidence that God was appalled by the actions of the Court of Oyer and Terminer. The judge grew increasingly despondent and, as the day of humiliation approached, he decided to make a greater sacrifice than had been requested. On the appointed day, Sewall, seated in his pew at Boston's Old South Church, passed up to the pulpit a note that he requested be publicly read. As the minister began, the old judge rose to stand in silent humiliation as the confession was announced:

> Samuel Sewall, sensible of the reiterated strokes of God upon himself and family; and being sensible that as to the guilt contracted upon the opening of the late Commission of Oyer and Terminer at Salem (to which the order for this day relates), he is, upon many

accounts, more concerned than any that he knows of, desires to take
the blame and shame of it; asking pardon of men, and especially
desiring prayers that God, who has unlimited authority, would
pardon that sin, and all other his sins, personal and relative; and
according to his infinite benignity and sovereignty, not visit the sin
of him, or of any other, upon himself or any of his, nor upon the
land; but that he would powerfully defend him against all temptations to sin for the future and vouchsafe him the efficacious saving
conduct of his word and spirit.

Sewall's penitence did not end with the church meeting. Each
year for the remainder of his life, the judge secluded himself for a day
of private prayer and contrition for his conduct at the witch trials.

No other officials chose to openly repent for their activities, but
the twelve Salem jurors did follow Sewall's example. In a public
proclamation, the twelve men admitted that their verdicts had been
in error. In asking forgiveness, the jurors announced that their action
had not been based in viciousness, but in ignorance and through the
influence of Satan. In conclusion they announced: "We do heartily ask
forgiveness of you all whom we have justly offended, and do declare
according to our present minds, we would, none of us, do such things
again on such grounds for the whole world. . . . "

Cotton Mather did not support those who believed contrition
should be shown, for the clergyman still maintained that witchcraft
presented a serious threat to New England. Instead of retribution for
the Salem trials, Mather believed that the series of calamities in Massachusetts had been sent by a God angered that "wicked sorceries"
were tolerated in the Bay. However, Mather did feel some guilt over
the hysteria that had characterized the prosecutions. In his private
journal, the minister noted that he feared "divine displeasure" might
be vented on his family for his failure to act "with vigor enough to
stop the proceedings of the judges when the inextricable storm from
the invisible world assaulted the country. . . . "

In 1706, Ann Putnam, leader of the afflicted girls, stepped forward to repent. Ann had been stricken for several years and, like
Judge Sewall, feared that her illnesses were the result of God's punishment. On August 26, Ann made a public apology as part of a service
conducted when she joined a local church. Some of Ann's past arro-

gance still remained, for she discounted all personal responsibility for the earlier allegations and insisted that she had been an innocent instrument of the devil:

> I can truly and uprightly say, before God and man, I did it not out of any anger, malice or ill-will to any person, for I had no such thing against one of them; but what I did was ignorantly, being deluded by Satan. And particularly, as I was a chief instrument of accusing of Goodwife Nurse and her two sisters, I desire to lie in the dust and to be humbled for it, in that I was a cause, with others, of so sad a calamity to them and their families. . . .

Ann, like her sisters of the circle, faded into obscurity. Mary Walcott and Elizabeth Booth married and presumably lived lives not far different from the normal routine of other colonial women of their class. But not all the accusers remained unscathed by the prosecutions. A reversal of attainder issued nearly two decades after the trials reported that some of the "principal accusers" had proven themselves "persons of profligate and vicious conversation." Thus were the afflicted girls of Salem finally transformed in the public eye to scandal-mongering gossips.

The dark days of Salem had not been forgotten by the survivors of those executed or imprisoned for witchcraft. In 1709, a group of relatives of persecuted citizens filed claims for compensation from the government. Along with requests for damages came pleas that the names and reputations of those tried might be formally cleared, so that shame would not be visited on future generations. This action was necessary, for although the Salem church had begun to revoke orders of excommunication, bills of civil attainder against the supposed witches were still in effect.

In accordance with an act of May, 1710, an official committee of claims of sufferers was appointed to deal with the complicated problems of recompense. The body was empowered to receive and evaluate all requests from persons connected with settlers who had been imprisoned, condemned, or executed during 1692.

The families of the twenty persons turned off at Salem found setting a financial value upon the loss of a relative a difficult proposition. For the children of Giles and Martha Corey, the damage was much greater than could be compensated for in pounds sterling. On

September 13, 1710, the Corey children submitted a statement that announced:

> That which breaks our hearts and for which we go mourning still is that our father was put to so cruel a death as being prest to death. Our mother was put to death also, though in another way. And we cannot sufficiently express our grief for the loss of our father and mother in such a way.
>
> So we cannot compute our expenses and costs but shall commit to your wisdom to judge of, but after our father's death, the sheriff threatened to seize our father's estate and for fear thereof, we complied with him and paid him eleven pounds six shillings in money by which we have been greatly damnified & impoverished by being exposed to sell creatures and other things for little more than half the worth of them to get the money to pay aforesaid and to maintain our father & mother in prison. But that which is grievous to us is that we are not only impoverished, but also reproached and so may be for all generations, and that wrongfully. . . .

Although nearly two decades had passed, the children of George Burroughs also felt the sting of Salem. Burroughs' daughter Rebecca requested that the commissioners complete their deliberations quickly so that the matter could be forgotten. She explained to the officials: "Every discourse on this melancholy subject doth but give a fresh wound to my bleeding heart. . . . "

The sorrow was no doubt partially prompted by the trying circumstances that had followed Burroughs' execution. The enchanter's seven children, the eldest aged sixteen, were turned out of their house following the hanging by an unscrupulous stepmother who confiscated the estate for her own use. Son Jeremiah Burroughs recalled the circumstances:

> Nothing thereof nor the household goods, &c., ever came into our hands; we were turn'd out into a wide world to shift for ourselves, having nothing to trust unto but Divine Providence and the generosity of friends . . . and some of us so young that we can give no account of particular circumstances of the family, nor capable, any of us, to give a particular account of the wrong done us any further than we are informed by others. But [I] can assure you we never had the value of a sixpence to remember our father with when dead and gone.

On December 17, 1711, the governor and council authorized payment of £578 12s to the claimants representing twenty-three persons condemned at Salem. The official payment coincided almost exactly with the claims filed by descendants and included:

	£	s.	d.
To Elizabeth Howe	12	0	0
George Jacobs	79	0	0
Mary Estey	20	0	0
Mary Parker	08	0	0
George Burroughs	50	0	0
Giles Corey & wife	21	0	0
Rebecca Nurse	25	0	0
John Willard	20	0	0
Sarah Good	30	0	0
Martha Carrier	7	6	0
Samuel Wardwell & wife	36	15	0
John Procter & wife	150	0	0
Sarah Wildes	14	0	0
Mary Bradbury	20	0	0
Abigail Faulkner	20	0	0
Abigail Hobbs	10	0	0
Ann Foster	6	10	0
Rebecca Eames	10	0	0
Dorcas Hoar	21	17	0
Mary Post	8	14	0
Mary Lacy	8	10	0

A petition to reverse the attainder of twenty-two of the thirty-one citizens convicted and condemned as a result of the trials was passed by the Massachusetts General Court in 1711. In 1957, The Commonwealth of Massachusetts reversed the stigma placed on all those not covered by earlier orders.

The ardor of Massachusetts witch-hunters was significantly cooled by the citizen opposition created by the Salem trials. After 1693, no further court actions were taken in the colony against supposed enchanters. A similar situation resulted in neighboring Connecticut. Although rumors relating to supposed incidents of witchcraft continued to circulate in Pennsylvania, the middle colonies, like the northeast, saw no formal court action. Grace Sherwood's 1706 trial ended the issue of enchantment in Virginia, and when Maryland's Virtue Violl was found not guilty of sorcery in 1712, the devil was effectively removed as a perpetrator of crimes in that colony.

Repugnance toward the manner in which justice temporarily waivered at Salem was not the only factor contributing to the decline of witchcraft as a factor in Early American life. A similar trend was taking place throughout the western world, where scientific reason rather than superstition was being used to explain events previously deemed "preternatural."

By the mid-1700s, those who entirely rejected the idea of witchcraft were well in control of English-speaking domains on both sides of the Atlantic. The last legal execution of a British Isle witch came in 1722, when a Scottish woman at Dornoch was burned for having cast damaging spells over her neighbors' pigs and sheep. Nearly three decades later, however, two "superannuated wretches" were seized by an unruly mob near Selborne. While being subjected to a water trial, both suspected sorcerers were accidentally drowned in a horse pond. The final execution of a witch in an English-speaking territory came in 1730, when a black slave, Sarah Bassett, was turned off in Bermuda. However, Sarah may have been executed under a petit treason decision, for her crime was murder of her master by witchcraft.

In 1736 the King James law was officially repealed and prosecution of any English citizen for "witchcraft, sorcery, enchantment, or conjuration" was forbidden. Formal repeal of colonial laws, however, was not automatic in all cases. Rhode Island, for example, did not officially eliminate hanging as the penalty for convicted witches until 1768.

Although England and the American colonies avoided the sorcery trials that continued in sections of the continent until well into the eighteenth century, all remnants of superstition did not immediately disappear. But, as time passed and as those who had lived during the witch-hunting era faded from the scene, fears of the supernatural world were replaced by simple curiosity. By the time the new American nation was established, the colonies' witchcraft prosecutions were viewed as almost-forgotten relics of a much more simple time.

Selected Readings

GENERAL BACKGROUND

John Ashton, *The Devil in Britain and America,* 1896; Grillot De Givry, *Witchcraft, Magic and Alchemy,* tr. by J. Courtenay Locke, 1931; *Encyclopaedia of Superstitions,* ed. by Christina Hale, 1961; *Materials Toward a History of Witchcraft,* col. by Henry Charles Lea, 1939; T.K. Oesterreich, *Possession, Demonical and Other,* 1930; Rossell Hope Robbins, *The Encyclopedia of Witchcraft and Demonology,* 1963; Montague Summers, *The History of Witchcraft* n.d. and *The Geography of Witchcraft,* 1927.

AMERICAN WITCHCRAFT

George Lincoln Burr, "New England's Place in the History of Witchcraft," Vol. XXI of the Proceedings of the American Antiquarian Society, 1911; Ezra Hoyt Byington, *The Puritan in England and New England,* 1896; Tom Peete Cross, "Witchcraft in North Carolina," Vol. XVI, Studies in Philology, 1919; Florence G. Danforth, *New England Witchcraft,* 1965; Samuel Adams Drake, *A Book of New England Legends and Folk Lore,* 1884; Samuel G. Drake, *Annals of Witchcraft in New England,* 1869, and *The Witchcraft Delusion in New England,* Vol. I–III, 1866; Samuel A. Green, *Groton in the Witchcraft Times,* 1883; George Lyman Kittredge, *Witchcraft in Old and New England,* 1929; Clyde Kluckhom, *Navajo Witchcraft,* 1944; *Narratives of the Witchcraft Cases, 1648–1706,* ed. by George Lincoln Burr, 1914; Francis Neal Parke, "Witchcraft in Maryland,'" The Maryland Historical Magazine, 1936; Allen Putnam, *Witchcraft of New England Explained by Modern Spiritualism,* 1888; Henry Shoemaker, "The Origins and Language of Central Pennsylvania Witchcraft," Vol. I. Publications of the Pennsylvania Folk-Lore Society; John M. Taylor, *The Witchcraft Delusion in Colonial Connecticut 1647–1697*, 1908; James Thacher, *An Essay on Demonology, Ghosts and Apparitions . . . , 1831; Mabel L. Todd, Witchcraft in New England*, n.d.; Justin Windsor, *The Literature of Witchcraft in New England*, 1896.

SALEM WITCHCRAFT

George M. Beard, *The Psychology of the Salem Witchcraft Excitement of 1692*, 1882; Sanford J. Fox, *Science and Justice: The Massachusetts Witchcraft Trials*, 1968; Chadwick Hansen, *Witchcraft at Salem*, 1969; William F. Poole, *Cotton Mather and Salem Witchcraft*, 1869; *Records of Salem Witchcraft Copied from the Original Documents*, compiled by W.E. Woodward, 1864; *Salem-Village Witchcraft—A Documentary Record of Local Conflict in Colonial New England*, ed. by Paul Boyer and Stephen Nissenbaum, 1972; Marion L. Starkey, *The Devil in Massachusetts, A Modern Inquiry into the Salem Witch Trials*, 1969; Charles Sutherland Tapley, *Rebecca Nurse—Saint but Witch Victim*, 1930; Charles W. Upham, *Salem Witchcraft*, Vol. I and II, 1867.

SPECIAL SUBJECTS

Fletcher S. Bassett, *Sea Phantoms or Legends and Superstitions of the Sea . . .*, 1892; Alice Morse Earle, *Curious Punishments of Bygone Days*, 1896; Thomas R. Forbes, "Midwifery and Witchcraft," Journal of the History of Medicine and Allied Sciences, April, 1962; Sir Walter Langdon-Brown, *From Witchcraft to Chemotherapy*, 1941; *Law and Authority in Colonial America*, ed. by George A. Billias, 1965; Eugenie Andruss Leonard, *The Dear-Bought Heritage*, 1965; Francis R. Packard, *History of Medicine in the United States*, Vol. I, 1931; Hugh F. Rankin, *Criminal Trial Proceedings in the General Court of Colonial Virginia*, 1965; Géza Róheim, *Magic and Schizophrenia*, 1955; Raphael Semmes, *Captains and Mariners of Early Maryland*, 1937, and *Crime and Punishment in Early Maryland*, 1938; Julia Cherry Spruill, *Women's Life & Work in the Southern Colonies*, 1938; *Strange Phenomena of New England in the Seventeenth Century, from the Writings of Cotton Mather*, col. by Henry Jones, 1846; Ilza Veith, *Hysteria, the History of a Disease*, 1965; *Witchcraft Confessions and Accusations*, ed. by Mary Douglas, 1970.

WRITINGS OF THE PERIOD

Richard Bernard, *A Guide to Grand-Jury Men*, 1627; Robert Calef, *More Wonders of the Invisible World*, 1700; R.C., *Lithobolia: or, The Stone-Throw-*

ing Devil, 1698; John Cotta, *The Triall of Witch-craft, Shewing the True and Right Methode of the Discovery,* 1616; Michael Dalton, *The Countrey Justice* . . . , 1643; John Hale, *A Modest Inquiry into the Nature of Witchcraft,* 1697; Sir Mathew Hale, *A Collection of Modern Relations of Matter of Fact, Concerning Witches & Witchcraft,* 1693; Francis Hutchinson, *An Historical Essay Concerning Witchcraft,* 1718; Thomas Hutchinson, *King Philip's War and Witchcraft in New England,* 1890, and *The Witchcraft Delusion of 1692,* 1870; John Josselyn, *An Account of Two Voyages to New-England,* 1674, and *New-England's Rarities Discovered,* 1672; Joseph Keble, *An Assistance to Justices of the Peace for the Easier Performance of their Duty* . . . , 1683; Deodat Lawson, *A Brief and True Narrative* . . . , 1692; Cotton Mather, *Magnalia Christi Americana,* 1702, *Memorable Providences Relating to Witchcrafts and Possessions* . . . , 1689, and *The Wonders of The Invisible World,* 1693; Increase Mather, *Cases of Conscience Concerning Evil Spirits,* 1693, *An Essay for the Recording of Illustrious Providences,* and *A Further Account of the Tryals of the New England Witches,* 1693; Reginald Scot, *The Discoverie of Witchcraft,* 1584; Sir Walter Scott, *Demonology and Witchcraft,* n.d.; John Webster, *The Displaying of Supposed Witchcraft,* 1677.

Index